THE FUTURE OF ARCHITECTURE

FRANK LLOYD WRIGHT

THE FUTURE OF ARCHITECTURE

BRAMHALL HOUSE · NEW YORK

CONTENTS

ILLUSTRATIONS

A CONVERSATION

A CONVERSATION

FRANK LLOYD WRIGHT: Come in, Hugh.

HUGH DOWNS: Hello, Mr. Wright.

WRIGHT: Glad to see you.

DOWNS: Glad to see you.

WRIGHT: What's that you have in your hand?

DOWNS: I have a book here I'm going to ask you a question about in just a moment. I thought in the brief space of a half hour which is the time we have, what we'd like to do, Mr. Wright, is get as clear a picture as possible, for our audience, of the essence of your thinking about architecture . . . about American architecture in American life.

WRIGHT: In a half hour?

DOWNS: Well, as much as we are able to do in a half hour. Would you identify this picture for us?

WRIGHT: The picture is that of the little house on Forest Avenue that I built when I was still with Adler & Sullivan in 1893. I think this Cheney house was built several years after—about 1900. The picture shows the house next door which gives you a pretty good idea of what, as an architect, I was born into. A little tree grew up, a little willow tree, between my own house and studio. There was a continual procession around the house to see where the tree grew up through the roof.

DOWNS: 1893.

WRIGHT: Yes.

DOWNS: I think many of our viewers will agree that this Cheney house looks like a house that could have been built last year, and I think that is as good a way as I can think of offhand to get into our subject, which is called "60 Years of Living Architecture."

When did you first decide to make architecture your life work?

WRIGHT: Well, fortunately for me I never had to decide. That was all decided for me before I was born. My mother was a teacher, you know—and, for some reason best known to her, she wanted an architect for a son. I happened to be the son and, of course, naturally an architect. I was so conditioned by her. The room into which I was born was hung with nine wood engravings made by Timothy Cole of the great old English Cathedrals. Remember those? So—I was born into architecture.

DOWNS: What was your first job as an architect, Mr. Wright?

WRIGHT: Well, Hugh, I think I really wanted to be an architect, as near as I could be. So—my first job in architecture was "to get into it" with Adler and Sullivan. In Madison we were a minister's family and so, very poor. We had no money to send me to an architectural school—but Madison, our home, had an engineering school at the University of Wisconsin and a very kind Dean of Engineering, Professor Allan D. Conover. He gave me a stipend to work for him and so pay my way through the engineering course at the University. I worked my way through it. Almost. If I had stayed three months longer I would have been given a degree as a civil engineer. But, I was anxious to be an architect, so I started on my own for Chicago—to go to work, for Adler and Sullivan, as it all turned out.

11

DOWNS: Would you say that any of Sullivan's ideas in architecture influenced you at any time?

WRIGHT: Naturally. They were influencing nearly everybody in the country.

DOWNS: How so?

WRIGHT: He was the real radical of his day. His thought gave us the present-day skyscraper. You see, when buildings first began to be tall, architects were confused—(no precedents)—didn't know how to make them *tall*. They would put one 2 or 3 story building on top of another until they had enough. I remember the master came in and threw something on my table—it was a "stretch" with the Wainwright building in St. Louis designed in outline upon it. He said, "Wright, this thing is *tall*. What's the matter with a tall building?" Well, there it was, *tall*! After that the skyscraper began to flourish—tall. The skyscraper you see today was the result of Louis Sullivan's initiative. That was his kind of mind, his type of thought. He saw the thing directly *for what it was*. You see?

DOWNS: Most people who are at all acquainted with your work know the fact that your work is organic and intimately bound up with the lives of people. When did this idea first begin to take shape in your work?

WRIGHT: That's pretty difficult to say.

Well, yes—difficult to say. But, of course, in my youth, nothing existed of the sort I wanted to see happen. It didn't exist anywhere. It had to be made, and it first happened out there around about the western prairies of Chicago: the first expression in humane terms of what we now call organic architecture.

DOWNS: You use the word organic. Is that any different from my use of the word modern architecture, in your opinion?

WRIGHT: Very different, because modern architecture is merely something—anything—which may be built today, but organic architecture is an architecture from within outward, in which *entity* is the ideal. We don't use the word organic as referring to something hanging in a butcher shop, you know.

Organic means intrinsic—in the philosophic sense, entity—wherever the whole is to the part as the part is to the whole and where the nature of the materials, the nature of the purpose, the *nature* of the entire performance becomes clear as a necessity. Out of that *nature* comes what character in any particular situation you can give to the building as a creative artist.

DOWNS: Well, now, with that in mind, what do you try to put into a house when you design one?

WRIGHT: First of all, the family it is designed for, as a rule—not always easy and not always successful, but usually so. And we try to put into that house a sense of unity—of the *altogether* that makes it a part of the site. If the thing is successful (the architect's effort) you can't imagine that house anywhere than right where it is. It is a gracious part of its environment. It graces its environment, rather than disgraces it.

DOWNS: A striking example of a site and house going together is, of course, Bear Run House. How do you relate the site to the house?

WRIGHT: There in a beautiful forest was a solid high rock-ledge rising beside a waterfall and the natural thing seemed to be to cantilever the house from that rock-bank over the falling water. You see, in the Bear Run House, the first house where I came into possession of concrete and steel with which to build, of course the grammar of that house cleared up on that basis. Then came (of course) Mr. Kaufmann's love for the beautiful site. He loved the site where the house was built and liked to listen to the waterfall. So that was a prime motive in the design.

I think you can hear the waterfall when you look at the design. At least
it is there and he lives intimately with the thing he loves.

DOWNS: Tell us about your own home, Mr. Wright. Taliesin.

WRIGHT: Well, here is Taliesin. Taliesin was first built in 1911—was a kind of refuge for me and mine at the time. I was getting a worm's eye view of society and needed to get out into the country. I found my mother had prepared this site for me. She asked me to come and take it. I did, and, of course, the countryside was Southern Wisconsin—low hills, protruding rock ledges—a wooded site, and the same thought applied to Taliesin that applied later to Bear Run. The site determined the features and character of Taliesin. Owing to tragic circumstances you are sitting here in the third house erected since then.

Taliesin really is now a stone house and it is a house of the North—really built for the North. I loved the icicles that came on the eaves, and in the winter the snow would sweep up over it and it would all look like a hill itself or one of the hills. Taliesin was built *to belong to the region.*

My grandfather came to the region with his family when the Indians were still there about 125 years ago, and the valley they always called "the valley," lovingly. It *was* a lovable place. And the valley was theirs by conquest. It was cleared by my grandfather and his sons. You see in Taliesin an instance of the third generation going back to the soil to really develop it, trying by every means to make something beautiful out of it.

DOWNS: Where did the name "Taliesin" come from, Mr. Wright?

WRIGHT: My people were Welsh. Mother's people were Welsh immigrants. My old grandfather was a hatter and a preacher in Wales. They were the cultivated element in our Iowa county here. All had Welsh names for their places—my sister's home was called Tanyderi "Under the Oaks," so I—too—chose a Welsh name for mine, and it was Taliesin. Taliesin, a Druid, was a member of King Arthur's Roundtable. He sang the glories of fine art—I guess he was about the only Britisher who ever did—so I chose Taliesin for a name—it means "shining-brow" and this place now called Taliesin is built like a brow on the edge of the hill—not on top of the hill—because I believe you should never build on top of anything directly. If you build on top of the hill, you lose the hill. If you build one side the top, you have the hill and the eminence that you desire. You see? Well, Taliesin is a brow like that.

DOWNS: In the case of Taliesin West, I wonder about some of the great contrasts between that and the other Taliesin, when it was built for the same person—since both are your homes. Why that difference?

WRIGHT: First of all, the terrain now changed absolutely. Here we came to the absolute desert where I first saw these astonishing and

exciting new forms—cactus and mountain. In Wisconsin erosion has, by way of age, softened everything. The landscape there was pastoral—sweet.

But out there everything was sharp, hard, clean and savage. Everything in the desert was armed, so it was all new experience. Following out the same feeling for structure, the same idea of building that we had in both instances you have mentioned, Taliesin West had to be absolutely according to the desert. So Taliesin there is according to its site again, according to its environment. The purpose, of course, in Arizona was much the same as in Wisconsin and hasn't changed much since.

DOWNS: What is the difference between organic architecture and conventional architecture?

WRIGHT: You mean structurally, I imagine?

DOWNS: Yes.

WRIGHT: You see the old post and beam construction—you can say

this is the post and beam—post and beam—was all a kind of superimposition, and if you wanted partitions, they cut, and they would butt—you

 see—cut, butt and slash—and if you wanted tension, you had to rivet

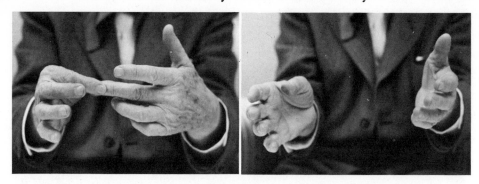

something to something and make a connection. It might give way.

Well, organic architecture brought these principles together so that

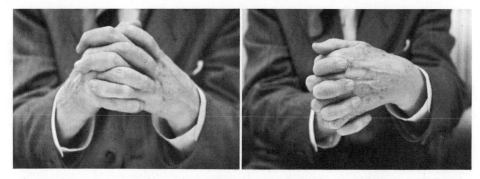

a building was more like this—you see—it had tension—you could pull

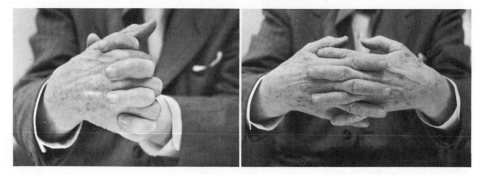

on the structure. It had tensile strength owing to steel—tenuity—and owing to steel it could span great spaces, and the great spaces could be protected with great clear sheets of glass. The Orientals, of course the Greeks, never had any such facility. If they had had steel and glass, why

20

we wouldn't have to do any thinking today—we'd be copying as usual. But now something had to be done with these new materials—these great new resources—glass and steel and the machine. They are tremendous. Because of that principle of tenuity in steel we could use the cantilever, and into structure by way of steel came this element of continuity. You see one thing merging into another and being of another rather than this old cut, butt and slash. This same element of strength it was that brought the Imperial Hotel through—intact—through the earthquake. That principle of tenuity and of flexibility, instead of rigidity which could be broken, was its new strength.

DOWNS: Would you recount for us some of the things which are fundamentally your own innovations in architecture?

WRIGHT: Well, it would be pretty tedious—a long story, too—perhaps too long for this occasion. First of all came this new sense of space, as the *reality* of the building—then came the countenance of that new sense of space which is more or less what I then termed streamlined— that word streamlined got into the language about that time through the nature of my effort. Then there was the open plan—instead of a building being a series of boxes and boxes inside boxes it became more and more open—more and more aware of space—the outside gradually came in more and more and the inside went outside more. That increased until we had practically a new floor plan. It has been referred to always as "the open-plan." That was one direct result. Then, of course, there were the structural implications which we hinted at a little while ago—of a building that had tenuity instead of a building without any, which could fall apart. The buildings built upon this plan are good for 300 years, I should think. Several centuries.

And in that structural dispensation, a great many new features arose, like, well perhaps the most important one was gravity heat (floor heat) where the heat is underneath the floor-slab, hot water pipes embedded in broken stone. With a thick rug on the floor you have a reservoir of heat underneath you. You sit warm, your feet are warm and you can open the windows and still be comfortable. The children may play on a nice warm surface. If you sit warm and your feet are warm, you are comfortably warm.

Oh, and I guess the corner-window is something we should mention in connection with innovation and you can judge from what happened by way of the corner-window what has happened to so many of the innovations. The corner-window is indicative of an idea conceived, early in my work, that the box is a Fascist symbol, and the architecture of freedom and democracy needed something basically better than the box. So I started out to destroy the box as a building.

Well, the corner-window came in as all the comprehension that was ever given to that act of destruction of the box. The light now came in where it had never come in before and vision went out. You had screens for walls instead of box-walls—here the walls vanished as walls, the box vanished as a box. The corner-window as a feature went around the world. But the idea of the thing I intended never followed it. The liberation of space became merely a window instead of the release of an entire sense of structure, a radical change in the idea of a building.

DOWNS: I've heard indirect lighting attributed to you.

WRIGHT: Yes, I did the first so-called indirect lighting very, very early. About fifty years ago, I guess. Incorporated light behind shelves, cast light from the floor on ceilings, then burying it in the ceiling in

various ways as recessed lighting shining on walls. Doing then, I suppose, nearly everything being done today. I don't know of anything radically new.

DOWNS: You have recently built a new church, and it is not typical of most churches in our experience. Could you tell us why?

WRIGHT: In Unity Church there, you see the Unitarianism of my forefathers found expression in a building by one of the offspring. The idea, "unitarian," was unity. Unitarians believed in the unity of all things. Well, I tried to build a building here that expressed that over-all sense of unity. The plan you see is triangular. The roof is triangular and out of this—triangulation—(aspiration) you get this expression of reverence without recourse to the steeple. The building itself, covering all, all in all and each in all, sets forth—says what the steeple used to say, but says it with greater reverence, I think, in both form and structure. I didn't like to build a church in the city. I sought to take it into the country and make it more like a country club in its aspects and be more interesting and inviting to the congregation. So I persuaded the trustees to go out. We went out but not far enough because before we got the church built, the town came out. And so we found ourselves suburban,

instead of in the country. If you're going to decentralize now, you will have to go far and go fast, because everything is swifter coming along. You can see decentralization growing everywhere, now. See the factory going to the country! You can also see the merchandiser impatient with the traffic problem moving out to the country—I think the gas station was the first act of decentralization. All these things are going on around you now whether you want to acknowledge them or not. Now decentralization must be planned for—better to plan for it than let it take place haphazardly as the cities themselves grew. New York, for instance, is just an overgrown crazed village, in plan. And so, more or less, it is with all our great cities.

What is supposed to be *the growth* of the city is really going to be seen finally as the death of the city.

DOWNS: If you were to plan and build an entire city, including elements of shelter, work, recreation and workshop, as we were just talking about, what would you intend to accomplish in doing this?

WRIGHT: Primarily the use of and sympathy with the site according to the nature of the ground, and the purpose of the city or town, whatever it might be and, of course, the character of the inhabitants would be no little consideration in that connection. In other words, it would be a native and natural performance. Organic architecture is a natural architecture. A natural architecture. Now, what would a natural architecture be? Indigenous, wouldn't it? It wouldn't be some eclecticism or other—something you picked up somewhere by way of taste and applied to the circumstances. You would go into the *nature-study* of the circumstances and come out with this thing from within, wouldn't you?

Well, it would apply to a town, apply to a city, apply to the planning of anything at all.

DOWNS: Even a factory? I wanted to ask—when you build a factory?

WRIGHT: Especially a factory.

DOWNS: Well, what do you consider the most important factors in this case, the building of a factory?

WRIGHT: I think the human values involved. I think the lives of the workers. I don't see why it isn't a more profitable thing to make those lives happy, they'll be more productive. Environment, as we found it to be when we built the Johnson administration building, results in a greatly increased efficiency on their part. If you make them proud of their environment, and happy to be where they are, and give them some dignity and pride in their environment, it all comes out to the good where the product is concerned.

The Johnson people have found that out. The Johnson people have a profit-sharing system with their employees and when they got into

that building, why, one of the first consequences was tea in the afternoon, and their people didn't like to go home. They loved to stay in the building, be there, come early, enjoy it, became themselves charming features of a very interesting, exciting environment. And it has proved *profitable*. It does (I think the phrase is) *"pay off,"* isn't it, in our country? And "the pay-off" of course is the criterion by which everything is decided? Well, even deciding it by way of the "pay-off," a healthful environment in which the workers can take pride is the "pay-off."

26

DOWNS: Over the years, Mr. Wright, the American press and sections of your own profession have not always treated you kindly. I just wonder if you have any comment about this.

WRIGHT: Well, Hugh, I don't see why they should have treated me kindly.

I was entirely contrary to everything they believed in and if I was right, they were wrong. Why should they treat me kindly? It was a question at one time, I suppose, of their survival or mine. In those circumstances you know what happens. Something always has to happen. It still is happening, by the way, but not so much now. But it is true that, still, the greatest appreciation of what we have done comes from European countries and from the Orient rather than from our own country. Education in our country today is not even on speaking terms with culture. We are very slow to take things on that occur at home. It has always been the idea of our people that culture came from abroad and it did, so you can't blame them for thinking so. They didn't want to hear of its developing out here in the tall grass of the western prairies. That was not exciting. In fact they rather resented hearing about it in that sense at all. So when it had gone abroad and Europeans came over here with it, they could sell it to the American people—the people would take it from them, when they didn't like to take it from me.

DOWNS: Through the span of your life there have been great changes in the world, economically, socially and ideologically. Through years of war and peace, through years that spelled great hope and great disasters for mankind. Have any of these changes influenced your work or your thinking?

WRIGHT: No, and it is a little unfortunate that my work couldn't have more influence on those changes. Probably if the work had been better understood, I might have had a very beneficial influence on many of those changes. But, I can't say those changes had any effect on my work. My ideal was pretty well-fixed—I was pretty sure of my ground and my star and I saw no occasion—you see—early in life I had to choose between honest arrogance and hypocritical humility. I chose honest arrogance, and have seen no occasion to change, even now.

We are pursuing the same center line of thought through all these changes and I am confident that the principles of our work (its heart and center line) are really the ideology of democracy. If democracy is ever to have a free architecture—I mean if it is ever to have freedom, have a culture of its own—architecture will be its basic effect and condition. Yes, I do believe we have the true center line of a great architecture—a natural architecture for freedom and for democracy.

DOWNS: Among other things, you are a teacher, Mr. Wright. In your years of experience, what conclusions have you reached of the roles and duties of the teacher and those of the students?

WRIGHT: I'm expected to answer that now, am I? I'm no teacher. Never wanted to teach, and don't believe in teaching an art. A science, yes; business, of course; but an art cannot be taught. You can only inculcate it. You can be an exemplar. You may be able to create an atmosphere in which it can grow. But I suppose I being exemplar would be called a teacher in spite of myself. So go ahead, call me a teacher.

DOWNS: Do you feel that American architecture has progressed generally over—well—the past several years?

WRIGHT: No, I'm afraid it has not. I think that the effects have been sought and multiplied and the "why" of the effect, the real cause at the center of the life of the thing, seems to have languished. If honest seekers once mastered the inner principle, infinite variety would result. No one would have to copy anybody else. My great disappointment—it always is—is to find, instead of emulation, what I see as a wave of imitation.

DOWNS: In your long life of practical and artistic endeavor, what do you consider as your most satisfactory achievement?

WRIGHT: Oh, my dear boy—the next one, of course. The next building I build.

DOWNS: Well, go on from there. What's that?

WRIGHT: I don't know. But whatever it is. That would be it.

DOWNS: What would you say is the greatest disappointment in your career?

WRIGHT: Well, I think I touched on it a moment ago when I said that instead of emulation I have seen chiefly imitation. Imitation by the imitators of imitation.

DOWNS: Might that not be the price that you pay for being ahead of your time?

WRIGHT: Well, I've had to think about it a good deal in recent years. Looking back now I suppose that is the way the thing we call progress always happens. Probably always has been so. A little more obvious in our day because of commercialized conditions, everybody being in a kind of free-for-all to pull out what he can as soon as he can and make the most of it. So I don't suppose it is any worse than it ever has been and maybe that is the way it has to come.

Maybe that is the way great ideas eventually obtain. By way of abuse. Well, it's a moot question. It is not to be settled here nor is it to be settled by me.

SOME ASPECTS OF THE PAST AND PRESENT OF ARCHITECTURE

SOME ASPECTS OF THE PAST AND PRESENT OF ARCHITECTURE

THE land is the simplest form of architecture.

Building upon the land is as natural to man as to other animals, birds or insects. In so far as he was more than an animal his buildings became what we call architecture.

In ancient times his limitations served to keep his buildings architecture. Splendid examples: Mayan, Egyptian, Greek, Byzantine, Persian, Gothic, Indian, Chinese, Japanese.

Looking back at these, what then is architecture?

It is man and more.

It is man in possession of his earth. It is the only true record of him where his possession of earth is concerned.

While he was true to earth his architecture was creative.

The time comes when he is no longer inspired by the nature of earth. His pagan philosophy is breaking down, owing to changing social conditions, to new science, new facilities, easy riches. The social world begins to turn upside down. Science takes the place of art. Things serve the man better than thoughts.

Nothing in his experience enables him to resist the disintegrating effect of money and machines. An enemy to his nature, likely to emasculate or destroy him, is embraced by him.

His creative faculties (art) are conditioned upon this earth. His possession of earth in this sense grows dim as his intellect (science and

34

invention) discovers ways to beat work. Money shows him new ways to cheat life. Power becomes exterior instead of interior. His own acts—which are vicarious—are no longer inherent.

In these circumstances architecture becomes too difficult, building too easy. New facilities are here for which he has no corresponding forms. He seems for the moment powerless to make them. He is lost to the source of inspiration, the ground. He takes any substitute. Neither the pagan ideal nor its counterpart, Christianity, any longer lead him.

In the stress of circumstance a new ideal appears capable of leading him out of bondage into life again. Again the ground comes into the light as a brighter sense of reality dawns. It is the sense and nature of that which is within—integrity.

The room or space within the building is man's reality instead of his exterior circumstance. Though as old as philosophy, the new ideal takes on fresh significance in the ideal of architecture as organic. It must be integral to a life lived as organic.

New sense of the whole enters the life of man to bring order out of chaos. The old—"classic," eclecticism—is chaos, restlessness.

The new—"integral," organic—is order, repose.

All materials lie piled in masses or float as gases in the landscape of this planet much as the cataclysms of creation left them.

At the mercy of the cosmic elements, these materials have been disintegrated by temperatures, ground down by glaciers, eroded by wind and sea, sculptured by tireless forces qualifying each other. They are all externally modified by time as they modify this earth in a ceaseless procession of change.

Stone is the basic material of our planet. It is continually changed by cosmic forces, themselves a form of change. Contrasted with these great mineral masses of earth structure—this titanic wreckage—are placid depths and planes of mutable water or the vast depth-plane of the immutable sky hung with evanescent clouds. And this creeping ground-cover of vegetable life, more inexorable than death, is rising from it all, over all, against all, texturing with pattern, infinite in resource, and inexhaustible in variety of effect. This is the earthly abode of the buildings man has built to work, dwell, worship, dance and breed in.

Change is the one immutable circumstance found in landscape. But the changes all speak or sing in unison of cosmic law, itself a nobler form of change. These cosmic laws are the physical laws of all man-built structures as well as the laws of landscape.

Man takes a positive hand in creation whenever he puts a building upon the earth beneath the sun. If he has birthright at all, it must consist in this: that he, too, is no less a feature of the landscape than the rocks, trees, bears or bees of that nature to which he owes his being.

Continuously nature shows him the science of her remarkable economy of structure in mineral and vegetable constructions to go with the unspoiled character everywhere apparent in her forms.

The long, low lines of colorful, windswept terrain, the ineffable dotted line, the richly textured plain, great striated, stratified masses lying noble and quiet or rising with majesty above the vegetation of the desert floor: nature-masonry is piled up into ranges upon ranges of mountains that seem to utter a form-language of their own.

Earth is prostrate, prostitute to the sun. All life we may know is sun life, dies sun death, as shadow, only to be born again. Evidence is everywhere.

Material forms are manifest in one phase today, to be found in another tomorrow. Everywhere around us creeps the eternally mysterious purpose of this inexorable ground-cover of growth. It is mysterious purpose, desperately determined, devouring or being devoured in due course upon this titanic battlefield. Growth seeks conquest by way of death.

To what end is all in pattern?

Always—eternally—pattern? Why?

Why this intrigue of eye-music to go with sensuous ear-music?

What is this inner realm of rhythm that dances in sentient beings and lies quiescent but no less sentient in pattern?

There seems to be no mortal escape, least of all in death, from this earth-principle which is again the sun-principle of growth. Earth becomes more and more the creative creature of the sun. It is a womb quickened by the passions of the master sun.

Nevertheless, every line and the substance of earth's rock-bound structure speak of violence. All is scarred by warring forces seeking reconciliation, still marred by conflict and conquest. But in our era violence has subsided, is giving way to comparative repose. Streamlines of the mountain ranges come down more gently to the plains. Geological cataclysm is subsiding or becoming subservient. Divine order creeps out and rises superior to chaos. Pattern asserts itself. Once more, triumph.

Ceaselessly, the rock masses are made by fire, are laid low by water, are sculptured by wind and stream. They take on the streamlines characteristic of the sweeping forces that change them.

Already matter lies quieted, and with it violence and discord. It is bathed in light that so far as man can see is eternal. Penetrating all, itself penetrated by itself, is mysterious eye-music: pattern.

Meantime in all this lesser building within greater building there is other animation, still another kind of building: these are creatures of creation patterned upon similar patterns until plant, animal creature and earth and man resemble each other for purpose malign or beneficent. Insect, reptile, fish, animal and bird are there in all the elements using gifts of life in this mysterious yet strangely familiar resemblance that we call our world. The seemingly senseless destruction goes on in each.

Some law of laws seems to keep in full effect the law of change in this world-workshop. The crevices and secret places of earth, shadows of the great underneath are swarming with fantastic insects, also singing, working, dancing and breeding.

But with this singular creature, man? Gaining dominion over all, what will he do to maintain his dominion? What will be his essential "pattern?" What does the vulnerable master of cause and effect know of instrumental cosmic law? What may he create?

Man by nature desired to build as the birds were meantime building their nests, as insects were building their cities, and as animals were seeking their dens, making their lairs, or burrowing into the ground.

And architecture became by way of this desire the greatest proof on earth of man's greatness, his right to be born, to inherit the earth.

If the man was poor and mean by nature he built that way. If he was noble and richly endowed then he built grandly, like a noble man. But high or low it was his instinct to build on this earth.

By innate animal instinct he got his first lessons. He got ideas of form from those nature-forms about him, native to the place where he lived. Consciously or unconsciously he was taught by birds and animals. Inspired by the way rock ledges were massed up against sky on the hills, he was taught by the stratified masses of the rock itself. Trees must have awakened his sense of form. The pagodas of China and Japan definitely resemble the pines with which they were associated. The constructions of the Incas married earth itself.

Man's faithful companion, the tree, lived by light. The building, man's own tree, lived by shadows. Therefore, early building masses naturally belonged to the sunlit landscape in which they stood. The stone constructions of the Incas belonged there. Those of the African, of the sea-islanders and of the cliff-dwellers belonged there. The more developed buildings of Persia, China, and Japan belonged there. Later a building had become consciously no less a child of the sun than trees themselves always were.

Probably man first lived in stone caves, when he did not live in trees, using selected sticks and seeking appropriate stones for tools. Concerning this point it is perhaps better to say he first lived sometimes in trees and sometimes in stone caves. As he moved north or south his type of dwelling changed with the climate. The north always demanded most from him in the way of building, if he was to preserve himself. And the Esquimaux learned to build their igloos of blocks of snow cemented with ice.

Farther south the builder was satisfied with some grass and leaves raised up on a platform of sticks, or with some kind of tent that he might fold up and take with him on his horse as he rode away While still dwelling in caves the man perhaps learned to make utensils out of wet clay. He burned them hard for use. These utensils he seems to have made with a higher faculty. His instinct became an aesthetic sense of environment. It taught him something of form. He learned from the animals, the serpents, the plants that he knew. Except for this faculty he was no more than another animal.

Still clinging to the cliffs, he made whole caves out of wet clay and let the sun bake the cave hard. He made them just as he had made the vessels that he had previously put into fire to bake and had used in the cave in the rocks. And so, once upon a time, man moved into his first earth-built house, of *earth*.

This large clay cave or pot of the cliff-dwellers, with a lid on it, was among the first man-made houses. The lid was troublesome to him then and has always been so to subsequent builders. But previously better forms of houses had come from the sticks that had been conferred upon him by his friendly companion, the tree. The lighter, more scientific house-shapes were at first conical, made so by leaning upright sticks together at the top. And the builder covered the sticks with skins of the animals he had eaten. But later man made more roomy houses by squaring the interior space and framing the walls upright. To make the walls he put sticks upright and crossed them at intervals with other horizontal sticks firmly lashed to the vertical sticks, finally covering all with various forms of mats woven of tall dried grasses or grasses lashed directly to the framework. Some forms of these earlier houses in certain parts of Africa and of the South Sea Islands are beautiful architecture to this day.

Then the builder had to contrive the lid—by now it may be called a roof—by framing much heavier sticks together, sloping the sticks across the interior spaces from wall to wall to carry overhead masses of tall dried grasses laid on smaller cross sticks in such a way as to run the water off. He covered this overhead wood framing in the manner of a thatch. The shape of this cover (or roof) was what most affected the general aspect of his building. Sometimes the roof stood up tall within the walls. Sometimes in shape it was a low protective mound. Sometimes it projected boldly. But it always showed its wood construction beneath the final covering.

Walls at first of earth, stone or wood stood up and out heavily as most important. The roof was seldom visible, especially where war was in man's mind, as it usually was. Later the sense of roof as shelter over-came the sense of walls, and great roofs were to be seen with the walls standing back in under them. Man soon came to feel that, if he had no roof in this sense, he had no house.

Later he came to speak of his house as "his roof" and was fond of inviting strangers to come and sit or stay "under his roof." If other men displeased him he drove them "from beneath his roof." His roof was not only his shelter, it was his dignity, as well as his sense of home.

Civilization proceeded. Unless man had war in mind (as he usually did) the roof-shelter became the most important factor in the making of the house. It became the ultimate feature of his building. This re-mains true to this late day when changes of circumstances have made it the roof that he needs to fortify instead of the walls. The real menace of attack is now from the air.

The real science of structure entered into building with this sense of the roof and of wood, or "the stick," because every roof had to be framed strongly enough to span the interior space from wall to wall Sometimes, as a confession of inability, perhaps, or a forced economy, the roof had to be supported on interior posts or partitions. Various pic-turesque roof forms arose as different materials were used to span the space below. More pains had to be taken with these spans than with anything else about the building. Although stone was used to imitate wood construction, the dome, the perfect masonry roof, soon arose among the myriad roofs of the world.

In all this work the principal tools in human hands were fire, the simple lever, and the wheel. But, in human hands, these soon grew into the might of the machine. Explosives soon came along to multiply the force of lever and wheel.

Early masonry buildings were mostly the work of men employing the simple leverage of inclined ways or using the bar as direct lever in human hands. The lever in some form (the wheel is the lever also) was used to make these early buildings.

Materials in primitive architecture were always most important. The character of all the earlier buildings was determined more by the materials available for construction than by any other one thing. Wood, brick, and stone always said "wood," "brick," or "stone," and acted it. Later the builder lost sight of nature in this integral sense. But these good limitations held until the so-called "Renaissance" or "Rebirth" of architecture.

Being craftsmen, because taught by experience with materials in actual construction, the early builders could find a right way to work whatever materials they found. They were ways that were best suited to the kind of buildings we can call architecture. Now the kind of building that we can call architecture today is the building wherein human thought and feeling enter to create a greater harmony and true significance in the whole structure. Shelter and utility in themselves were never enough. The edifice was the highest product of the human mind. Man always sought reflection in it of his sense of himself as God-like. Man's imagination made the gods, and so he made a God-like building. He dedicated it to the God he had made. His architecture was something out of his practical self to his ideal self.

The gods were various, but as the God he made was high or low, so the buildings he made were noble or relatively mean.

As we view the widely different kinds of buildings built by red, yellow, white, or black men, we see that all were clustered into various aggregations under many different conditions. These aggregations we call cities, towns, and villages. In primitive times these clusters of buildings were occasioned by animal fear and social need of daily human contacts, or by obedience to rule. So we see buildings in clusters great, and clusters small. No doubt the cluster once represented a certain social consensus. The village once satisfied a real human need.

The warlike tribe had its village. The peaceful tribe tilling the ground also went to its village for the night. It was necessary to go for protection on one hand, and offense or defense on the other. And always, for the convenience of the chieftain as well as of his subjects, all was closed in around him. Man, the animal, has always sought safety first. As a man, he continually seeks permanence. As an animal he wishes to endure his life long. As a man he has invented immortality. Nowhere is this yearning for continuity or permanence so evident as in his architecture. Perhaps architecture is man's most obvious realization of this persistent dream he calls immortality.

Animal instinct has reached upward and found a higher satisfaction.

These various clusters of buildings grew from tribal villages into towns, from towns to cities, and from lesser to greater cities until a few cities had something of the might and character of great individual building. Sometimes a city became as various in its parts as any building, and similar in greatness.

But usually the city was an accretion not planned beyond the placing of a few features. These features probably were not designedly placed. The city happened much as any crowd will gather about centers of interest wherever the centers of interest happen to be. Sometimes a circumstance of transport or historical consideration changed this center.

And, usually, there was a difference in degree only between the village, town, and great city. The one often grew into the other so that original spacing suitable to the village became a serious fault in the subsequent city. Populous crowding took what places it could find. It often took them by force of circumstance. Real freedom of human life in such circumstances soon became a farce.

In early times cities and towns were surrounded by fortified walls because cities and towns were forts. When might made right, the chieftain, the baron, the pirate and the bandit throve. Often the most successful robber became baron, sometimes monarch. The ruffian could rule in feudal times and often did rule, as he often rules in our own time.

The "divine right of kings" was a relatively modern improvement. It was an assumption that wore itself out by attrition. But meantime, by way of baron and monarch, we see architecture more and more undertaken as the great emprize of the rich and powerful rather than a service to the genius of a whole people or as the expression of race. Architecture became self-conscious. It began to be pretentious, affected and petty. Oftentimes as the robber chieftain became the baron and baron became monarch, the desire to build became vainglorious.

42

It far outran necessity. All the great buildings thus built—many palaces and tombs, even churches, baths, theaters, and stadiums—were built as monuments to the powerful individuals under whose patronage they were erected. But conquering races were always coming down from the north as potentate rose against potentate. While baron contended with baron, neighboring cities were razed or enslaved by vandals, as they were called. This vandalism put new vandals into the places of weaker, older vandals. They called the weaker ones vassals. This is reflected in what remains of the architecture of periods when conquering mainly consisted in tearing down whatever the enemy might have built up. The more laborious and painstaking the building up had been, the more satisfactory was the pulling down.

In time, by way of the popular desperation caused by kingly discord and the baronial jealousies that employed men more for destruction than construction, government gradually became republican in form until in our day the people have subscribed to the idea of democratic government. This shows, at least, that the ultimate rise and progress of the whole people towards self-determination was proceeding, if slowly, through the human wreckage that we are viewing as ancient architecture. And however far away a satisfactory result may be, or however difficult it may be to imagine an indigenous architecture as its own expression, this struggle to rise does still go on among the peoples of the world. It is a seething in the mass. This, too, has affected the spirit that we call architecture. It is about to appear in new and more harmonious ways of building. Because they are more direct and natural, we are learning to call the new ways of building "organic." But to use the term in its biological sense only would be to miss its significance. The word organic should signify architecture as living "entity" and "entity" as individuality.

Let us now go nearer to the grand wreckage left by this tremendous energy poured forth by man in quest of his ideal, these various ruined cities and buildings built by the various races to survive the race. Let us go nearer to see how and why different races built the different buildings and what essential difference the buildings recorded.

Whether yellow, red, black, or white race took precedence in the buildings that followed down the ages is not known. We have many authorities ready in this respect to cancel each other. History, necessarily post mortem, must be some kind of internal evidence discerned within what remains of the building itself. Remains of each separate race have for the most part totally disappeared. Some subsist merely as cuneiform writing on stone or as porcelain tablets. So conjecture has wide limits within which to thrive. But architecture appears, more and more with every fresh discovery, to have had common origin in the civilizations of the past. It seems now to be on the way out rather than on the way in.

In the evolution of the kind of building that we may call architecture, such primitive civilizations as remain have a high place. We may not neglect the contributions from the South Sea Islanders, from far south to the north, or of the Pacific savages who already made their implements look and feel stronger as utensils through the decoration they put upon them. The old Persian, the Dorian, and Ionic, and the old Byzantine all are architectures of vast importance. Their origins are lost to view. And all are tributary in our view of architecture. They proceed from one common human stock. But we begin with those great architectures in view from about 1000 B.C. to 1300 A.D. This is a period of time in which the greatest buildings of the world, traces of which are still visible to us, arose out of the soul and the soil of civilization. Civilizations are original cultural impulses whether they converge on some downward road or not.

Uncertain scholarship places the Mayan civilization centuries later than the height of Egyptian civilization. It was, say, 600 B.C., Germans and others dissenting. However that may be, Mayan and Egyptian both have more in common where elemental greatness is concerned than other cultures, unless we include the great work of the To, Cho, and Han periods of Chinese culture. These we may also place from 600 B.C. to 600 A.D. And as we have seen, architecture was in point of style relative to all that was used in it or in relation to it, that is to say, utensils, clothes, ornaments, arts, literature, life itself. All, manifestly, were of a family. They served a common purpose converging to a common end.

The Egyptian of that period was already more sophisticated than either early Mayan or early Chinese, and so might well have arisen at an earlier period in human development than either. Or, if primitive character is the more ancient, then the Mayan might be the elder. In Maya we see a grand simplicity of concept and form. Probably it is greater elemental architecture than anything remaining on record anywhere else. Next would come the early Chinese, especially their stone and bronze sculptures. In both Mayan and Chinese there was an assertion of form that could only have proceeded from the purest kinship to elemental nature and from nature forms of the materials used by both. Egyptian architecture, pyramid and obelisk excepted (they probably belong to an earlier period), had a sensuous smoothness and comparative elegance inspired by the sensuous human figure. Egyptian architecture was a noble kind of stone *flesh*. In the Egyptian dance, as contrasted with the Greek form of the dance, you may see this verified. The background of the architecture, the Egyptian landscape, was the sweeping simplicity of deserts relieved by greenery of the oasis. By his industry in the agrarian arts the Egyptian grew. He was astrological. He was a God-maker through myth. Egyptian individuality seems rounded. Its reward seems completely recorded by architecture. It is the most sophisticated of survivals from ancient origins.

But the Mayan lived amidst rugged rock formations. He contended with a vast jungle-like growth in which the serpent was a formidable figure. The Mayan grew by war. He was a great ritualist. He was a God-maker through force. Flesh lives in his architecture only as gigantic power. Grasp the simple force of the level grandeur of the primal Mayan sense of form and the Mayan enrichment of it. Grasp the cruel power of his crude Gods (to objectify one, a sculptured granite boulder might suffice), then relate that to the extended plateaux his terraces made and to the mighty scale of his horizontal stone constructions. You will have in these trabeations the sense of might in stone. Even a Mayan "decoration" was mighty. It was mostly stone built.

Yet, both Egyptian and Mayan races seem children of a common

45

motherland. With a broad grasp compare the might and repose of the Mayan outlines with the primitive Egyptian form in its almost human undulations; so rounded and plastic is the Egyptian architecture against the endless levels of the undulating sands surrounding it that it is the pagan song in an architecture of human profiles cut in stone. Though it is modeled in stone like the human nude, it finds great and similar repose in the ultimate mass.

Then compare both Mayan and Egyptian architecture with primal Chinese nature-worship as seen in the outlines of early Chinese forms. They are influences, no doubt, coming in from the mysterious Pacific. A sense of materials is there. It is seeking qualities. It is form qualified always by the profound sense of depth in the chosen substance and in the working of it. You will then see that what the early Chinese made was not so much made to be looked at as it was made to be looked into. In whatever the Chinese made there was profundity of feeling that gave a perfect kinship to the beauty of the natural world as it lived about man, and that was China. It is an architecture wherein flesh as flesh lives not at all. The early art work of China is ethereal. And yet altogether these architectures seem to acknowledge kinship to each other, whether Mayan, Egyptian, Dorian or Chinese.

Early stone buildings—perhaps earlier than Egyptian or Greek—in the hands of the Byzantines became buildings quite different from Incan, Egyptian, or Chinese stone buildings. The arch was Byzantine and is a sophisticated building act resulting in more sophisticated forms than the lintel of the Mayan, Egyptian or Greek. Yet it is essentially primitive masonry. Byzantine architecture lived anew by the arch. The arch sprung from the caps of stone posts and found its way into roofing by way of the low, heavy, stone dome. Its haunches were well down within heavy walls. It was a flat crown showing above the stone masses punctured below by arches. St. Sophia is a later example. The stone walls of Byzantium often became a heavy mosaic of colored stone. The interiors above, roundabout and below, were encrusted with mosaics of gold, glazed pottery and colored glass. The Byzantines carved stone much in exfoliate forms, but the forms preserved the sense of stone mass in whatever they carved. Heavy wooden beams, painted or carved, rested on carved bolsters of stone or were set into the walls. Roof surfaces were covered with crude tiles. The effect of the whole was robust nature. It was worship by way of heavy material, masterful construction and much color.

The Romanesque proceeded from the Byzantine. And among the many other influences today our own country—so long degenerate where architecture is concerned—in the work of one of its greater architects, Henry Hobson Richardson, shows Romanesque influence.

St. Sophia is probably the greatest remaining, but a late example, of the architecture of Byzantium. In point of scale, at least, it is so. The Byzantine sense of form seems neither East nor West but belongs to both. It is obviously traditional architecture, the origins of which are lost in antiquity. Eventually becoming Christian, the Byzantine building was more nobly stone than any Gothic architecture. It was no less truly stone, though less spiritually so, than Mayan architecture. Into Byzantine buildings went the riches of the East in metals, weaving, images and ritual. Byzantium grew most by merchandising. Notwithstanding the dominance of the merchant class, a robust spirit lived in Byzantine work. It still grappled earth forcefully with simple purpose and complete individuality.

In the domed buildings of Persia we see the Byzantine arch still at work. Their buildings were the work of an enlightened people. Their architecture was probably the pinnacle of the civilizations that proceeded to the valley of the Euphrates and the Tigris from the supposed cradle of the white race. Persian architecture lifted its arches and domes to full height, in full flower, when great medieval Western architecture was beginning to point its arches in stone. The Persian loved masonry. By the most knowing use on record of clay and the kiln he achieved enormous building scale by way of bricks and mortar. He worked out his roof by way of the kiln as a great masonry shell domed and encrusted with extraordinary tile mosaics. He made his brick domes strong by placing their haunches well down into massive brick walls. His masonry dome was erected as an organic part of the whole structure.

And lifting this sky-arch high, with gently sensuous, swelling sides, he humanized it completely. The Persian liked his dome so much that he turbaned his head, we may imagine, to match it, and robed himself from shoulders to the ground in keeping with the simple walls to carry the patterned enrichment. As ceramic efflorescence it flowed over his buildings, and as weaving and embroidery it overflowed upon his garments and carpets.

The Persian was born, or had become, a true mystic. And because he was a mystic, this particularly developed man of the white race naturally loved blue. He put blue within blue, blue to play again with blues in a delicate rhythmical pattern displaying divine color in all and all over his wall surfaces. He kept his wall surfaces unbroken, extended, and plain, so that he might enrich them with these sunlit inlays of his spirit evident in glazed colored pottery tile. His jars, less elegant than the Greek, were shapely and large and blue as no blue—not even Ming blue—has ever been blue. His personal adornments and ornaments were blue and gold. Subtle in rhythm and color, indelible in all, were rhythms as varied as those of the flowers themselves. Under his thought, walls became sunlit gardens of poetic thought expressed as geometric forms loving pure color. So also were the woven carpets under his feet with which he covered the red and blue mosaics of his floors.

And then the Persian surrounded his buildings by avenues of cypress trees and acres of living flower gardens. He mirrored his domes and minarets in great, placid, rectangular adjacent pools of fresh water coming flush with the ground and rimmed from the gardens by a narrow rib of stone.

Yes, the Persian liked his domed buildings so well that he not only dressed his head likewise but was continually making out of brass or silver or gold or enamel, similar buildings, in miniature, and he domed them too. Filling their basements with oil he would hang these little buildings by hundreds inside his buildings as lamps to softly light the glowing spaciousness of his wonderfully dignified interiors. His sense of scale was lofty, and he preserved it by never exaggerating the scale of his exquisite details. So these edifices stood out upon the plains, blue-domed against the sky among the rank and file of Persian cities as complete in themselves as the cypress trees around them were complete.

No ruffian ever ruled the Persians, but one did conquer them. His name was Alexander.

In the works of this imaginative race, sensitive to inner rhythms, superlative craftsmanship by way of the greatest scientific masonry the world has ever seen is yet to be found in the remains of the period ending about the eleventh and thirteenth centuries. The workman was the potential artist. He was not yet the time-bound slave of a wage system. And the architect was grandly and usefully a poet.

The *quality* of a man's work was then still his honor. These noble buildings were made of and made for well-made bodies, tall of stature, fine minds. Black heads and deep dark eyes were the perfect complement for this poetic sense of building and the garden, and of blue. So the Persian of old made his God of Beauty and passionately dreamed his life away godward.

What a romantic of the race was this Persian, what mystic romance this Persia! Aladdin with the wonderful lamp? The wonderful lamp was Persian imagination.

In these creations of Persian life the upward growth of imaginative philosophic building had come far toward us, far beyond primitive walls and roofs of mankind. It came probably as far as it was ever to come with the exterior sense of form. Yet it was much more developed than the pagan sense of mass which preceded it.

The opulent Arabian wandered, striking his splendid, gorgeous tents to roam elsewhere. He learned much from the Persian; the Hindu, learning from the same origins, was himself seemingly more involved. He raised his complex but less spiritual temples to his God in the manifold tiers and terraces and domes of masonry or copper or gold. They even rivaled the Persian in exuberance but seemed to lack the pure and simple synthesis of form and clear pattern and color achieved by the Persian. This architecture traveled South and East, by way of its genius, Buddha. It influenced China, Java, Bhutan, and Thibet.

The Hindu carved and grooved, fluted his groovings with moldings. Then he loaded his architecture with images where the Persian held his surfaces true, as he inlaid them with precious materials to give them sun-glory as strong walls. But a Persian building sang in sunshine as the nightingale sings in shadow.

Perhaps Persian architecture was the end of a quality of the spirit, a feeling for the abstract as form in architecture. Probably it was gradually lost, never to be surpassed unless the ideal of architecture as organic now reaches logical but passionate expression in years to come. These simple masses of noble mind and the exquisite tracery of fine human sensibilities remain in our grand vista to remind us of this phase of human architecture, called Persian. It is the natural dome among the more self-conscious roofs of the world of architecture.

Somber, forest-abstract made in stone, the architecture we call Gothic is much nearer to us and has taken to itself a long course of time in which to die. To the development of architecture in "Le Moyen Age" came stone embodying all earlier wood forms of architecture. The wood forms became more and more implicate and complicated as Gothic masonry perfected its science.

Stone craft as organic structure rose to its highest level. In the beautiful cathedral constructions of the Gothic builders, the "Gothic" of the Teuton, the Frank, the Gaul, the Anglo-Saxon, not only did the architect decorate construction but he constructed decoration. Some of this was not integral to structure. No stone arris was left unmolded. Stone itself had now blossomed into at least an affair of human skill, usually into a thing of the human spirit. The "Gothic" cathedral seems an expiring wave of creative impulse seizing humanity by way of stone. The noble material, becoming mutable as the sea, rose into lines of surge, peaks of foam that were all human symbols. In it images of organic life were caught and held in cosmic urge. It was the final movement in the great song of stone as in ages past we see man singing it in architecture. The human spirit, as organic or living entity, seems here to have triumphed over organic matter.

But this great architecture grew by feudal strength. The spirit called Gothic at this time pervaded the baron, the merchant, the guild, the peasant. In a religious age Mariolatry, the devil and hell became articulate in architecture, a dream of heaven. Flesh remained the rough, salty romance of the people. The merchant rapidly grew in power.

In all these great periods of human history the buildings themselves, in point of style, were related to everything put into them for human use or for beauty. They were related to anything else that was in any way related to them, even clothes and ornaments, the way of wearing them and of wearing the hair, the grooming of eyebrows, even making up the face. We may reasonably see these architectures altogether as having common origin, all flowing in the same direction. The features of all are truly the features of humankind. Human nature is their nature and human limitation their limitation. For, not only were ancient popular customs in perfect harmony with ancient buildings, utensils, and ornaments, but even human personal manners were affected likewise by environment and affected or reflected environment. Better to say that environment and architecture were one with nature in the life of the people at the time, whenever and wherever it existed as architecture.

This is the great fact in this great human-scape called architecture: architecture is simply a higher type and expression of nature by way of human nature where human beings are concerned. The spirit of man enters into all, making of the whole a God-like reflection of himself as creator.

In all buildings that man has built out of earth and upon the earth, his spirit, the pattern of him, rose great or small. It lived in his buildings. It still shows there. But common to all these workmanlike endeavors in buildings great or small, another spirit lived. Let us call this spirit, common to all buildings, the great spirit, architecture. Today we look back upon the endless succession of ruins that are no more than the geological deposits washed into shore formation by the sea, landscape formed by the cosmic elements. These ancient buildings were similarly formed by the human spirit. It is the spirit elemental of architecture. The buildings are now dead to uses of present-day activity. They were sculptured by the spirit of architecture in passing, as inert shapes of the shore were sculptured by cosmic forces. Any building is a by-product of eternal living force, a spiritual force taking forms in time and place appropriate to man. They constitute a record to be interpreted, no letter to be imitated.

We carelessly call these ancient aggregations "architecture." Looking back upon this enormous deposit to man's credit, and keeping in mind that just as man was in his own time and place so was his building in its time and place, we must remember that architecture is not these buildings in themselves but far greater. We must believe architecture to be the living spirit that made buildings what they were. It is a spirit by and for man, a spirit of time and place. And we must perceive architecture, if we are to understand it at all, to be a spirit of the spirit of man that will live as long as man lives. It begins always at the beginning. It continues to bestrew the years with forms destined to change and to be strange to men yet to come.

We are viewing this valid record of the inspired work of the red men, yellow men, black men or white men of the human race in perspective outline. What we see is a vast human expression having a common ground of origin. It is more a part of man himself than the turtle's shell is part of the turtle. A great mass of matter has been eroded by man's spirit. These buildings were wrested by his tireless energy from the earth and erected in the eye of the sun. It was originally the conscious creation, out of man himself, of a higher self. His building, in order to be architecture, was the true spirit of himself made manifest (objective) whereas the turtle had no freedom of choice or any spirit at all in the making of his shell.

Considering this, we may now see wherein architecture is to be distinguished from mere building. Mere building may not know "spirit" at all. And it is well to say that the spirit of the thing is the essential life of that thing because it is truth. Such, in the retrospect, is the only life of architecture.

Architecture is abstract. Abstract form is the pattern of the essential. It is, we may see, spirit in objectified forms. Strictly speaking, abstraction has no reality except as it is embodied in materials. Realization of form is always geometrical. That is to say, it is mathematic. We call it pattern. Geometry is the obvious framework upon which nature works to keep her scale in "designing." She relates things to each other and to the whole, while meantime she gives to your eye most subtle, mysterious and apparently spontaneous irregularity in effects. So, it is through the embodied abstract that any true architect, or any true artist, must work to put his inspiration into ideas of form in the realm of created things. To arrive at expressive "form" he, too, must work from within, with the geometry of mathematic pattern. But he so works only as the rug maker weaves the pattern of his rug upon the warp. Music, too, is mathematic. But the mathematician cannot make music for the same reason that no mere builder can make architecture. Music is woven with art, upon this warp that is mathematics. So architecture is woven with a super-sense of building upon this warp that is the science of building. It also is mathematical. But no study of the mathematic can affect it greatly. In architecture, as in life, to separate spirit and matter is to destroy both.

Yet, all architecture must be some formulation of materials in some actually significant pattern. Building is itself only architecture when it is essential pattern significant of purpose.

We may look back now upon the character of the great works of man called architecture and see how, by way of instinctive abstraction, the hut of the African sometimes became in the sun very tree-like or flower-like or much like the more notable animal forms or hill-shapes round about it; how the cliff dwellers raised the clay up from under their feet into great square vessels for the sun to bake; and how they put smaller vessels into them, fire-baked into admirable shapes, for daily use or for fire-worship; how their vessels were marked by imaginative patterns, and how meanwhile they were making small human images to go into them or go along with them. We have seen how the Incas carried along earlier traditions, extending back to lost civilizations, and completed the rock strata of their region by noble structures of stone adorned by crude stone human images, and how they put stone and metal and pottery into them all and shaped them for use. Both buildings and their contents were enriched by adornment. They may be the record of greater, more ancient civilizations from which they were themselves only migrations.

We have seen how the Byzantines lifted stone up into the arch and then on up into the dome, asking their materials, even so, to be no better or worse than they were. We have seen how the Egyptians, another migration, worked stone ledges into buildings, and buildings into stone ledges; how they knew metals, pottery and weaving and adorned their buildings with the human image by way of painting and sculpture. Upon their walls, those pages of stone, were their hieroglyphics. But their buildings were in themselves hieroglyphs of truths coming to them from some ancient source of origin that seems common to all. This feeling seeps through all ancient architecture to us of the present day.

And we see how the later Greeks consciously evolved flower shapes in stone, but worked stone also as wood. After the Dorians and Ionians they seemed to have less sense of materials than other peoples. But the Greeks developed painting far and sculpture still further and put the building into the vase, as into the building they put the vase and the manuscript. The vase was the result of their search for the elegant solution, their supreme contribution to culture.

We have seen how the Persians came from similar distant origins, how they blue-domed their buildings under the canopy of blue and emblazoned them with blue and purple ceramic flower gardens, making their buildings flower gardens within flower gardens, and put into them illuminated enamels, pottery and weaving. They omitted human images except when illustrating their books.

We have seen how, more recently, the cathedral builders put the somber uprising forest into stone, until stone triumphant could endure no more and began to fall. But meantime they had been weaving into their stone forest great glass paintings and wood carvings, and finishing them with pictured woolen and linen textiles, painted wood and stone images, great music, stately ritual and many books.

We have seen how the pagoda of the Orientals grew to resemble the fir trees, and how their shrines harmonized with the pines around them, and how within their buildings was a wealth of nature-worship in gold and painting and sculpture. Writing and myriad crafts were at home among them, and these buildings too were loaded with images.

And now, finally, we may see how all this was man's sense of himself: how it all came to be by the simple way of human use and purpose, but how also, in all ages and all races, it was man's greatest work wherein his five senses were all employed and enjoyed. By way of eye, ear, and finger, by tongue and even by nostril he was creating out of himself greater delights for a super-self, finding deep satisfactions far beyond those he could ever know were he merely a good animal.

But we are compelled to see, looking back upon this vast homogeneous human record, that the human race built most nobly when limitations were greatest and, therefore, when most was required of imagination in order to build at all. Limitations seem to have always been the best friends of architecture. The limitation in itself seems to be the artist's best friend in the sum of all the arts, even now. Later, we must see how subjugation, sophistication, easy affluence and increasing facility of intercourse began to get things all mixed up until nothing great in architecture lived any more. All architecture became bastardized. Finally the great arch of the Persian dome was fatuously invited by a "greatest artist" in the name of art to live up in the air. It was tossed against the sky to stand on top of round columns. Unnecessary columns were placed against sturdy walls for mere appearance's sake. Roofs likewise became more ornamental than useful. Wood got to be used like stone, and stone like wood. Pottery began to be used like anything else but seldom used as itself. In short, mere appearance became enough. Integrity was given no thought. Also we are compelled to see how, when greater facilities of machinery came into use in the nineteenth century, the great art of building soon became utterly confused, degraded by mere facilities. The people began putting into their buildings so much piping and wiring, and so many sanitary appliances of every kind, that architecture of the earlier sort may be said to have died. Building had become so easy that architecture became too difficult.

No stream rises higher than its source. Whatever man might build could never express or reflect more than he was. It was not more than what he felt. He could record neither more nor less than he had learned of life when the buildings were built. His inmost thought lives in them. His philosophy, true or false, is there.

Inevitably, certain races were more developed than others. Some were more favorably situated. And we see that the influence in architecture of certain races profoundly or superficially affected other races. An instance: the artificial cornices and necessary columns of the Greeks still shape our public acts in the useless cornices and unnecessary columns of modern architecture "à la mode." Later work of the middle ages, called Gothic, still shapes our modern educational institutions and churches, and the modern homes of opulent tradesmen. They mark our public money-boxes called banks. It may be that the heights of architecture were reached so long ago that the various subsequent styles we now call "classic" and practice regardless, were already degenerate when they occurred.

Throughout this authentic human record, inscribed in the countless buildings erected by man's labor, now fallen or falling back again upon the earth to become again earth, a definite character may be discerned determining man's true relationship to time and place. The sum of man's creative impulses, we find, took substance in architecture as his creative passion rose and fell within it. It always was creative. We have now reached the point in time when such original impulses subside or cease. Inspiration is no more. Go back 500 years and nothing can be found in architecture worthy to be called creation, as architecture has been creative, except as folklore, folkways, folk building.

The last original impulse, called Gothic, has subsided and the "Renaissance," a period of rebirth of original forms that were also "rebirth" when first born, begins. Creative impulses grow dim, are all but lost. Only rebirth is possible to the culture of the period we are now to consider. It is probably an over-cultured period. Apparently, humanity had gone as far with its pagan ideal of architecture as it could go. The hitherto vast, uninspired merchant class has been gradually gaining the upper hand in society and will soon outbid the higher classes for power. It will then proceed to foreclose upon a decayed, uninspired higher class.

56

The handmaidens of architecture—music, painting, sculpture--during these 500 years are going on their way. Music, young, healthy, is growing up independently into Mozart, Bach and Beethoven. Painting based upon the work of Giotto and the early Italians begins to set up in this world of the "Reborn" as an art complete in itself. By way of many schools and phases it is to eventuate into the easel picture or the bogus mural. Sculpture begins the struggle for liberation from architecture that began with Buonarrotti. Undergoing many transformations it ends in realism or in imitation of the primitive. At this period handicraft, still active and essential, is yet to die because men have found an easier way to accomplish the work of the world. Having found it, it is easier now for them to "immortalize" themselves.

From Italian sources, chiefly gathered together at Florence, where degeneration and regeneration of all arts were interlocked, Italian revivals of ancient Graeco-Roman architecture begin to reach the various European capitals as patterns. By importation or export these patterns are later to be exploited among the various Western nations. Ancient Greek, itself a derivation, becomes the standard of a new "low" in Western culture. The artificial cornice, the column and entablature, become the common refuge of a growing impotence.

Derivations of derivations, commercialized as Georgian "Colonial," or what not, are soon exports (or imports) to the new world, America. Later, all styles of all periods of "rebirth" were exported or imported by the Americans, as the Romans imported them and as the Japanese now import them, to be mingled, soon mangled, by the new machinery of endless reproduction. The saws, lathes, planers of modern mills are soon to strew the empty carcasses of these erstwhile styles far and wide until Queen Anne comes in and all sense goes out.

Where the primitive and splendid sense of structure or building construction was going on down the ages, the reality of all buildings for human occupation was found in the enclosing, supporting walls. But a deeper sense of architecture has come to light. This is due to a new philosophy, to the invention of new machines, and to the discovery of new materials. The new architecture finds reality in the space within the walls to be lived in. The new reality of the building is the interior space which roofs and walls only serve to enclose. This reality was not felt by primitive builders. Nor is it yet known to the pseudo-classic members of our academies today. Slowly dawning as the exterior or pagan sense of building dies, this interior ideal, or inner sense of the building as an organic whole, grows. It grows more consistent, carries more genuine culture with it as it develops: culture indigenous.

In modern building this ideal of structural cause as organic effect is destined to be the center line of man's modern culture. An organic architecture will be the consequence.

Ancient builders went to work "lavishly" upon the walls and roofs themselves as though they were the reality of the building, cutting holes in the walls for light and air. In the name of art they made such holes ornamental by putting molded caps over them, or by putting up unnecessary columns beside them, or by working needless moldings and insignificant ornament into or onto the walls. They built cornices. They surrounded all openings with more moldings to heal the breaches that had to be made in the walls to let in light and air, and to get in and out of. An architect worked with his building, then, much as a sculptor would work with his solid mass of clay. He strove to mold and enrich the mass. He tried to give to it some style that he had learned or happened to like. Exterior modeling and featuring thus became, by adoption, the so-called western academic concept of architecture. This academic—"classic"—concept was chiefly based upon Greek and Roman buildings. But meantime the Chinese, Japanese, Persians and the Moors, Orientals all, developed a somewhat different sense of building. Their sense of the building was also the mass of solid matter sculptured from the outside, but the Oriental sense of the building was more plastic, therefore more a thing of the spirit.

Being "plastic," the building was treated more consistently as a unit or consistent whole. It was less an aggregation of many features and parts, all remaining separate features, by, and for, themselves. In organic building nothing is complete in itself but is only complete as the part is merged into the larger expression of the whole. Something of this had begun to find its way into many Oriental buildings.

During these later periods of various "renaissances," even the Pope's authority at Rome, the religious capital, has been rivaled by the authority of the Italian artist and workman, as the Italian Renaissance grew upon Europe. And so the remarkable Italian city of Florence grew to be the artist capital if not the cultural capital of a world.

But it became the artist capital of a western world that could only buy or sell. Already it was prostitute to imitation. It was a world prostitute to imitation because, with the exception of music and painting, and always excepting the newly born literature, society was unable to distinguish between birth and rebirth. It was unable to create anything much above the level of technique, scientific process or mechanical invention. The new world was learning to buy and sell its way to whatever it wanted in this matter of culture. By way of commercial reproductions of the styles affected by these European cultures society gratified such creative aspiration as remained.

Upon this prevalent rising tide that is called "commerce" comes the printed page, "letters," the book. Society becomes consciously literate as the printed book absorbs ever more of the cultural energies of mankind. Upon any large scale this scientific art of printing was the first application of the machine to human affairs. It is the machine that brings the book to humanity. And men, by means of the book, grew more literal. Life itself became and continues to grow more and more vicarious.

Human nature always seeks an easier way to do its work, or seeks a substitute. Human effort finds this "easiest way," or a substitute. The nineteenth century, especially, found both in machine development. As a consequence of this easy release all life, therefore all architecture, became less and less from within until society became content that art be something purchasable, something to be applied. The tendency of art in such circumstances is to become uncreative. It appears as some perverted form of literature or at least as no more than something literal. Realistic is the word. Machine power increased the deluge of literature and ready-made European "objets d'art." A newly literalized humanity becomes obvious to commerce as the new facility for exploitation. Yes, "realistic" is the proper word for the art work of the period. It was really no great art at all. Photography could take over the popular "art interest" of the period. It proceeded to do so.

Yet, the machine is to make opportunity new. The science of printing is to make the book a medium for human expression more facile than building and the book is to become a means of recording life perhaps more enduring than the great edifice ever was.

But, meantime, the printed word accelerates. An increasingly vicarious life and servile art is becoming universal in the western world. Foregathering to listen, to stand, to watch, or to ride is now sufficient. Fifty thousand people watch a football game. Ninety thousand watch a prize fight. A remittance man sits at the steering wheel of a hundred and twenty-five horse-power car, with the airs, and sensation, too, that the power is his own—is, in fact, him. Connection with the soil is giving way to machinery. Contacts between men are increasingly had by electrical devices. Intercommunication becomes instantaneous and far reaching, but actual human contacts become fewer and more feeble. Superficial release is provided by literature, now ubiquitous, and new ways and means to beat work are found. Culture as architecture and architecture as culture is on the way down and out. Structure no longer finds beauty by way of integral evolution. Nor does society think to ask for such.

The place where this great integrity was wont to be is fast becoming an empty place.

The machine can exploit externality. But as we have set it up the machine can do nothing nor let much be done from within. The machine reduces and reproduces such forms of old-fashioned representation in art as are most salable. Those most salable are naturally those most realistic or superficially elegant. Grandomania flourishes in consequence. Architecture as something ready-made is in the hand of the highly specialized and speculative salesman. Characteristic of this show-window period, architecture can only be a thing of mixed origins and haphazard applications. We may see it around us everywhere. Styles now abound. But nowhere is there genuine style. These are the days of the General Grant Gothic and the Pseudo-Classic. When Michelangelo piled the Pantheon upon the Parthenon and called it

60

St. Peter's, he, a painter, had committed architectural adultery. It was destined to bring forth a characteristic monstrosity, namely, an arch set up into plain air on posts to shift for itself. It is an imitative anachronism that characterizes our public acts, as illustrated by our capitols, court houses, and town halls. A noble thing, the Persian dome has become ignoble. Now it is base. The same depravity sees a Greek temple as fitting memorial to Abraham Lincoln. He is the Greek antithesis. Nothing is Greek about his life or work or thought. A Gothicized French Chateau, incongruous pattern, is the unsuitable stall for some urban fire engine. Any Roman bath or sarcophagus will do to lend prestige to the sacrosanct bank on any town sidewalk anywhere. A Gothicized cathedral is set up at Yale to throw a glamour over college athletics. Another may serve to memorialize the grandmother of a successful speculator. All serve, unchallenged, this commercialized assumption or provincial gesture that the period calls culture.

In short, in this present time only the bastard survives even as a temple for the work of the Supreme Court of the United States. Stale survivals of every sort are "modern." Business turns to help itself liberally to "the classic." The "classic" goes to market as diamonds go.

Art and religion, in this inversion of human circumstances, lose prestige. Both these resources of the human spirit become purchasable and, as a natural consequence, life itself becomes purchasable. Meantime, science, far more useful to trade than either art or religion, grows in dominion. Neither art nor religion is longer a necessity to the people. The people have sought a replica. They have found and bought a substitute. The merchant has become the ruler for the time being of man's singing, dancing, dwelling and breeding. And the creative individual in the arts must become pauper, at a time when a Joseph Duveen is a knight, Andy Mellon a prince, and a Rockefeller, king.

In the preceding era, men of Florence were the guiding spirits and the light on the horizon, such as that light was. So, now in the twentieth century, social, economic, and artistic forms are determined by outward rather than by inner factors. Today the "civilized" world has come to the consequences of "renaissance." It has tried to live on a decadent precedent. Architecture and its kindred, as a matter of course, are divorced from nature in order to make of art the merchantable thing of texts, classroom armchairs and, above all, of speculative "price," that it now is. It is a speculative commodity.

The artist, now no more than the designing partner, the official streamliner, the interior decorator, the industrial designer, is entirely outside. Nothing could be more external than an interior decorator. Nothing could be more irrelevant than the exterior architect. Nothing could be more remote from life at the moment than citizens content to live in what either of them produces. Perspective is in reverse. The cart is before the horse.

A new type of patron of the arts has grown up out of this perversity. He is a Frick, a Widener, a Morgan, a Henry Ford, or a Bendix. Perhaps he is a Hart, Shaffner and Marx or Metro-Goldwyn-Mayer. He is, and he must be, some success in speculation upon some grand scale. Not for nothing was Joseph Duveen a knight.

By money power democracy has been perverted to inverted aristocracy. The new world has made social parasitism and vulgarity academic. What by nature can only be grown, may by such modern improvements be mere artifice freely bought to change hands at a price. Life itself must now be standardized because it is to be prefabricated, show-windowed, and eventually sold. Yes, and sold even now.

Trade and machine production are having their way and their say in the standardizations of our day. How can the young escape? As for the architect, who consents to buy and sell indulgences for his people, indulgences unwittingly provided by the traffic in foreign cultures to which he himself helped educate them: with him standardization has had its way too. Unwittingly, the Cass Gilberts, Ray Hoods, Corbetts and Walkers, the McGonigles and Popes carry on the work of the McKim, Mead and Whites, the D. H. Burnhams, Richard M. Hunts and the Henry Hardenbergs. They are merely useful tools of this devastating power.

The great and liberal arts that man nourished because they nourished him have gone. They have gone by this same route to the mill which is this remorseless standardization for profit. And the tide of literal representation by way of the press, radio and cinema, all rapacious maws for more fodder of the sort, rises unsteadily to new monopolies.

At this moment, any ideal at all organic in character becomes impractical if not slightly absurd: shopkeepers all. All in all are ruled by the expedient.

Only petty specialists in architecture and the sister arts are needed on the job made by our order of "business." Its wholly artificial power must be maintained upon an artificial basis. It is engendered and kept by indiscriminate use of indiscriminate increment. The whole man can no longer be used. He too is a "job"

Let us frankly admit it:

The universal modern "art" is really salesmanship.

Showmanship is perihelion. Everywhere, it is at a premium.

The show-window is the most important form of all artistry in these United States. Let it stand for the symbol of this era.

The mother of the arts, architecture, in such circumstances could have little or no issue. Neither impregnation nor conception upon any social scale is possible. And a restless movement begins the world over. Action is inevitable. It has now begun because, long ago, it was time.

In this human restlessness the new order of culture, structure to emerge as "organic," lies concealed as the child in the womb. Meanwhile, cultural decay of the individual proceeds by way of the commercialized mass-education we have learned to call academic.

Has this modern restlessness anything to turn to? Has it recourse? Yes. Organic architecture with its sense of structure, the sense of the whole, is one great recourse. Religion might be another. These two, now as always.

We have been describing what has happened to art. What, then, has happened to religion so far as it relates to art?

Religion, in its present form, is become "Christianity," the church. The church was the last great client of architecture. The last great urge of human creative energy, upward thrust of human creative power, flowered into stone as it built the great cathedrals. The church was Christianity. What of Christianity, now, as it passes for religion in this general confusion and debauchery of the creative powers of mankind? Neither the teaching nor character of Christianity was such as to inspire the nature-worship of the creative mind.

Christianity took the church to man as a substitute for that law and order of the universe which should have been worked out by him from within himself, law and order made his own by way of the arts. But, as Christianity had it, the man was to be saved by his beliefs, not saved by his works. So, the church substituted beatitudes for beauty. Spiritually the man was invited to become a parasite upon the Lord. That quality in the man that stood tall inside him up against the roof of his mind, which must ever be his true self, can no longer be much encouraged even by the church.

And the ideals of Jesus, the gentle anarchist, remain generally feared because generally misunderstood or yet unknown.

This failure to see God and man as one has disaffected all art for it has betrayed architecture. There is no longer general realization of matter and spirit as the same thing. This is a fatal division of the house against itself. A great wave of ugliness has followed in the wake of this error. Bogus sanctuaries to God stand propped against the sky by steel, as though it were necessary to prove to some court of last resort that the final period of creative impulse on earth is dying of imitation or already dead by mutilation.

With Christianity for tenant today, architecture is a parasite, content with an imitation of an imitation like the spurious St. John the Divine in New York City. To go along with the imported cathedral are such inversions as the Lincoln Memorial, such aberrations as our capitols, such morgues as our museums, monuments, and such grandomania as our city halls. Abortions of sentiment, like the "Great White Whale" at Princeton, a Rockefeller cathedral on Riverside Drive are proof enough that the spirit of architecture has fled from a social era. Corpses encumber the ground. As for religion or art, a pig may live in a palace: any cat can scratch the face of a king.

Upon this, the American scene, emerges the new ideal-structure as organic architecture becomes interpretation of life itself. From within outward is no longer remote ideal. It is everywhere becoming action. With new integrity action insists upon indigenous culture. The new reality.

64

FIRST UNITARIAN CHURCH, INTERIOR, MADISON, WISCONSIN

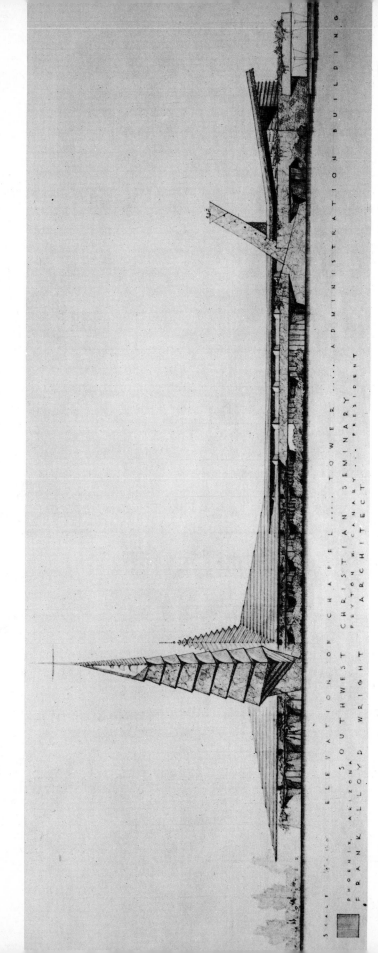

SOUTHWEST CHRISTIAN SEMINARY, ELEVATION, PHOENIX, ARIZONA

MODERN ARCHITECTURE

1: MACHINERY, MATERIALS AND MEN

AN ARCHITECTURE for these United States will be born "modern," as were all the architectures of the peoples of all the world. Perhaps this is the deep-seated reason why the young man in architecture grieves his parents, academic and familiar, by yielding to the fascination of creation, instead of persisting as the creature of ancient circumstance. This, his rational surrender to instinct, is known, I believe, as "rebellion."

I am here to aid and comfort rebellion insofar as rebellion has this honorable instinct—even though purpose may not yet be clearly defined—nor any fruits, but only ists, isms or istics be in sight. Certainly we may now see the dawning of a deeper insight than has for the past thirty years characterized so-called American architecture. In that length of time American architecture has been neither American nor architecture. We have had instead merely a bad form of surface-decoration.

This "dawn" is the essential concern of this moment and the occasion for this series of "lectures." We, here at Princeton, are to guard this dawning insight and help to guide its courage, passion and patience into channels where depth and flow is adequate, instead of allowing youthful adventure to ground in shallows all there beneath the surface in the offing, ready to hinder and betray native progress.

In this effort I suppose I am to suffer disadvantage, being more accustomed to saying things with a hod of mortar and some bricks, or with a concrete mixer and a gang of workmen, than by speaking or writing. I like to write, but always dissatisfied, I, too, find myself often staring at the result with a kind of nausea . . . or is it nostalgia?

I dislike to lecture, feeling something like the rage of impotence. With a small audience hovering over my drawing-board, there would be better feeling on my part and a better chance for the audience. But a lecturer may, in fact must, make his own diversion, indulge his "malice" as he goes along, or get no entertainment at all out of the matter.

So here at my hand I have some gently malicious pamphlets or leaflets issued, as myth has it, by that mythical group to which careless reference is sometimes made, by the thoughtless, as the "New School of the Middle West." From these rare, heretical pamphlets, from time to time as I may have occasion, I shall quote. Among them are such titles as: "Palladio turns in his grave and speaks," another, "Groans from Phidias": the author's original title—it would be beside our mark to mention it—was suppressed by the group as just that much too much. One solitary "New School" scholar, himself having, under painful economic pressure, degenerated to the practice of mere architectural surgery—blaming Vitruvius for his degradation—wrote bitterly and much under the title of "Vitruviolic Disorders."

A number of these leaflets are given over by several and sundry of the "New School" to the ravages of the "Vignola"—an academic epidemic showing itself as a creeping paralysis of the emotional nature—creeping by way of the optic nerve.

During the course of our afternoons, from among these modestly profane references we may have occasion to hear from a rudely awakened Bramante, an indignant Sansovino, a gently aggrieved Brunelleschi, perhaps even from robustious "Duomo" Buonarrotti himself, all, plucked even of their shouds, frowning up from their graves on their pretentious despoilers . . . our own American classicists. These time-honored Italians in these wayward and flippant leaflets, are made to speak by way of a sort of motor-car Vasari. His name deserves to be lost—and as certainly will be.

Unfortunately and sad to say, because their names and individualities are unknown to us, so close were they, as men, to the soil or to man—we shall be unable to hear from the ancient builders of "Le Moyen Age," those dreamers in cloisters, guild-masters, gardeners, worshipers of the tree, or the noble stone-craftsmen of still earlier Byzantium, who were much like the cathedral builders in spirit. No—we shall hear from them only as we, ourselves, are likewise dreamers, gardeners, or worshipers of the tree and by sympathetic nature, therefore, well qualified to understand the silence of these white men. And those human nature-cultures of the red man, lost in backward stretch of time, almost beyond our horizon—the Maya, the Indian—and of the black man, the African—we may learn from them. Last, but not least, come the men of bronze, the Chinese, the Japanese—profound builders of the Orient—imaginative demons, their art of earth winging its way to the skies: Dragons with wings—their fitting symbol. Of their art—much. The ethnic eccentricity of their work makes it safe inspiration for the white man, who now needs, it seems, aesthetic fodder that he cannot copy or reproduce. I am not sure but there is more for us in our modern grapple with creation, in their sense of the living thing in Art, than we can find in any other culture. Profundity of feeling the men of bronze could encourage. Their forms we should have to let alone.

In order that we may not foregather here in this dignified atmosphere of Princeton without due reference to authority, we will go far back for our text on this, our first afternoon together. Go so far back that we need fear no contradiction. Go without hesitation, to Rameses the Great, to find that: "All great architecture"—Rameses might have used the hieroglyph for art instead of the one for architecture—"*All great architecture is true to its architects' immediate present,*" and seal it with the regal symbol. And in this connection comes the title of our discourse—the "MACHINERY, MATERIALS AND MEN" of our immediate present.

Long ago—yes, so long ago that the memory of it seems to join with recent echoes from Tut-Ank-Amen's ancient tomb—I passionately swore that the machine was no less, rather more, an artist's tool than any he had ever had or heard of, if only he would do himself the honor to learn to use it. Twenty-seven years old now, the then offensive heresy

70

has been translated and published, I am told, in seven or more foreign languages, English excepted, which means said in seven or more different ways. But just what the seven different ways each exactly mean, I can have no idea. At the time, I knew no better than to make the declaration—it seemed so sensibly obvious in the vast cinderfield in which I then stood—our enormous industrial Middle West.

Today, twenty-seven years later, the heresy is become truism, at least "truistic," therefore sufficiently trite to arouse no hostility even if said in several or even seven different ways. And yet: a Pompeian recently come back and struggling for nourishment on French soil has reiterated one-quarter of the matter, made more stark, with signs of success right here in our own country. The reiteration reaches us across the Atlantic—more machine-made than the erstwhile cry in the cinderfield, but with several important omissions—most important, at least, to us. Or perhaps, who knows, they may not really be omissions but evasions. First among these probable evasions is the nature of materials; second, is that characteristic architectural element, the third dimension; and third, there is integral ornament. This neglected trinity, it seems to me, constitutes the beating heart of the whole matter of architecture so far as art is concerned.

Surface and mass, relatively superficial, however machine-made or however much resembling machinery, are subordinate to this great trinity. Surface and mass are a by-product, or will be when architecture arises out of the matter. If proof is needed we shall find it as we go along together. . . .

Machinery, materials and men—yes—these are the stuffs by means of which the so-called American architect will get his architecture, if there is any such architect and America ever gets any architecture of her own. Only by the strength of his spirit's grasp upon all three—machinery, materials and men—will the architect be able so to build that his work may be worthy the great name "architecture." A great architecture is greatest proof of human greatness.

The difference, to the architect and his fellow artists, between our era and others, lies simply enough in the substitution of automatic machinery for tools, and (more confusing), instead of hereditary aristocracy for patron, the artist now relies upon automatic industrialism, conditioned upon the automatic acquiescence of men, and conditioned not at all upon their individual handicraftsmanship.

At first blush an appalling difference, and the more it is studied, the more important the difference becomes. And were we now to be left without prophet—that is, without interpretation—and should we, among ourselves, be unable to arouse the leadership of supreme human imagination—yes, then we should be at the beginning of the end of all the great qualities we are foregathered here to cherish: namely, the arts which are those great *qualities* in any civilization. This republic has already gone far with very little of any single one of these great *saving* qualities, yet it goes further, faster and safer; eats more, and eats more regularly; goes softer, safer, is more comfortable and egotistic in a more universal mediocrity than ever existed on earth before. But who knows where it is going? In this very connection, among the more flippant references referred to as at hand, there is also heavy matter and I have here serious original matter, saved several years ago from the flames by a miracle. The first pages were blackened and charred by fire, of this original manuscript, first read to a group of professors, artists, architects and manufacturers at Hull House, Chicago. To show you how it all seemed to me, back there, twenty-seven years ago in Chicago, I shall read into the record, once more, from its pages. Should its clumsy earnestness bore you—remember that the young man who wrote, should, in that earlier day, as now, have confined himself to a hod of mortar and some bricks. But passionately he was trying to write—making ready to do battle for the life of the thing he loved. And I would remind you, too, that in consequence he has been engaged in eventually mortal combat ever since.

Here is the manuscript. We will begin, twenty-seven years later, again, at the beginning of—

The Art and Craft of the Machine

No one, I hope, has come here tonight for a sociological prescription for the cure of evils peculiar to this machine age. For I come to you as an architect to say my word for the right use upon such new materials as we have, of our great substitute for tools—machines. There is no thrift in any craft until the tools are mastered; nor will there be a worthy social order in America until the elements by which America does its work are mastered by American society. Nor can there be an art worth the man or the name until these elements are grasped and truthfully idealized in whatever we as a people try to make. Although these elemental truths should be commonplace enough by now, as a people we do not understand them nor do we see the way to apply them. We are probably richer in raw materials for our use as workmen, citizens or artists than any other nation—but outside mechanical genius for mere contrivance we are not good workmen, nor, beyond adventitious or propitious respect for property, are we as good citizens as we should be, nor are we artists at all. We are one and all, consciously or unconsciously, mastered by our fascinating automatic "implements," using them as substitutes for tools. To make this assertion clear I offer you evidence I have found in the field of architecture. It is still a field in which the pulse of the age throbs beneath much shabby finery and one broad enough (God knows) to represent the errors and possibilities common to our time-serving time.

Architects in the past have embodied the spirit common to their own life and to the life of the society in which they lived in the most noble of all noble records—buildings. They wrought these valuable records with the primitive tools at their command and whatever these records have to say to us today would be utterly insignificant if not wholly illegible were tools suited to another and different condition stupidly forced to work upon them; blindly compelled to do work to which they were not fitted, work which they could only spoil.

In this age of steel and steam the tools with which civilization's true record will be written are scientific thoughts made operative in iron and bronze and steel and in the plastic processes which characterize this age, all of which we call machines. The electric lamp is in this sense a machine. New materials in the man-machines have made the physical body of this age what it is as distinguished from former ages. They have made our era the machine age—wherein locomotive engines, engines of industry, engines of light or engines of war or steamships take the place works of art took in previous history. Today we have a scientist or an inventor in place of a Shakespeare or a Dante. Captains of industry are modern substitutes, not only for kings and potentates, but, I am afraid, for great artists as well. And yet—man-made environment is the truest, most characteristic of all human records. Let a man build and you have him. You may not have all he is, but certainly he is what you have. Usually you will have his outline. Though the elements may be in him to enable him to grow out of his present self-made characterization, few men are ever belied by self-made environment. Certainly no historical period was ever so misrepresented. Chicago in its ugliness today becomes as true an expression of the *life* lived here as is any center on earth where men come together closely to live it out or fight it out. Man is a selecting principle, gathering his like to him wherever he goes. The intensifying of his existence by close contact, too, flashes out the human record vividly in his background and his surroundings. But somewhere —somehow—in our age, although signs of the times are not wanting, beauty in this expression is forfeited—the record is illegible when not ignoble. We must walk blindfolded through the streets of this, or any great modern American city, to fail to see that all this magnificent resource of machine-power and superior material has brought to us, so far, is degradation. All of the art forms sacred to the art of old are, by us, prostitute.

On every side we see evidence of inglorious quarrel between things as they were and things as they must be and are. This shame a certain merciful ignorance on our part mistakes for glorious achievement. We believe in our greatness when we have tossed up a Pantheon to the god of money in a night or two, like the Illinois Trust Building or the Chicago National Bank. And it is our glory to get together a mammoth aggregation of Roman monuments, sarcophagi and temples for a post office in a year or two. On Michigan Avenue Montgomery Ward presents us with a nondescript Florentine palace with a grand campanile for a "farmer grocery" and it is as common with us as it is elsewhere to find the giant stone Palladian "orders" overhanging plate glass shop fronts. Show windows beneath Gothic office buildings, the office-middle topped by Parthenons, or models of any old sacrificial temple, are a common sight. Every commercial interest in any American town, in fact, is scurrying for respectability by seeking some advertising connection, at least, with the "classic." A commercial renaissance is here; the renaissance of "the ass in the lion's skin." This much, at least, we owe to the late Columbian Fair—that triumph of modern civilization in 1893 will go down in American architectural history, when it is properly recorded, as a mortgage upon posterity that posterity must repudiate not only as usurious but as forged.

In our so-called "skyscrapers" (latest and most famous business-building triumph), good granite or Bedford stone is cut into the fashion of the Italian followers of Phidias and his Greek slaves. Blocks so cut are cunningly arranged about a structure of steel beams and shafts (which structure secretly robs them of any real meaning), in order to make the finished building resemble the architecture depictured by Palladio and Vitruvius—in the schoolbooks. It is quite as feasible to begin putting on this Italian trimming at the cornice, and come on down to the base as it is to work, as the less fortunate Italians were forced to do, from the base upward. Yes, "from the top down" is often the actual method employed. The keystone of a Roman or Gothic arch may now be "set"—that is to say "hung"—and the voussoirs stuck alongside or "hung" on downward to the haunches. Finally this mask, completed, takes on the features of the pure "classic," or any variety of "renaissance" or whatever catches the fancy or fixes the "convictions" of the designer. Most likely, an education in art has "fixed" both. Our Chicago University, "a seat of learning," is just as far removed from truth. If environment is significant and indicative, what does this highly reactionary, extensive and expensive scene-painting by means of hybrid collegiate Gothic signify? Because of Oxford it seems to be generally accepted as "appropriate for scholastic purposes." Yet, why should an American university in a land of democratic ideals in a machine age be characterized by second-hand adaptation of Gothic forms, themselves adapted previously to our own adoption by a feudalistic age with tools to use and conditions to face totally different from anything we can call our own? The public library is again asinine renaissance, bones sticking through the flesh because the interior was planned by a shrewd library

75

board—while an "art-architect" (the term is Chicago's, not mine) was "hired" to "put the architecture on it." The "classical" aspect of the sham-front must be preserved at any cost to sense. Nine out of ten public buildings in almost any American city are the same.

On Michigan Avenue, too, we pass another pretentious structure, this time fashioned as inculcated by the École des Beaux Arts after the ideals and methods of a Graeco-Roman, inartistic, grandly brutal civilization, a civilization that borrowed everything but its jurisprudence. Its essential tool was the slave. Here at the top of our culture is the Chicago Art Institute, and very like other art institutes. Between lions —realistic—Kemyss would have them so because Barye did—we come beneath some stone millinery into the grandly useless lobby. Here French's noble statue of the republic confronts us—she too, imperial. The grand introduction over, we go further on to find amid plaster casts of antiquity, earnest students patiently gleaning a half-acre or more of archaeological dry-bones, arming here for industrial conquest, in other words to go out and try to make a living by making some valuable impression upon the machine age in which they live. Their fundamental tool in this business about which they will know just this much less than nothing, is—the machine. In this acre or more not one relic has any vital relation to things as they are for these students, except for the blessed circumstance that they are more or less beautiful things in themselves— bodying forth the beauty of "once upon a time." These students at best are to concoct from a study of the aspect of these blind reverences an extract of antiquity suited to modern needs, meanwhile knowing nothing of modern needs, permitted to care nothing for them, and knowing just as little of the needs of the ancients which made the objects they now study. The tyros are taught in the name of John Ruskin and William Morris to shun and despise the essential tool of their age as a matter commercial and antagonistic to art. So in time they go forth, each armed with his little Academic extract, applying it as a sticking-plaster from without, wherever it can be made to stick, many helplessly knowing in their hearts that it should be a development from within—but how? And this is an education in art in these United States.

Climb now the grand monumental stairway to see the results of this cultural effort—we call it "education"—hanging over the walls of the exhibition galleries. You will find there the same empty reverences to the past at cost to the present and of doubtful value to the future, unless a curse is valuable. Here you may see fruits of the lust and pride of the patron-collector but how shamefully little to show by way of encouraging patronage by the artist of his own day and generation. This is a temple of the fine arts. A sacred place! It should be the heart-center, the emotional inspiration of a great national industrial activity, but here we find tradition not as an *inspiring* spirit animating progress. No. Now more in the *past* than ever! No more, now, than an ancient mummy, a dead letter. A "precedent" is a "hang over" to copy, the copy to be copied for machine reproduction, to be shamelessly reproduced until demoralized utterly or unrecognizable.

More unfortunate, however, than all this fiasco, is the fiasco al fresco. The suburban house-parade is more servile still. Any popular avenue or suburb will show the polyglot encampment displaying, on the neatly kept little plots, a theatrical desire on the part of fairly respectable people to live in châteaux, manor houses, Venetian palaces, feudal castles, and Queen Anne cottages. Many with sufficient hardihood abide in abortions of the carpenter-architect, our very own General Grant Gothic perhaps, intended to beat all the "lovely periods" at their own game and succeeding. Look within all this typical monotony-in-variety and see there the machine-made copies of handicraft originals; in fact, unless you, the householder, are fortunate indeed, possessed of extraordinary taste and opportunity, all you possess is in some degree a machine-made example of vitiated handicraft, imitation antique furniture made antique by the machine, itself of all abominations the most abominable. Everything must be curved and carved and carved and turned. The whole mass a tortured sprawl supposed artistic. And the floor-coverings? Probably machine-weavings of oriental rug patterns—pattern and texture mechanically perfect; or worse, your walls are papered with paper-imitations of old tapestry, imitation patterns and imitation textures, stamped or printed by the machine; imitations under foot, imitations overhead and imitations all round about you. You are sunk in "imitation." Your much-molded woodwork is stained "antique." Inevitably you have a white-and-gold "reception-room" with a few gilded chairs, an overwrought piano, and withal, about you a general cheap machine-made "profusion" of—copies of copies of original imitations. To you, proud proprietors—do these things thus degraded mean anything aside from vogue and price? Aside from your sense of quantitative ownership, do you perceive in them some fine fitness in form, line and color to the purposes which they serve? Are the chairs to sit in, the tables to use, the couch comfortable, and are all harmoniously related to each other and to your own life? Do many of the furnishings or any of the window-millinery serve any purpose at all of which you can think? Do you enjoy in "things" the least appreciation of truth in beautiful guise? If not, you are a victim of habit, a habit evidence enough of the stagnation of an outgrown art. Here we have the curse of stupidity—a cheap substitute for ancient art and craft which has no vital meaning in your own life or our time. You line the box you live in as a magpie lines its nest. You need not be ashamed to confess your ignorance of the meaning of all this, because not only you, but every one else, is hopelessly ignorant concerning it; it is "impossible." Imitations of imitations, copies of copies, cheap expedients, lack of integrity, some few blind gropings for simplicity to give hope to the picture. That is all.

Why wonder what has become of the grand spirit of art that made, in times past, man's reflection in his environment a godlike thing? *This* is what has become of it! Of all conditions, this one at home is most deplorable, for to the homes of this country we must look for any beginning of the awakening of an artistic conscience which will change this parasitic condition to independent growth. The homes of the people will change before public buildings can possibly change.

Glance now for a moment behind this adventitious scene-painting passing, at home, for art in the nineteenth century. Try to sense the true conditions underlying all, and which you betray and belie in the name of culture. Study with me for a moment the engine which produces this wreckage and builds you, thus cheapened and ridiculous, into an ignoble record.

Here is this thing we call the machine, contrary to the principle of organic growth, but imitating it, working irresistibly the will of man through the medium of men. All of us are drawn helplessly into its mesh as we tread our daily round. And its offices—call them "services"—have become the commonplace background of modern existence; yes, and sad to say, in too many lives the foreground, middle distance and future. At best we ourselves are already become or are becoming some cooperative part in a vast machinery. It is, with us, as though we were controlled by some great crystallizing principle going on in nature all around us and going on, in spite of ourselves, even in our very own *natures*. If you would see how interwoven it is, this thing we call the machine, with the warp and the woof of civilization, if indeed it is not now the very basis of civilization itself, go at nightfall when all is simplified and made suggestive, to the top of our newest skycraper, the Masonic temple. There you may see how in the image of material man, at once his glory and his menace, is this thing we call a city. Beneath you is the monster stretching out into the far distance. High overhead hangs a stagnant pall, its fetid breath reddened with light from myriad eyes endlessly, everywhere blinking. Thousands of acres of cellular tissue outspread, enmeshed by an intricate network of veins and arteries radiating into the gloom. Circulating there with muffled ominous roar is the ceaseless activity to whose necessities it all conforms. This wondrous tissue is knit and knit again and inter-knit with a nervous system, marvelously effective and complete, with delicate filaments for hearing and knowing the pulse of its own organism, acting intelligently upon the ligaments and tendons of motive impulse, and in it all is flowing the impelling electric fluid of man's own life. And the labored breathing, murmur, clangor, and the roar—how the voice of this monstrous force rises to proclaim the marvel of its structure! Near at hand, the ghastly warning boom from the deep throats of vessels heavily seeking inlet to the waterway below, answered by the echoing clangor of the bridge bells. A distant shriek grows nearer, more ominous, as the bells warn the living current from the swinging bridge and a vessel cuts for a moment the flow of the nearer artery. Closing then upon the great vessel's stately passage the double bridge is just in time to receive in a rush of steam the avalanche of blood and metal hurled across it; a streak of light gone roaring into the night on glittering bands of steel; an avalanche encircled in its flight by slender magic lines, clicking faithfully from station to station—its nervous herald, its warning and its protection.

Nearer, in the building ablaze with midnight activity, a spotless paper band is streaming into the marvel of the multiple-press, receiving indelibly the impression of human hopes and fears, throbbing in the pulse of this great activity, as infallibly as the gray-matter of the human brain receives the impression of the senses. The impressions come forth as millions of neatly folded, perfected news-sheets, teeming with vivid appeals to good and evil passions; weaving a web of intercommunication so far-reaching that distance becomes as nothing, the thought of one man in one corner of the earth on one day visible on the next to all men. The doings of all the world are reflected here as in a glass—so marvelously sensitive this simple band streaming endlessly from day to day becomes in the grasp of the multiple-press.

If the pulse of this great activity—automatons working night and day in every line of industry, to the power of which the tremor of the mammoth steel skeleton beneath your feet is but an awe-inspiring response—is thrilling, what of the prolific, silent obedience to man's will underlying it all? If this power must be uprooted that civilization may live, then civilization is already doomed. Remain to contemplate this wonder until the twinkling lights perish in groups, or follow one by one, leaving others to live through the gloom; fires are banked, tumult slowly dies to an echo here and there. Then the darkened pall is gradually lifted and moonlight outlines the shadowy, sullen masses of structure, structure deeply cut here and there by half-luminous channels. Huge patches of shadow in shade and darkness commingle mysteriously in the block-like plan with box-like skylines—contrasting strangely with the broad surface of the lake beside, placid and resplendent with a silver gleam. Remain, I say, to reflect that the texture of the city, this great machine, is the warp upon which will be woven the woof and pattern of the democracy we pray for. Realize that it has been deposited here, particle by particle, in blind obedience to law—law no less organic so far as we are concerned than the laws of the great solar universe. That universe, too, in a sense, is but an obedient machine.

Magnificent power! And it confronts the young architect and his artist comrades now, with no other beauty—a lusty material giant without trace of ideality, absurdly disguised by garments long torn to tatters or contemptuously tossed aside, outgrown. Within our own recollection we have all been horrified at the bitter cost of this ruthless development —appalled to see this great power driven by greed over the innocent and defenseless—we have seen bread snatched from the mouths of sober and industrious men, honorable occupations going to the wall with a riot, a feeble strike, or a stifled moan, outclassed, outdone, outlived by the machine. The workman himself has come to regard this relentless force as his nemesis and combines against machinery in the trades with a wild despair that dashes itself to pieces, while the artist blissfully dreaming in the halls we have just visited or walking blindly abroad in the paths of the past, berates his own people for lack luster senses, rails against industrial conditions that neither afford him his opportunity, nor, he says, can appreciate him as he, panderer to ill-gotten luxury, folding his hands, starves to death. "Innocuous martyr upon the cross of art!" One by one, tens by tens, soon thousands by thousands, handicraftsmen and parasitic artists succumb to the inevitable as one man at a machine does the work of from five to fifty men in the same time, with all the art there is meanwhile prostituting to old methods and misunderstood ideals the far greater new possibilities due to this same machine, and doing this disgracefully in the name of the beautiful!

American society has the essential tool of its own age by the blade, as lacerated hands everywhere testify!

See the magnificent prowess of this unqualified power—strewing our surroundings with the mangled corpses of a happier time. We live amid ghostly relics whose pattern once stood for cultivated luxury and now stands for an ignorant matter of taste. With no regard for first principles of common sense the letter of tradition is recklessly fed into rapacious maws of machines until the reproduction, reproduced *ad nauseam,* may be had for five, ten or ninety-nine cents although the worthy original cost ages of toil and patient culture. This might seem like progress, were it not for the fact that these butchered forms, the life entirely gone out of them, are now harmful parasites, belittling and falsifying any true perception of normal beauty the Creator may have seen fit to implant in us on our own account. Any idea whatever of fitness to purpose or of harmony between form and use is gone from us. It is lacking in these things one and all, because it is so sadly lacking in us. And as for making the best of our own conditions or repudiating the terms on which this vulgar insult to tradition is produced, thereby insuring and rectifying the industrial fabric thus wasted or enslaved by base imitation—the mere idea is abnormal, as I myself have found to my sorrow.

And among the few, the favored chosen few who love art by nature and would devote their energies to it so that it may live and let them live—any training they can seek would still be a protest against the machine as the creator of all this iniquity, when (God knows) it is no more than the creature.

But, I say, usurped by greed and deserted by its natural interpreter, the artist, the machine is only the creature, not the creator of this iniquity! I say the machine has noble possibilities unwillingly forced to this degradation, degraded by the arts themselves. Insofar as the true capacity of the machine is concerned it is itself the crazed victim of artist-impotence. Why will the American artist not see that human thought in our age is stripping off its old form and donning another; why is the artist unable to see that this is his glorious opportunity to create and reap anew?

But let us be practical—let us go now afield for evident instances of machine abuse or abuse by the machine. I will show you typical abuses that should serve to suggest to any mind, capable of thought, that the machine is, to begin with, a marvellous simplifier in no merely negative sense. Come now, with me, and see examples which show that these craft-engines may be the modern emancipator of the creative mind. We may find them to be the regenerator of the creative conscience in our America, as well, so soon as a stultified "culture" will allow them to be so used.

First—as perhaps wood is most available of home-building materials, naturally then the most abused—let us now glance at wood. Elaborate machinery has been invented for no other purpose than to imitate the wood-carving of early handicraft patterns. Result? No good joinery. None salable without some horrible glued-on botchwork meaning nothing, unless it means that "art and craft" (by salesmanship) has fixed in the minds of the masses the elaborate old hand-carved chair as ultimate ideal. The miserable tribute to this perversion yielded by Grand Rapids alone would mar the face of art beyond repair, to say nothing of the weird or fussy joinery of spindles and jig-sawing, beamed, braced and elaborated to outdo in sentimentality the sentiment of some erstwhile overwrought "antique." The beauty of wood lies in its qualities as wood, strange as this may seem. Why does it take so much imagination—just to see that? Treatments that fail to bring out those qualities, foremost, are not *plastic,* therefore no longer appropriate. The inappropriate cannot be beautiful.

The machine at work on wood will itself teach us—and we seem so far to have left it to the machine to do so—that certain simple forms and handling serve to bring out the beauty of wood, and to retain its character, and that certain other forms and handling do not bring out its beauty, but spoil it. All wood-carving is apt to be a forcing of this material likely to destroy the finer possibilities of wood as we may know those possibilities now. In itself wood has beauty of marking, exquisite texture, and delicate nuances of color that carving is likely to destroy. The machines used in woodwork will show that by unlimited power in cutting, shaping, smoothing, and by the tireless repeat, they have emancipated beauties of wood-nature, making possible, without waste, beautiful surface treatments and clean strong forms that veneers of Sheraton or Chippendale only hinted at with dire extravagance. Beauty unknown even to the Middle Ages. These machines have undoubtedly placed within reach of the designer a technique enabling him to realize the true nature of wood in his designs harmoniously with man's sense of beauty, satisfying his material needs with such extraordinary economy as to put this beauty of wood in use within the reach of everyone. But the advantages of the machines are wasted and we suffer from a riot of aesthetic murder and everywhere live with debased handicraft.

Then, at random, let us take, say, the worker in marbles—his gang-saws, planers, pneumatic-chisels and rubbing-beds have made it possible to reduce blocks ten feet long, six feet deep, and two feet thick to sheets or thin slabs an inch in thickness within a few hours, so it is now possible to use a precious material as ordinary wall covering. The slab may be turned and matched at the edges to develop exquisite pattern, emancipating hundreds of superficial feet of characteristic drawing in pure marble colors that formerly wasted in the heart of a great expensive block in the thickness of the wall. Here again a distinctly new architectural use may bring out a beauty of marbles consistent with nature and impossible to handicraft. But what happens? The "artist" persists in taking dishonest advantage of this practice, building up imitations of solid piers with molded caps and bases, cunningly uniting the slabs at the edge until detection is difficult except to the trained eye. His method does not change to develop the beauty of a new technical possibility; no, the "artist" is simply enabled to "fake" more architecture, make more piers and column shafts because he can now make them hollow! His architecture becomes no more worthy in itself than the cheap faker that he himself is, for his classical forms not only falsify the method which used to be and belie the method that is, but they cheat progress of its due. For convincing evidence see any public library or art institute, the Congressional Library at Washington, or the Boston Library.

In the stone-cutting trade the stone-planer has made it possible to cut upon stone any given molded surface, or to ingrain upon that surface any lovely texture the cunning brain may devise, and do it as it never was possible to do it by hand. What is it doing? Giving us as near an imitation of hand tooth-chiselling as possible, imitating moldings specially adapted to wood, making possible the lavish use of miles of meaningless molded string courses, cornices, base courses—the giant power meanwhile sneered at by the "artist" because it fails to render the wavering delicacy of "touch" resulting from the imperfections of hand-work.

No architect, this man! No—or he would excel that "antique" quality by the design of the contour of his sections, making a telling point of the very perfection he dreads, and so sensibly designing, for the prolific dexterity of the machine, work which it can do so well that hand-work would seem insufferably crude by comparison. The deadly facility this one machine has given "book architecture" is rivalled only by the facility given to it by galvanized iron itself. And if, incontinently, you will still have tracery in stone, you may arrive at acres of it now consistently with the economy of other features of this still fundamental "trade." You may try to imitate the hand-carving of the ancients in this matter, baffled by the craft and tenderness of the originals, or you may give the pneumatic chisel and power-plane suitable work to do which would mean a changed style, a shift in the spiritual center of the ideal now controlling the use of stone in constructing modern stone buildings.

You will find in studying the group of ancient materials, wood and stone foremost among them, that they have all been rendered fit for *plastic* use by the machine! The machine itself steadily making available for economic use the very quality in these things now needed to satisfy its own art equation. Burned clay—we call it terra cotta—is another conspicuous instance of the advantage of the "process." Modern machines (and a process is a machine) have rendered this material as sensitive to the creative brain as a dry plate is to the lens of the camera. A marvelous simplifier, this material, rightly used. The artist is enabled to clothe the steel structure, now becoming characteristic of this era, with modestly beautiful, plastic robes instead of five or more different kinds of material now aggregated in confused features and parts, "composed" and supposedly picturesque, but really a species of cheap millinery to be mocked and warped by the sun, eventually beaten by wind and rain into a variegated heap of trash. But when these great possibilities of simplicity, the gift of the machine, get to us by way of the architect, we have only a base imitation of the hand-tooled blocks—pilaster-cap and base, voussoirs and carved spandrils of the laborious man-handled stonecrop of an ancient people's architecture!

The modern processes of casting in metal are modern machines too, approaching perfection, capable of perpetuating the imagery of the most vividly poetic mind without hindrance—putting permanence and grace within reach of every one, heretofore forced to sit supine with the Italians at their Belshazzar-feast of "renaissance." Yes, without exaggeration, multitudes of processes, many new, more coming, await sympathetic interpretation, such as the galvano-plastic and its electrical brethren—a prolific horde, now cheap makers imitating "real" bronzes and all manner of metallic antiques, secretly damning all of them in their vitals, if not openly giving them away. And there is electro-glazing, shunned because its straight lines in glasswork are too severely clean and delicate. Straight lines it seems are not so susceptible to the traditional designer's lack of touch. Stream lines and straight lines are to him severely unbeautiful. "Curved is the line of beauty"—says he! As though nature would not know what to do with its own rectilinear!

The familiar lithograph, too, is the prince of an entire province of new reproductive but unproductive processes. Each and every one has its individualities and therefore has possibilities of its own. See what Whistler made and the Germans are making of the lithograph: one note sounded in the gamut of its possibilities. But that note rings true to process as the sheen of the butterfly's wing to that wing. Yet, having fallen into disrepute, the most this particular "machine" did for us, until Whistler picked it up, was to give us the cheap imitative effects of painting, mostly for advertising purposes. This is the use made of machinery in the abuse of materials by men. And still more important than all we have yet discussed here is the new element entering industry in this material we call steel. The structural necessity which once shaped Parthenons, Pantheons, cathedrals, is fast being reduced by the machine to a skeleton of steel or its equivalent, complete in itself without the artist-craftsman's touch. They are now building Gothic cathedrals in California upon a steel skeleton. Is it not easy to see that the myriad ways of satisfying ancient structural necessities known to us through the books as the art of building, vanish, become history? The mainspring of their physical existence now removed, their spiritual center has shifted and nothing remains but the impassive features of a dead face. Such is our "classic" architecture.

For centuries this insensate or insane abuse of great opportunity in the name of culture has made cleanly, strengthy and true simplicity impossible in art or architecture, whereas now we might reach the heights of creative art. Rightly used the very curse machinery puts upon handicraft should emancipate the artist from temptation to petty structural deceit and end this wearisome struggle to make things seem what they are not and can never be. Then the machine itself, eventually, will satisfy the simple terms of its modern art equation as the ball of clay in the sculptor's hand yields to his desire—ending forever this nostalgic masquerade led by a stultified culture in the name of art.

Yes—though he does not know it, the artist is now free to work his rational will with freedom unknown to structural tradition. Units of construction have enlarged, rhythms have been simplified and etherealized, space is more spacious and the sense of it may enter into every building, great or small. The architect is no longer hampered by the stone arch of the Romans or by the stone beam of the Greeks. Why then does he cling to the grammatical phrases of those ancient methods of construction when such phrases are in his modern work empty lies, and himself an inevitable liar as well?

Already, as we stand today, the machine has weakened the artist to the point of destruction and antiquated the craftsman altogether. Earlier forms of art are by abuse all but destroyed. The whole matter has been reduced to mere pose. Instead of joyful creation we have all around about us poisonous tastes—foolish attitudes. With some little of the flame of the old love, and creditable but pitiful enthusiasm, the young artist still keeps on working, making miserable mischief with lofty motives: perhaps, because his heart has not kept in touch or in sympathy with his scientific brother's head, being out of step with the forward marching of his own time.

Now, let us remember in forming this new Arts and Crafts Society at Hull House that every people has done its work, therefore evolved its art as an expression of its own life, using the best tools; and that means the most economic and effective tools or contrivances it knew: the tools most successful in saving valuable human effort. The chattel slave was the essential tool of Greek civilization, therefore of its art. We have discarded this tool and would refuse the return of the art of the Greeks were slavery the terms of its restoration, and slavery, in some form, would be the terms.

But in Grecian art two flowers did find spiritual expression—the acanthus and the honeysuckle. In the art of Egypt—similarly we see the papyrus, the lotus. In Japan the chrysanthemum and many other flowers. The art of the Occident has made no such sympathetic interpretation since that time, with due credit given to the English rose and the French fleur-de-lis, and as things are now the West may never make one. But to get from some native plant an expression of its native character in terms of imperishable stone to be fitted perfectly to its place in structure, and without loss of vital significance, is one great phase of great art. It means that Greek or Egyptian found a revelation of the inmost life and character of the lotus and acanthus in terms of lotus or acanthus life. That was what happened when the art of these people had done with the plants they most loved. This imaginative process is known only to the creative artist. Conventionalization, it is called. Really it is the dramatizing of an object—truest "drama." To enlarge upon this simple figure, as an artist, it seems to me that this complex matter of civilization is itself at bottom some such conventionalizing process, or must be so to be successful and endure.

Just as any artist-craftsman, wishing to use a beloved flower for the stone capital of a column-shaft in his building must conventionalize the flower, that is, find the pattern of its life-principle in terms of stone as a material before he can rightly use it as a beautiful factor in his building, so education must take the natural man, to "civilize" him. And this great new power of the dangerous machine we must learn to understand and then learn to use as this valuable, *"conventionalizing"* agent. But in the construction of a society as in the construction of a great building, the elemental conventionalizing process is dangerous, for without the inspiration or inner light of the true artist—the quality of the flower—its very life—is lost, leaving a withered husk in the place of living expression.

Therefore, society, in this conventionalizing process or culture, has a task even more dangerous than has the architect in creating his building forms, because instead of having a plant-leaf and a fixed material as ancient architecture had, we have a sentient man with a fluid soul. So without the inner light of a sound philosophy of art (the educator too, must now be artist), the life of the man will be sacrificed and society gain an automaton or a machine-made moron instead of a noble creative citizen!

If education is doomed to fail in this process, utterly—then the man slips back to rudimentary animalism or goes on into decay. Society degenerates or has a mere realistic creature instead of the idealistic creator needed. The world will have to record more "great dead cities."

To keep the artist-figure of the flower *dramatized for human purposes*—the socialist would bow his neck in altruistic submission to the "harmonious" whole; his conventionalization or dramatization of the human being would be like a poor stone-craftsman's attempt to conventionalize the beloved plant with the living character of leaf and flower left out. The anarchist would pluck the flower as it grows and use it as it is for what it is—with essential reality left out.

The hereditary aristocrat has always justified his existence by his ability, owing to fortunate propinquity, to appropriate the flower to his own uses after the craftsman has given it life and character, and has kept the craftsman too by promising him his flower back if he behaves himself well. The plutocrat does virtually the same thing by means of "interests." But the true democrat will take the human plant as it grows and—in the spirit of using the means at hand to put life into his conventionalization—preserve the individuality of the plant to protect the flower, which is its very life, getting from both a living expression of essential man-character fitted perfectly to a place in society with no loss of vital significance. Fine art is this flower of the man. When education has become creative and art again prophetic of the natural means by which we are to grow—we call it "progress"—we will, by means of the creative artist, possess this monstrous tool of our civilization as it now possesses us.

Grasp and use the power of scientific automatons in this *creative sense* and their terrible forces are not antagonistic to any fine individualistic quality in man. He will find their collective mechanistic forces capable of bringing to the individual a more adequate life, and the outward expression of the inner man as seen in his environment will be genuine revelation of his inner life and higher purpose. Not until then will America be free!

This new American liberty is of the sort that declares man free only when he has found his work and effective means to achieve a life of his own. The means once found, he will find his due place. The man of our country will thus make his own way, and *grow* to the natural place thus due him, promised—yes, promised by our charter, the Declaration of Independence. But this place of his is not to be made over to fit him by reform, nor shall it be brought down to him by concession, but will become his by his own use of the means at hand. He must *himself* build a new world. The day of the individual is not over—instead, it is just about to begin. The machine does not write the doom of liberty, but is waiting at man's hand as a peerless tool, for him to use to put foundations beneath a genuine democracy. Then the machine may conquer human drudgery to some purpose, taking it upon itself to broaden, lengthen, strengthen and deepen the life of the simplest man. What limits do we dare imagine to an art that is organic fruit of an adequate life for the individual! Although this power is now murderous, chained to botchwork and bunglers' ambitions, the creative artist will take it surely into his hand and, in the name of liberty, swiftly undo the deadly mischief it has created.

Here ends the early discourse on the art and craft of the machine.

You may find comfort in the reflection that truth and liberty have this invincible excellence, that all man does for them or does against them eventually serves them equally well. That fact has comforted me all the intervening years between the first reading of the foregoing discourse and this reading at Princeton . . . the last reading, for I shall never read it again. Tomorrow afternoon there will be—I am afraid—heavy matter also because the question of qualifying the "machine-made" in American industries by human elements of style will be, in detail, our subject. There may be matter more subjective and difficult but I do not know what it may be.

It will be necessary for us all to give close attention and considerable thought to the subject, "STYLE IN INDUSTRY." We shall see that any hope of such style will mean a crusade against *the* styles.

90

2: STYLE IN INDUSTRY

Where certain remarks I have made concern nature and romance on the one hand, and the machine upon the other, I am accused of inconsistency—also in several or seven different languages. But if the word nature, and the word romance too, are understood in the sense that each is used we can find little to correct, although the last analysis is never to be made.

The machine is that mathematical automaton or automatic power contrived in brass and steel by men, not only to take the place of man-power, but to multiply man-power—the brainless craftsman of a new social order.

Primarily the word nature means the principle at work in everything that lives and gives to life its form and character. All lives, so we may refer to the nature of two plus two equals four, if we like, or to the nature of tin, or to the nature of a disease or of the chromatic seventh. The word has nothing to do with realistic or realism, but refers to the essential *reality* of all things—so far as we may perceive reality. We cannot conceive life, we do not know what it is, but we can perceive the nature of its consequences and effects and so enter into creation with some intelligence. If we have occasion to refer to the visible world we will use the term "external nature." The word "organic" too, if taken too biologically, is a stumbling-block. The word applies to "living" structure—a structure or concept wherein features or parts are so organized in form and substance as to be, applied to purpose, *integral*. Everything that "lives" is therefore organic. The inorganic—the "unorganized"—cannot *live*.

While we are at the, perhaps unnecessary, pains of explaining, let us say also what we should understand by romance. True romanticism in art is after all only liberalism in art, and is so understood, I believe, by all great poets. Romance is the essential joy we have in living, as distinguished from mere pleasure; therefore we want no narrow conventions, as preventions, to rise up from small minds and selfish hands, no intolerant "modes" to grow up in the modern world; it is to be our privilege to build up on new fertile ground. Yes, we are to build in the arts upon this great ground fertilized *by* the *old* civilizations—a new liberty.

We, so beset by educational advantages as are Americans, cannot say too often to ourselves or others that "toleration and liberty are the foundations of this great republic." We should keep it well in the foreground of our minds and as a hope in our hearts that liberty in art as well as liberty in society *should* be, and therefore *must* be, the offspring of political liberty.

Then to us all, so minded, let the artist come. He has a public. And as we have already seen in "Machinery, Materials and Men," the artist now has both the "making and the means." Let him arise in our industry. For a new people a new art!

Liberty, however, is no friend to license. So, for our text in connection with difficult "Style in Industry," for due reference to authority suppose we again go far back in history—again to avoid all contradiction—this time to the birth of old Japan—and there, to safeguard liberty, take for text, simply, "An artist's limitations are his best friends," and dedicate that text to Jimmu Tenno.

At least the ancient civilization of his slowly sinking stretch of pendulous island, arising from the sea in the snows of perpetual winter and reaching all the way south to perpetual summer, affords best proof of the text anywhere to be found. "Limitations," in this sense, were, I take it, those of materials, tools and specific purpose.

In Jimmu's island perfect style in industry was supreme and native until "Japan" was discovered within range of our own Commodore Perry's guns. That Western contacts have destroyed this early style—if not the industry—only enhances the value of that early style. *Certainly*, the arts and crafts, as developed in Nippon during her many centuries of isolation in happy concentration, afford universal object lessons incomparable in style.

92

Industry and style there—before the "peaceful" comercial invasion by the West—were supremely natural. Nor in Jimmu Tenno's time was there anywhere to be found separate and contrasted existence between art and nature. Nowhere else in the world can we so clearly see this nor so well inform ourselves in considering this matter of style in our own native automatic industries. This notwithstanding the fact that our industries are conditioned upon automatic acquiescence of men instead of upon the craftsmanship of the man. By giving our attention to the ease and naturalness with which things Japanese originally achieved style, we may learn a valuable lesson.

Our industry must educate designers instead of making craftsmen —for our craftsmen are machines, craftsmen ready-made, efficient and obedient. So far as they go—mechanical power stripped clean. How to get these formidable craft-engines the work to do they may do well? Then, beyond mechanical skill, the cadences of form?

The first answer will seem generalization beyond any immediate mark, for that answer is—by means of imagination. Imagination superior and supreme. Supreme imagination is what makes the creative artist now just as it made one then. And imagination is what will make the needed designer for industry now—no less than then or ever before. But, strange to say, it is of the true quality of great imagination that it can see wood as wood, steel as steel, glass as glass, stone as stone, and make limitations its best friends. This is what Jimmu Tenno's busy people proved so thoroughly well and what may be so useful to us to realize. Our machine-age limitations are more severe and more cruelly enforced than limitations were in this severely disciplined island-empire of Japan. Nevertheless, though more difficult in important ways, in other more important directions, we have marvelously more opportunity than ever Japan had.

Principles which made the art and craft of old Japan a living thing —living, that is, for old Japan—will work as well now as then. The same principles in art and craft either of the East or the West, wherever similar truths of being went into effect with some force in the lives of their peoples, need no change now. Secrets of cause and effect in work and materials in relation to life as lived are the same for the coming designer for machines as they were for the bygone craftsman designers. But when a man becomes a part of the machine that he moves—the man is lost.

We Americans, too, *do live*—in a way—do we not? But we differ. We do live and, notwithstanding all differences, our souls yet have much in common with all souls. The principles, therefore, on which we must work our modern style for ourselves will not change the while our interpretation and applications will utterly change. Results in American industry will be simpler, broader, more a matter of texture and sublimated mathematics as music is sublimated mathematics; therefore our designs will be more subjective than before. Our applications will be more generalized but our derivations not more limited than in the days of ancient handicraft.

Provided the limitations of any given problem in the arts do not destroy each other by internal collision and so kill opportunity, limitations are no detriment to artist endeavor. It is largely the artist's business—all in his day's work—to see that the limitations do *not* destroy each other. That is to say, it is up to him to get proper tools, proper materials for proper work. Speaking for myself, it would be absurd if not impossible to take advantage of the so-called "free-hand." To "idealize" in the fanciful sketch is a thing unknown to me. Except as I were given some well defined limitations or requirements—the more specific the better—there would be no problem, nothing to work with, nothing to work out; why then trouble the artist? Perhaps that is why "fairs" are so universally uncreative and harmful—the hand is too free, the quality of imagination, therefore, too insignificant.

No—not until American industrial designers have grown up to the point where they have known and made friends with the limitations characteristic of their job, will America have any style in industry. What are these limitations?

Automatic industrial fabrication is not the least of them. But—to reiterate from the matter of our first chapter, "MACHINERY, MATERIALS AND MEN"—the American designers' hope lies in the fact that as a consequence of the automaton, already machinery can do many desirable things, "by hand" prohibited or impossible. Now, mixed up with

"MACHINERY, MATERIALS AND MEN," in our first chapter, was the word plasticity used as machine-aesthetic in modern designing for wood-working, stone-work, metal-casting and reproductive processes. Some practical suggestions were made to indicate how and wherein this new "aesthetic" which the machine has given to us may enable the artist to make new use of old materials, and new use of new materials instead of making abuse of both.

"Plasticity" is of utmost importance. The word implies total absence of constructed effects as evident in the result. This important word, "plastic," means that the quality and nature of materials are seen "flowing or growing" into form instead of seen as built up out of cut and joined pieces. "Composed" is the academic term for this academic process in furniture. "Plastic" forms, however, are *not* "composed" nor set up. They, happily, inasmuch as they are produced by a "*growing*" process, must be developed . . . *created.* And to shorten this discourse we may as well admit that if we go far enough to find cause in any single industry like furniture for this matter of style, we will have the secret of origin and growth of style in any or in all industries. After getting so far, there would come only specialization in differences of materials and machinery in operation.

Repeatedly and freely too we are to use this word style—but if intelligently, what, then, is style? Be sure of one thing in any answer made to the question—style *has nothing to do with "the" styles!* "The great styles" we call them. "Styles" have been tattered, torn and scattered to the four winds and all the breezes that blow between them as a form of mechanical corruption in industry, and yet, we have no style. The more "styles" in fact, the less style, unless by accident—nor anything very much resembling the stimulating quality. Our designers for various industries—still busy, unfortunately, trying to imitate "styles" instead of *studying the principles* of style intelligently—are at the moment jealously watching France as they see her products go from Wanamaker's on down the avenue and out along the highways of these United States as far as the Pacific Ocean. And yet, if you will take pains to compare the best of French products, say in textiles, with the products of the ancient Momoyama of Japan you will see the industrial ideas of old Japan at work in new French industry as direct inspiration. The French product is not Japanese and nearly all of the textiles are within the capacity of the machine; most of the product is good. But France, in all her moments of movement in art and craft, and no less at this "modern" moment in this "modernistic" particular, helps herself liberally if not literally from Japanese sources, and creditably. She it was who discovered the Japanese print by way of the De Goncourts. That discovery bore significant fruit in French painting. And there are more valuable brochures in the French language on the art of Japan in all its phases available for reference than in all other languages put together, the Japanese language included. France, the inveterate discoverer, must discover "l'esprit de l'art Japonais—à la Japon," to her great honor be it said. Holland arrived at Nagasaki first, but France is probably further along today in profitable industrial results in present arts and crafts from the revelations she found when she got to Yedo by way of Yokohama than is any other country, Austria excepted— unless our own country should soon prove formidable exception.

This does not mean that France or Austria copies Japan or that America may do so. It does mean that France is, only now, beginning to do approximately well what Japan did supremely well four centuries ago in the great Momoyama period of her development—yes, about four hundred years ago!

Any principle is fertile, perhaps it is fertility itself! If its application is once understood in any branch of design, it will go on blooming indefinitely, coordinately, in as many different schools and schemes as there are insects, or in forms as varied as the flowers themselves, or for that matter be as prolific of pattern as the fishes or the flora of the sea.

We should, were we going into the matter at length, get to nature forms later on as the best of all references for the working of the principles we are here seeking, and I should have preferred to go to them at once as is my habit. But for the purposes of this hour I have preferred tradition because Japan has already done, in her own perfect way, what now lies for study before us. And I believe it well to know what humanity has accomplished in the direction we must take, if we are strong enough to profit by tradition—the spirit of principle—and leave traditions—the letter, or form—alone, as not our own. Even so, having finished with tradition, we will still have before us and forever, as an open book of creation, that natural appeal to the nature court of last resort.

Remember, however, that long before France rationalized and vitalized her industries, during the period when she was still sickened and helpless in the serpentine coils of l'art nouveau (derived from her own deadly rococo), you may find in the "secession" of Middle Europe an application earlier than the present application by France of the vital principles we are discussing on behalf of our subject.

I came upon the secession during the winter of 1910. At that time Herr Professor Wagner, of Vienna, a great architect, the architect Olbrich, of Darmstadt, the remarkable painter Klimt of Austria and the sculptor Metzner of Berlin—great artists all—were the soul of that movement. And there was the work of Louis Sullivan and of myself in America. Many Europeans accounted for this secession—their own early contribution to modern art—as a "Mohammedan renaissance." (It was natural by that time to believe in nothing but some kind of renaissance.) But later, when the secession—though frowned upon by the royal academies—was in full swing in the products of the Wiener Werkstätte, seen today similarly in the products of French art and craft, we find the ancient art and craft of Japan's great Momoyama often approximated in effect.

Nothing at this "modern" moment could be more ungracious nor arouse more contumacious "edge" than thus looking the "gift horse" or the "modernistic" in the teeth. Nevertheless, I believe it valuable to our future to raise this unpopular issue.

Artists, even great ones, are singularly ungrateful to sources of inspiration—among lesser artists ingratitude amounts to phobia. No sooner does the lesser artist receive a lesson or perceive an idea or even receive the objects of art from another source, than he soon becomes anxious to forget the suggestion, conceal the facts, or, if impossible to do this, to minimize, by detraction, the "gift." And as culture expands, we soon, too soon, deny outright the original sources of our inspiration as a suspected reproach to our own superiority. This you may quite generally find in the modern art world. At this moment in our development Japan particularly is thus the "great insulted." Cowardly evasion seems unworthy of great artists or great causes, and certainly is no manner in which to approach great matter for the future. Ignorance of origins is no virtue—nor to keep fresh thought ill-advised concerning them. So let us pursue still further this quest as to what is style by digging at the root of this ancient culture where I imagine there was more fertile ground and the workman had severer discipline than he ever had anywhere else in the world. Thus we may interpret a ready-made record that is unique. Let us study for a moment the Japanese dwelling, this humble dwelling that is a veritable sermon on our subject, "style in industry."

It became what it is owing to a religious admonition. "Be clean!" "Be clean" was the soul of Shinto—Jimmu Tenno's own ancient form of worship. Shinto spoke not of a good man, nor spoke of a moral man, but spoke of a clean man. Shinto spoke not only of clean hands, but of a clean heart. "Be clean" was the simple cry from the austere soul of Shinto. Japanese art heard the cry, and therefore posterity has one primitive instance where a remarkably simple religious edict or ideal made architecture, art and craftsmanship the cleanest, in every sense, of all clean workmanship the world over.

This simple ideal of cleanliness, held by a whole people, came to abhor waste as matter out of place, saw it as ugly—therefore as what we call "dirt."

Here you have a kind of spiritual ideal of natural and hence organic, simplicity. Consequently all Japanese art with its imaginative exuberance and organic elegance (no fern-frond freshly born ever had more) was a practical study in elimination of the insignificant. All phases of art expression in the Momoyama period were organic. There was no great and no small art. But there lived the profound Sotatzu, the incomparable Korin, the brilliant Kenzan and their vital schools, as, later in the Ukioyé, we find Kiyonobu, Toyonobu, Harunobu, Kiyonaga, Utamaro, Hokusai and Hiroshigé—a small student group gathered about each—all springing from the industrial soil thus fertilized by the school of the great Momoyama masters. Instinctive sense of organic quality qualified them as artists, *all*. Again, a kind of spiritual gift of

S. C. JOHNSON AND SON, INC., RESEARCH CENTER, RACINE, WISCONSIN

S. C. JOHNSON AND SON, INC., RESEARCH CENTER, RACINE, WISCONSIN

significance. Here, as a saving grace in one civilization on earth, feeling for significance, simplicity in art was born, becoming soon an ideal naturally attained by organic means. Here, in this "plastic-ideal" *attained by organic means,* we touch the secret of great style. Wood they allowed to be wood, of course. Metal they allowed—even encouraged—to be metal. Stone was never asked to be less or more than stone. Nor did the designer of that day try to make any thing in materials or processes something other than itself. Here is a sound first principle that will go far to clear our encumbered ground for fresh growth in "art in industry."

Also the modern process of standardizing, as we now face it on every side, sterilized by it, prostrate to it, was in Japan known and practiced with artistic perfection by freedom of choice many centuries ago, in this dwelling we are considering. The removable (for cleaning) floor mats or "tatami" of Japanese buildings were all of one size, 3' 0" by 6' 0". The shape of all the houses was determined by the size and shape of assembled mats. The Japanese speak of a nine, eleven, sixteen or thirty-four mat house. All the sliding interior partitions occur on the joint lines of the mats. The "odeau"—polished wood posts that carry ceilings and roof—all stand at intersections of the mats. The light sliding paper shoji or outside wall-screens are likewise removable—for cleaning. The plan for any Japanese dwelling was an effective study in sublimated mathematics. And the house itself was used by those who themselves made it for themselves with the same naturalness with which a turtle uses his shell. Consider too that, "be clean"—"the simplest way without waste"—was dignified as *ceremonial* in old Japan. The ceremonies of that ancient day were no more than the simple offices of daily life raised to the dignity of works of art. True culture, therefore. Ceremonials, too, it seems, may be organic, integral though symbolic. For instance what is the important tea-ceremony of the Japanese but the most graciously perfect way, all considered, of serving a cup of tea to respected or beloved guests? Grace and elegance, as we may see—*of the thing itself*—organic elegance. Not *on* it Greek-wise as the "elegant solution." It was in easy, simple, spontaneous expression of nature that the Japanese were so perfect—contenting themselves with humble obedience to nature-law.

Naturally enough, disorder, too, in this "clean" house built by Jimmu Tenno's people is in the same category as dirt. So everything large or little of everyday use, even the works of art for humble and profound admiration, have appropriate place when in use and are carefully put away into safekeeping when not in use.

All designed for kneeling on soft mats on the floor you say? Yes —but the same ideal, in principle, would work out just as well on one's feet.

With this Shinto ideal of "be clean" in mind the Japanese dwelling in every structural member and fiber of its being means something fine, has genuine significance and straightway does that something with beautiful effect. Art, for once, is seen to be supremely natural.

Yes—here is definite root of style in industry. Also in every other country and period where style developed as genuine consequence of natural or ethnic character, similar proofs may be found as to the origin of style.

Today, it seems to me, we hear this cry "be clean" from the depths of our own need. It is almost as though the machine itself had, by force, issued edict similar to Shinto—"be clean." Clean lines—clean surfaces—clean purposes. As swift as you like, but clean as the flight of an arrow. When this edict inspires organic results and not the mere picture-making that curses so-called "modernism," we will here find the basic elements of style in our own industry to be the same by machine as they were by hand back there in the beginning of the history of a unique civilization. To give this edict of the machine human significance there is the command of the creative artist to keep a grip upon the earth in use of the architectural planes parallel to earth, and to make new materials qualify the new forms of the new methods, so that all is warmly and significantly human in the result. The human equation is the art equation in it all. "Clean," in human sense, does not mean "plain" but it does mean significant. Nor does it mean hard, nor mechanical nor mechanistic, nor that a man or a house or a chair or a child is a machine, except in the same sense that our own hearts are suction pumps.

Style in our industries will come out of similar, natural, "clean" use of machines upon "clean" material, with similar, unaffected, *heart-felt* simplicity instead of *head-made* simplicity. The nature of both machine and material for human use must be understood and mastered so they may be likewise in our case plastic interpretations by great imagination. We will learn how to use both machinery and materials and perhaps men as well in the coming century. But we must learn how to use them all not only for qualities they possess in themselves, but to use each so that they may be beautifully as well as scientifically related to human purpose in whatever form or function we humanly choose to put them. Then let us take all as much further along beyond the implications of "be clean," as our superior advantages in aesthetics permit.

To get nearer to the surface. We started to speak of textiles: having during the discourse of our first chapter touched upon woodworking, stonework and metalworking, let us now go back for a moment to the Rodier fabrics for an example of present-day, successful design for the loom. Textures, infinite in variety, are the natural product of the loom. Pattern is related to, and is the natural consequence of, the mechanics of these varying textures. Large, flat patterns involved with textures, textures qualifying them or qualified by them, picturesque but with no thought of a picture, as in this product, are entirely modern in the best sense. And I would emphasize for you, in this connection, the fact that the ancient art we have just been interpreting was never, in any phase of its industries, ruined by childish love of the picture. The "picture" sense in art and craft came in with the renaissance, as one consequence of the insubordination of the arts that disintegrated architecture as the great art. And before we can progress in our own machine products as art, we, too, will have to dispose of the insufferable insubordination of the picture. Summarily, if need be. I should like to strike the pictorial death blow in our art and craft. Of course I do not mean the picturesque.

Because of this insubordination of the picture few tapestries except the "Mille-fleurs" (and then very early ones) exist as good textile designs on account of the complex shading essential to the foolish picture as designed by the undisciplined painter. The insubordination of painting, setting up shop on its own account, divorced from architecture (architecture being the natural framework and background of all ancient, as it will be of any future, civilization), has cursed every form of art endeavor whatsoever with similar abuses of the *pictorial*. "Toujours la peinture," *ad libitum, ad nauseam*—the *picture*. We live in the pictorial age. We do not have childlike imagery in simplicity but are "childish" in art, and whatever form our great art and craft in future may take, one thing it will not be, and that thing is "pictorial." Even a Japanese print, the popular form of imagery illustrating the popular life of Japan in all its phases, as the French well know, never degenerated to the mere picture. Let us be thankful that the machine by way of the camera today takes the pictorial upon itself as a form of literature. This gratifying feat has, already, made great progress in the cinematograph. Let the machine have it, I say, on those terms and keep it active there and serviceable in illustration as well, for what it may be worth—and it is worth much. But let us henceforth consider literature and the picture as one—eliminating both from the horizon of our art and craft—and for all time.

Let us now, in passing, glance at glassmaking: the Leerdam glass products for which artists are employed to make designs upon a royalty basis, similar to authors writing for publishers, then the special art of Lalique, and finally, the great, clear plates of our own commercial industry, the gift of the machine, . . . great glass sheets to be cut up and used with no thought of beauty, valuable only because of their usefulness.

Here again let us insist that the same principle applies to glass as to wood, stone, metal or the textiles just mentioned. But how far variety may go can be seen in the range of the Holland product from the simple glass-blown forms of De Basle, Copius and Berlage at Leerdam to the virtuosity of French pieces by the genius Lalique. Certain characteristics of glass are properties of these designs: a piece by Lalique, being specialized handicraft, is useful as indicating the super-possibilities of glass as a beautiful material. Concerning our own "commercial" contribution (contributions so far are all "commercial") to glass—glass, once a precious substance, limited in quantity, costly in any size—the glass industry has grown so that a perfect clarity in any thickness, quality or dimension up to 250 square feet from 1/8" in thickness to 1/2" thick, is so cheap and desirable that our modern world is drifting towards structures of glass and steel.

The whole history of architecture would have been radically different had the ancients enjoyed any such grand privileges in this connection as are ours. The growing demands for sunshine and visibility make walls—even posts—something to get rid of at any cost. Glass did this. Glass alone, with no help from any of us, would eventually have destroyed classic architecture, root and branch.

Glass has now a perfect visibility, thin sheets of air crystallized to keep air currents outside or inside. Glass surfaces, too, may be modified to let the vision sweep through to any extent up to perfection. Tradition left no orders concerning this material as a means of perfect visibility; hence the sense of glass as crystal has not, as poetry, entered yet into architecture. All the dignity of color and material available in any other material may be discounted by glass in light, and discounted with permanence.

Shadows were the "brush-work" of the ancient architect. Let the "modern" now work with light, light diffused, light reflected, light refracted—light for its own sake, shadows gratuitous. It is the machine that makes *modern* these rare new opportunities in glass—new experience that architects so recent as the great Italian forebears, plucked even of their shrouds, frowning upon our "renaissance," would have considered magical. They would have thrown down their tools with the despair of the true artist. Then they would have transformed their cabinets into a realm, their halls into bewildering vistas and avenues of light—their modest units into unlimited wealth of color patterns and delicate forms, rivaling the frostwork upon the window-panes, perhaps. They were creative enough to have found a world of illusion and brilliance, with jewels themselves only modest contributions to the splendor of their effects. And yet somehow Palladio, Vitruvius, Vignola, seem very dead, far away and silent in this connection, Bramante and Brunelleschi not so far, nor Sansovino, though we must not forget that the great Italians were busy working over ancient forms. There was Buonarrotti. Where should he be in all this, I wonder?

The prism has always fascinated man. We may now live in prismatic buildings, clean, beautiful and new. Here is one clear "material" proof of modern advantage, for glass is uncompromisingly modern. Yes—architecture is soon to live anew because of glass and steel.

And so we might go on to speak truly of nearly all our typical modern industries at work upon materials with machinery. We could go on and on until we were all worn out and the subject would be still bright and new, there are so many industrial fields—so much machinery, so many processes, such riches in new materials.

We began this discussion of art in industry by saying, "toleration and liberty are the foundations of a great republic." Now let the artist come. Well—let him come into this boundless new realm so he be a liberal, hating only intolerance and especially his own. As said at the beginning of this discourse, true romanticism in art is after all only liberalism in art. This quality in the artist is the result of an inner experience and it is the essential poetry of the creative artist that his exploring brother, tabulating the sciences, seems never quite able to understand nor wholly respect. He distrusts that quality in life itself.

But the sense of romance cannot die out of human hearts. Science itself is bringing us to greater need of it and unconsciously giving greater assurance of it at every step. Romance is shifting its center now, as it has done before and will do constantly—but it is immortal. Industry will only itself become and remain a machine without it.

Our architecture itself would become a poor, flat-faced thing of steel-bones, box-outlines, gas-pipe and hand-rail fittings—as sun-receptive as a concrete sidewalk or a glass tank without this essential *heart* beating in it. Architecture, without it, could inspire nothing, and would degenerate to a box merely to *contain* "objets d'art"—objects it should itself create and *maintain*. So beware! The artist who condemns romance is only a foolish reactionary. Such good sense as the scientist or philosopher in the disguise of "artist" may have is not creative, although it may be corrective. Listen therefore and go back with what you may learn, to live and be true to romance.

Again — there is no good reason why objects of art in industry, because they are made by machines in the machine age, should resemble the machines that made them, or any other machinery whatever. There might be excellent reason why they should *not* resemble machinery. There is no good reason why forms stripped clean of all considerations but function and utility should be admirable beyond that point: they may be abominable from the human standpoint, but there is no need for them to be so in the artist's hands.

The negation naturally made by the machine, gracefully accepted now, may, for a time, relieve us of sentimental abortion and abuse, but it cannot inspire and recreate humanity beyond that point. Inevitably the negation proceeds upon its own account to other abuses and abortions, even worse than sentimentality. Again, let us have no fears of liberalism in art in our industries, but encourage it with new understanding, knowing at last that the term romanticism never did apply to make-believe or falsifying, except as it degenerated to the artificiality that maintained the renaissance.

The facts confronting us are sufficiently bare and hard. The taste for mediocrity in our country grows by what it feeds on.

Therefore the public of this republic will, more than ever now, find its love of commonplace elegance gratified either by the sentimentality of the "ornamental" or the sterility of ornaphobia. The machine age, it seems, is either to be damned by senseless sentimentality or to be sterilized by a factory aesthetic. Nevertheless, I believe that romance—this quality of the *heart*, the essential joy we have in living—by human imagination of the right sort can be brought to life again in modern industry. Creative imagination may yet convert our prosaic problems to poetry while modern Rome howls and the eyebrows of the Pharisees rise.

And probably not more than one-fifth of the American public will know what is meant by the accusation, so frequently made in so many different languages, that the American is uncreative, four-fifths of the accused pointing to magnificent machinery and stupendous scientific accomplishment to refute the impeachment. So while we are digesting the nationalities speaking those same languages within our borders, such culture as we have in sight must assist itself with intelligence to materialize for Americans out of everyday common places—and transcend the commonplace.

So finally, a practical suggestion as to ways and means to grow our own style in industry.

The machine, as it exists in every important trade, should without delay be put, by way of capable artist interpreters, into student hands —for them, at first, to play with and, later, with which to work. Reluctantly I admit that to put the machine, as the modern tool of a great civilization, to any extent into the hands of a body of young students, means some kind of school—and naturally such school would be called an art school, but one in which the fine arts would be not only allied to the industries they serve, but would stand there at the center of an industrial hive of characteristic industry as inspiration and influence in design-problems.

Sensitive, unspoiled students (and they may yet be found in this unqualified machine that America is becoming) should be put in touch with commercial industry in what we might call industrial "style" centers, workshops equipped with modern machinery, connected perhaps with our universities, but endowed by the industries themselves, where the students would remain domiciled working part of the day in the shop itself.

Machinery-using crafts making useful things might through such experiment centers discover possibilities existing in the nature of their craft—which the present industries know nothing about and might never discover for themselves. In such a school it would be the turn of the fine arts to serve machinery in order that machinery might better serve them and all together better serve a beauty-loving and appreciative United States.

Let us say that seven branches of industrial arts be taken for a begining (a number should be grouped together for the reason that they react upon one another to the advantage of each). Let us name glassmaking, textiles, pottery, sheet metals, woodworking, casting in metal, reproduction. Each industry so represented should be willing to donate machinery and supply a competent machinist and to a certain extent endow its own craft, provided such industries were certain of proper management under safe auspices, and assured of a share in results which would be directly theirs—sharing either in benefit of designs or presently in designers themselves, both adapted to their particular field.

Such experiment centers intelligently conducted could do more to nationalize and vitalize our industries than all else, and soon would make them independent of France, Austria or any other country, except as instruction by international example from all countries would help work out our own forms. There is no reason why an experiment center of this character, each center confined to forty students or less, should not make its own living and produce valuable articles to help in "carrying-on." As compared with the less favorably circumstanced factories, and owing to the artists at the head of the group, each article would be of the quality of a work of art and so be a genuine missionary wherever it went.

Such a school should be in the country, on sufficient land so that three hours a day of physical work on the soil would insure the living of the students and the resident group of seven artist workers, themselves the head of the student group. There would remain, say, seven hours of each day for forty-seven individuals in which to unite in production. A well directed force of this sort would very soon have considerable producing power. Thus belonging to the school each month there would be beautifully useful or usefully beautiful things ready for market and influence—stuffs, tapestries, table linen, new cotton fabrics, table glassware, flower holders, lighting devices, window glass, mosaics, necklaces, screens, iron standards, fixtures, gates, fences, fire irons, enameled metals for house or garden purposes, cast metal sculpture for gardens, building hardware. All sorts of industrial art in aluminum, copper, lead, tin. Practical flower pots, architectural flower containers on large scale, water jars, pots and sculpture. Paintings for decoration suitable for reproduction and designs for new media—for process-reproductions. Modern music, plays, rhythm, designs for farm buildings, the characteristic new problems like the gasoline station, the refreshment stand, food distribution, town and country cottages and objects for their furnishings, and factories, too, of various sorts.

The station might broadcast itself. Issue brochures, illustrated by itself, of pertinent phases of its work. Devote a branch to landscape studies on conservation and planting and town planning. In short, the station would be a hive of inspired industry. Architecture, without hesitation, or equivocation, should be the broad essential background of the whole endeavor—again strong in modern life as it ever was in ancient times. It is logical to say that again it must be the background and framework of civilization. Such stations or centers could be alcoves in connection with standard university courses in the history of art, architecture and archaeology. And it would not matter where the centers were located, were they sufficiently isolated in beautiful country. They should not be too easy of access.

No examinations, graduations or diplomas. But so soon as a student worker showed special competence in any branch of industry he would be available as teacher in the university or for a place in that industry, manufacturers who were contributors to the school having first right to use him or her. The body of inspirational talent and the trade machinists should be of such character that outside students would enjoy and seek points of contact with the work going on at the school—helpful to them and to the school as well.

I believe the time has come when art must take the lead in education because creative faculty is now, as ever, the birthright of man—the quality that has enabled him to distinguish himself from the brute. Through tricks played upon himself by what he proudly styles his intellect, turning all experience into arrogant abstractions and applying them as such by systems of education, he has all but sterilized himself. Science has been tried and found to be only a body. Science, and philosophy, too, have known but little of those inner experiences of the soul we call art and religion.

This creative faculty in man is that quality or faculty in him of getting himself born into whatever he does, and born again and again with fresh patterns as new problems arise. By means of this faculty he has the gods if not God. A false premium has been placed by education upon will and intellect. Imagination is the instrument by which the force in him works its miracles. Now—how to get back again to men and cultivate the creative quality in man is the concern of such centers as here suggested. What more valuable step looking toward the future could any great institution take than to initiate such little experiment stations in out of the way places, where the creative endeavor of the whole youth is coordinate with the machinery, and where the technique of his time is visible at work, so that youth may win back again the creative factor as the needed vitalizing force in modern life?

We know, now, that creative art cannot be taught. We know, too, that individual creative impulse is the salt and savor of the natural ego as well as the fruit and triumph of any struggle we call work. Civilization without it can only die a miserable death. To degrade and make hypocritical this quality of the individual by imposing mediocrity upon him in the name of misconceived and selfishly applied democracy is the modern social crime. Too plainly we already see the evil consequences of sentimentalized singing to Demos—foolishly ascribing to Demos the virtues of deity. Concentration and sympathetic inspiration should be isolated and concentrated in experimental work of this kind in order to hasten the time when art shall take the lead in education, and character be a natural consequence. Were this to be put into effect on even a small scale in various units scattered over the surface of these United States, this indispensable ego might be strengthened and restored to a sanity compared to which "egotism," as we now know it in education, would only be a sickly disease of consciousness—highly improbable because manifestly absurd.

Thus given opportunity truly liberal, American youth might soon become the vital medium through which the spirit of man may so appear to men in their own work that they might again see and realize that great spirit as their own.

This liberal opportunity to work and study is a practical suggestion for the growth of that quality of style in industry we have been seeking this afternoon.

Behind personality tradition should stand—behind tradition stands the race.

We have put tradition before personality—and made tradition as a fatal hurdle for race.

3: THE PASSING OF THE CORNICE

Instinctively, I think, I hated the empty, pretentious shapes of the renaissance. When sixteen years old, I used to read the great "modern" of his day—Victor Hugo. Reading his discursive novel, *Notre-Dame*, I came upon the chapter, "Ceci Tuera Cela." That story of the decline of architecture made a lasting impression upon me. I saw the renaissance as that setting sun all Europe mistook for dawn; I believed Gutenberg's invention of the shifting types would kill the great edifice as architecture. In fact, as we all may now see, printing *was* the first great blow to art by the machine. I saw the life-blood of beloved architecture slowly ebbing, inevitably to be taken entirely away from the building by the book, the book being a more liberal form of expression for human thought. This mechanical invention was to become the channel for thought—because more facile and more direct. In place of the art of architecture was to come literature made ubiquitous.

I saw that architecture, in its great antique form, was going to die. Ghastly tragedy—I could hardly bear the thought of the consequences.

About this time, too—catastrophe! As the new west wing of the old Wisconsin State Capitol at Madison fell, I happened to be passing in the shade of the trees that bordered the green park in which the building stood. Suddenly I heard the roar of collapse—saw the clouds of white lime-dust rise high in the air—heard the groans and fearful cries of those injured and not killed—some forty workmen dead or seriously hurt. I remember clinging to the iron palings of the park in full view of the scene, sick with horror as men plunged headlong from the basement openings—some seeming to be still madly fighting off falling bricks and timbers, only to fall dead in the grass outside, grass no longer green but whitened by the now falling clouds of lime.

The outer stone walls were still standing. Stone basement-piers carrying the iron interior supporting columns had given way and the roof took all the floors, sixty men at work on them, clear down to the basement. A great "classic" cornice had been projecting boldly out from the top of the building, against the sky. Its moorings partly torn away, this cornice now hung down in places, great hollow boxes of galvanized iron, hanging up there suspended on end. One great section of cornice I saw hanging above an upper window. A workman hung, head downward, his foot caught, crushed on the sill of this window, by a falling beam. A red line streaked the stone wall below him and it seemed as though the hanging box of sheet-iron that a moment before had gloomed against the sky as the "classic" cornice, must tear loose by its own weight and cut him down before he could be rescued.

The spectacle of that sham feature hanging there, deadly menace to the pitifully moaning, topsy-turvy figure of a man—a working man—went far to deepen the dismay planted in a boy's heart by Victor Hugo's prophetic tale. This terrifying picture persisting in imagination gave rise to subsequent reflections. "This empty sheet-iron thing . . . a little while ago it was pretending to be stone, . . . and doing this, mind you, for the capitol of the great state of Wisconsin, . . . what a shame!

"Somebody must have been imposed upon!

"Was it the state or perhaps the architect himself?

"Had the architect been cheated in that too, as well as in the collapsed piers that had let the structure down? Or was it all deliberate and everybody knew about it, but did nothing about it—did not care? Wasn't this the very thing Victor Hugo meant?"

I believed it was what he meant and began to examine cornices critically. "Why was it necessary to make them 'imitation'? If it was necessary to do that, why have them at all? Were they really beautiful or useful anyway? I couldn't see that they were particularly beautiful—except that a building looked 'strange' without one. But it looked more strange when the roof fell in and this thing called the cornice hung down endwise and was 'thin.' But that was it. . . . No matter how 'thin' it was, the cornice was put there regardless of reality, to make the building familiar. It had no other meaning. Well, then, Victor Hugo saw this coming, did he, so long ago? . . . He foresaw that architecture would become a sham? . . . Was it all now sham or was it just the cornice that was shamming? . . . And if they would lie about the cornice, or lie with it this way in matters of state, why wouldn't they lie about other parts of the building too . . . perhaps as a matter of taste?" And then came critical inquests held by the boy-coroner . . . the pilaster found to be another nauseating cheat. Others followed thick and fast, I remember.

It was early disillusionment and cruel, this vision of the life-blood of idolized architecture ebbing slowly away, vividly pointed and finally driven home by the horror of the falling building, showing the sham architecture, a preposterous bulk, threatening to take the very life of the workman himself, his life-blood already dripping away down the wall, just beneath. The poor workman became significant, himself a symbol. Both experiences, "Ceci Tuera Cela" and the wreck of the capitol by internal collapse, did something to me for which I have never ceased to be grateful. If the old order is to be preserved—regardless—it is not well for boys to read the great poets nor see classic buildings fall down.

Soon after this, Viollet-le-Duc's *Dictionnaire Raisonné de l'Architecture Française* fell into my hands by way of a beloved school-teacher aunt of mine and the work was finished, ready for the master to whom I came some four years later, Louis H. Sullivan—Beaux-Arts rebel. I went to him, for one thing, because he did not believe in cornices.

Now if the "pseudo-classic" forms of the renaissance had had more life in them they would have died sooner and long ago have been decently buried. Renaissance architecture, being but the dry bones of a life lived and dead, centuries before, the bones were left to bleach. For text, then, on this our third afternoon, our reference to authority is hereby inscribed to Moti, ancient Chinese sage.

This inscription: "In twilight, light of the lantern, or in darkness, worship no old images nor run after new. They may arise to bind you, or, being false, betray you into bondage wherein your own shall wither." (Twilight probably meaning partial understanding; lantern-light, glamor; darkness, ignorance.) Or another translation—Chinese is far from English:

"Except in full light of day bow down to no images, cast, graven, or builded by another, lest they, being false, betray and bind you powerless to earth."

Still another:

"Without full knowledge worship no images, lest being false they bind thee powerless to make thine own true."

And finally we have reached the title of the discourse—"THE PASSING OF THE CORNICE," the image of a dead culture.

There was a Graeco-Roman feature advocated by the American Institute of Architects to finish a building at the top. This authentic feature was called the cornice. Not so long ago no building, great or small, high or low, dignified and costly or cheap and vile, was complete without a cornice of some sort. You may see accredited cornices still hanging on and well out over the busy streets in any American city for no good purpose whatsoever . . . really for no purpose at all. But to the elect no building looked like a building unless it had the brackets, modillions, and "fancy" fixings of this ornamental and ornamented pseudo-classic "feature." Cornices were even more significantly insignificant than it is the habit of many of the main features of our buildings to be. The cornice was an attitude, the ornamental gesture that gave to the provincial American structure the element of hallowed "culture." That was all the significance cornices ever had—the worship of a hypocritical theocratic "culture." Usually built up above the roof and projecting well out beyond it, hanging out from the top of the wall, they had nothing in reason to do with construction—but there the cornice had to be. It was, somehow, become "manner"—something like lifting our hat to the ladies, or, in extreme cases, like the "leg" an acrobat makes as he kisses his hand to the audience after doing his "turn." The cornice, in doing our "turn," became our commonplace concession to respectable "form," thanks again to the Italians thus beset—and disturbed in their well earned architectural slumber.

But, have you all noticed a change up there where the eye leaves our buildings for the sky—the "sky-line," architects call it? Observe! More sky! The cornice has gone. Gone, we may hope, to join the procession of foolish "concessions" and vain professions that passed earlier. Gone to join the "corner-tower," the "hoop-skirt," the "bustle" and the "cupola."

Like them—gone! This shady-shabby architectural feature of our middle distance, the 'seventies, 'eighties and 'nineties, has been relegated to that mysterious scrap-heap supposedly reposing in the back-yard of oblivion. Look for a cornice in vain anywhere on America's new buildings high or low, cheap or costly, public or private. You will hardly find one unless you are looking at some government "monument." Government, it seems, is a commitment, a rendezvous with traditions that hang on.

But for a time no skyscraper—yes, it is all that recent—was complete without the cornice. The Belmont Hotel and the Flatiron Building in New York City perhaps said the last word, took the last grand stand and made the final grand gesture in behalf of our subject. For about that time the hidden anchors that tied the pretentious feature back on some high Chicago buildings began to rust off and let this assumption-of-virtue down into the city streets to kill a few people on the sidewalks below. The people killed, happened to be "leading citizens." But for "accident" what would modern American cities be looking like, by now? Cornices cost outrageous sums, cornices shut out the light below, but that didn't seem to hurt cornices, much, with us. Not until cornices became dangerous and "pseudo-classic" by way of the A.I.A. ("Arbitrary Institute of Appearances") began to crash down to city streets—did the city fathers talk "ordinance" to the Institute. The learned architects listened, read the ordinances, and though indignant, had no choice but to quit. Observe the relief!

Nor dare we imagine they would have dared to quit the cornice on their own account!

Shall we see the stagey, empty frown of the cornice glooming against the sky again? Has this cultured relic served its theatrical "turn" or are appearances for the moment *too* good to be true? Periodic "revivals" have enabled our aesthetic crimes to live so many lives that one may never be sure. But since we've learned to do without this particular "hangover" in this land of free progress and are getting used to bareheaded buildings, find the additional light agreeable, the money saved extremely useful, and as, especially, we are for "safety first," we are probably safe from the perennial renaissance for some years to come. At any rate for the moment "the glory that was Greece, the grandeur that was Rome," ours by way of Italy, may cease turning in ancient and honorable graves. O Palladio! Vitruvius! Vignola!—be comforted—the twentieth century gives back to you your shrouds!

Ye Gods! And *that* was the American architecture of liberty! Yes, it was unwarranted liberty that American architecture took.

We may well believe there is some subjective wave, that finally, perhaps blindly, gets buildings, costumes and customs all together in effect as civilization marches on. At least it would so seem as we look about us, for in the umbrageous cornice-time immediately behind us, hats were extravagant cornices for human heads, just as the cornices were extravagant hats for buildings. And what about puffed sleeves, frizzes, furbelows and flounces? Didn't they go remarkably well with pilasters, architraves and rusticated walls? In fact, weren't they exactly the same thing? Even the skirts of the cornice-period were extravagant cornices upside down over feet. And there was the "train" trailing the floor on occasion, the last word in cornices. Nor was "dinner" in those days complete without its own peculiar "cornice." They called it "dessert." Many brave and agreeable men died of that less obvious "cornice," but "cornice" nevertheless.

And the manners of that period of grandomania! Were they not emulation of the "cornice" when really manner? And top-heavy too, with chivalry and other thinly disguised brutalities? Now? No hat brim at all. Just a close sheath for the head. Skirts? None. Instead, a pair of silken legs sheer from rigid stilted heel to flexing knees; something scant and informal hung round the middle from above. What would

117

have barely served as underwear in the late cornice-days, now costume for the street. No "manner" in our best manners.

Study, by contrast, the flamboyant human and architectural silhouettes of the cornice-period just past with the silhouettes of today. After the comparison, be as grateful as it is in your nature to be—for escape, for even the *appearance* of simplicity.

Here comes "fashionable" penchant for the clean, significant lines of sculptural contours. Contrast these silhouettes in cars, buildings, clothing, hair dressing of today with those of the 'nineties. Even in the flower arrangements of the period of our "middle distance" and that of our immediate foreground you may see great difference. The "bokay" was what you remember it was. Now, a bouquet is a few long-stemmed flowers with artful carelessness slipped into a tall glass, or "au naturel," a single species grouped in close sculptural mass over a low bowl. Consider, too, that modern music no longer needs the cornice. It, too, can stop without the crescendo or the grand finale, the flourish of our grandfathers, which was "classic." Yes, the cornice was "flourish" too. Curious! Jazz, all too consistently, belongs to this awakening period, to the "youth" that killed the cornice, awakening to see that nothing ever was quite so pretentious, empty, and finally demoralizing as that pompous gesture we were taught to respect and to call the "cornice." It had much—much too much—foreign baggage in its train, ever to be allowed to come back to America.

Should we now clearly perceive what the cornice really meant in terms of human life, especially of our own life as dedicated to liberty, we *would* be rid of cornices forever. Turning instinctively from the cornice shows our native instincts healthy enough. But we require *knowledge* of its fatality, where freedom is concerned, to insure protection from the periodic "aesthetic revival" that is successfully put over every few years just because of enterprising salesmanship and our own aimlessness. We must have a standard that will give us protection. If we know *why* we hate the cornice now, it may never rise again to ride us or smite us some other day.

Suppose, for the sake of argument, once upon a time we *did* live in trees, lightly skipping from branch to branch, insured by our tails as we pelted each other with nuts. We dwelt sheltered from the sun and rain by the overhanging foliage of upper branches—grateful for both shelter and shade. Gratitude for that "overhead"—and the sense of it—has been with us all down the ages as the cornice, finally become an emblem—a symbol—showed. Instinctive gratitude is of course fainter now. But whenever the cornice, true to that primeval instinct, was *real shelter* or even the sense of it, and dropped roof-water free of the building walls—well, the cornice was not a cornice then but was an overhanging *roof*. Let the overhanging roof live as human shelter. It will never disappear from architecture. The sense of architecture as human shelter is a very fine sense—common sense, in fact.

But as soon as this good and innocent instinct became a habit, original meaning, as usual, lost by the time *usefulness* departed, the ancient and no less fashionable doctor-of-appearances took notice, adopted the "look" of the overhang, began to play with it, and soon the citizen began to view the overhang from the street, as *the* cornice. If ever "the doctor" knew or ever cared what meaning the overhang ever had, the doctor soon forgot. He became "cornice-conscious." The roof-water now ran back from the cornice on to the flat roof of the building and down inside down-spouts. But why should the doctor worry? Has the doctor of aesthetics ever worried about structural significances? No. So through him, although all had been reversed, this now obsession of the "overhead," for mere aesthetic effect, an aesthetic that had got itself into Greek and, therefore, into Roman life as art for art's sake, this arbitrary convention, became our accepted academic pattern. It was all up with us then—until now.

The net result of it all is that no culture is recognizable to us as such without the cornice. But just eliminate the troublesome and expensive feature from Greek and Roman buildings and see what happens by way of consequence. Then when you know what it meant in their buildings, just take that same concession to the academic artificiality of tradition from their lives and see, as a consequence, what happens to "culture." You will see by what is lost, as well as by what is left, that the cornice, as such, originally *was* Graeco-Roman culture and to such an extent that—"pasticcio-Italiano"—it has been our own "American pseudo-classic" *ever since.* Inasmuch as nearly everything institutional in our much over-instituted lives is either Roman or Graeco-Roman, we couldn't have had our chosen institutions without this cherished symbol. No, we had to do the precious cornice too. So we did the cornice-lie with the best of them, to the limit and far and away beyond any sense of limit at all.

Amazing! Utter artificiality become a more or less gracefully re-fined symbolic *lie,* the "culture" we Americans patterned and tried our best to make our own classic, too, and adored for a long, long time. Thomas Jefferson himself was blameworthy in that. George Washington no less so.

But pragmatic as the Romans were in all other matters, we may comfort ourselves a little, if there is any comfort in the fact that these same Romans, great jurists and executives, too, when it came to "culture," denied their own splendid engineering invention of the arch for centuries in order to hang on to the same cornice—or more correctly speaking, to hang the cornice on.

Not until the Roman doctors-of-appearances (their names are lost to us, so we cannot chastely and becomingly insult them) could conceal the arch no longer, did they let the arch live as the arch. Even then, in order to preserve "appearances," the doctors insisted upon running a cornice—in miniature—around over the arch itself and called the little cornice on the curve an archivolt. They then let the matter go at that. Yes, the noble arches themselves now had to have the cornices, and renaissance arches have all had cornices on their curves for several centuries or more, in fact had them on until today. Roofs were mostly now become flat or invisible. The roof-water ran back the other way. But here was the cornice, derived from and still symbolic of the over-hanging roof, continuing to hang over just the same. Yes, it was now great "art." In other words, the cornice was secure as academic aesthetic. No one dared go behind the thing to see how and what it *really* was. It no longer mattered what it was.

Another human instinct had left home and gone wrong, but civilization sentimentalized and made the degradation into prestige—irresistible. Professors taught the cornice now as "good-school." Every building, more or less, had to defer to this corniced authority to be habitable or valuable. Only a radical or two in any generation dared fight such authority and usually the fight cost the radical his economic life.

But now you may look back, although the perspective is still insufficient, and see what a sham this undemocratic fetish really was, what an imposition it became, how pompously it lied to us about itself; realize how much social meanness of soul it hid and what poverty of invention on the part of great architects it cleverly concealed for many centuries. And you may now observe as you go downtown that the worst is over. Only very sophisticated doctors-of-appearances dare use the cornice any more, and then the dead living dare use it only for national monuments to honor the living dead; especially have they done so for a monument to Abraham Lincoln who would have said, with Emerson, "I love and honor Epaminondas—but I do not wish to be Epaminondas. I hold it more just to love the world of this hour, than the world of *his* hour."

Here the cornice, being by nature and derivation so inappropriate to the "great commoner," gave to the doctor his opportunity for final triumph. The doctor has now succeeded in using it where most awful— too insulting. When we see this, almost any of us—even the "best" of us—may fully realize *why* cornices had to die, for at least "let us desire not to disgrace the soul!"

Now, for some time to come, democratic governmental departments being what they are, it may be that America will continue to be-cornice her dead heroes, dishonor them by its impotence. But there is ample evidence at hand on every side that the "quick," at least, have shed the cornice. The sacred symbol is worn out—to be soon obliterated by free thought.

It is time man sealed this tradition under a final monument. I suggest as admirable "project" for the students in architecture at Princeton a design for this monument, and by way of epitaph:

"Here lies the most cherished liar of all the ages—rest, that we may find peace."

For the first six thousand years of the world, from the pagodas of Hindustan to the Cathedral of Cologne, architecture was the great writing of mankind. Whoever then was born a poet became an architect. All the other arts were the workmen of the great work. The "symbol" unceasingly characterized, when it did not dogmatize, it all. Stability was an ideal—hence a general horror of progress. What consecration there then was, was devoted to a conservation of previous primitive types.

According to the great modern poet, neglected now, quoted at the outset of this discourse—in the Hindoo, Egyptian and Roman edifices it was always the priest . . . in the Phoenician, the merchant . . . in the Greek, the aristocratic republican . . . in the Gothic, the bourgeois. In the twentieth century—says our prophet—an architect of genius may happen, as the accident of Dante happened in the thirteenth, although architecture will no longer be the social art, the collective art, the dominant art. The great work of humanity it will be no longer.

But to Victor Hugo, when he spoke, architecture was the grand residue of the great buildings that wrote the record of a theocratic, feudalistic humanity, theologic, philosophic, aristocratic. Concerning that architecture his prophecy has come true. He foresaw democracy as a consequence, but did not foresee the consequences of its engine—the machine—except as that engine was symbolized by printing. He seems not to have foreseen that genius and imagination might find in the machine mightier means than ever with which to create anew a more significant background and framework for twentieth century civilization than was ever known before. Nor foreseen an architect who might create anew in genuine liberty—*for* great liberty—on soil enriched by the very carcasses of the ancient architectures. So let us take heart . . . we begin anew.

But instead of ourselves indulging in prophecy against prophecy, let us take hold of the cornice at the source from which it came to us, and take it apart—in order to see what the feature actually was. It may give us something useful in our own hard case. Perhaps we may find in it something valuable to the "modern"—in the sense that we ourselves are to be modern or die disgraced. Of course I visited Athens—held up my hand in the clean Mediterranean air against the sun and saw the skeleton of my hand through its covering of pink flesh—saw the same translucence in the marble pillars of the aged Parthenon, and realized what "color" must have been in such light. I saw the yellow stained rocks of the barren terrain. I saw the ancient temples, barren, broken, yellow stained too, standing now magnificent in their crumbling state, more a part of that background than ever they were when born—more stoic now than allowed to be when those whose record they were had built them—more heroic, as is the Venus of Melos more beautiful without her arms. Like all who stand there, I tried to re-create the scene as it existed when pagan love of color made it come ablaze for the dark-skinned, kinky-haired, black-eyed Greeks to whom color must have been naturally the most becoming thing in life. I restored the arris of the moldings, sharpened and perfected the detail of the cornices, obliterated the desolate grandeur of the scene with color, sound, and movement. And gradually I saw the whole as a great painted, wooden temple. Though now crumbling to original shapes of stone, so far as intelligence went at that time there were no stone forms whatever. The forms were only derived from wood! I could not make them stone, hard as I might try. Nor had the Greeks cared for that stone-quality in their buildings, for if traces found are to be trusted, and nature too, not only the forms but the marble surfaces themselves were all originally covered with decoration in gold and color. Marble sculpture was no less so covered than was the architecture.

All sense of materials must have been lost or never have come alive to the Greeks. No such sympathy with environment as I now saw existed for them, nor had any other inspired them. No—not at all. These trabeated stone buildings harked back to what? A little study showed the horizontal lines of wooden beams, laid over vertical wooden posts, all delicately sculptured to refine and make elegant the resemblance. The pediments, especially the cornices, were the wooden projections of the timber roofs of earlier wooden temples, sculptured here in stone. Even the *method* of that ancient wood-construction was preserved in the more "modern" material, by way of the large, wooden beam ends that had originally rested on the wooden lintels, and by the smaller wooden beam ends that rested above those; even such details as the wooden pins that had fastened the beam structure together were here as sculptured stone ornament. Here then in all this fibrous trabeation was no organic stone building. Here was only a wooden temple as a "tradition" embalmed—in noble material. Embalmed, it is true, with grace and refinement. But beyond that, and considering it all as something to be taken for itself, in itself, all was false—arbitrarily to preserve for posterity a tradition as arbitrary. Thought, then, in this life of the Greeks, was not so free? The grand sculptured stone cornices of their greatest building had originally been but the timber edges and projections of an overhanging roof that was intended to drop roof-water free of the walls. Elegant refinements of proportion were not lost upon me, but there was small comfort to see recorded in them—for ever-more—that liberty had not gone very far in thought in ancient Greece. Here at this remote day architecture had been merely prostitution of the new as a servile concession to the high-priest of the old order. In the hands of the impeccable Greeks here was noble, beautiful stone insulted and forced to do duty as an imitation enslaved to wood. Well, at any rate, the beautiful marble was itself again falling back from the shame of an artificial glory upon its own, once more. Here too, then, in this triumph was tragedy!

Was all this symbolic—a mere symptom of an artificial quality of thought, an imposition of authority that condemned this high civilization of the Greeks to die? Their "elegant solutions" and philosophic abstractions beneath the beautiful surface—were they as sinister? Were they too as false to nature as their architecture was false? Then why had it all to be born, reborn and again and yet again—confusing, corrupting and destroying, more or less, all subsequent chance of true organic human culture? Here it seemed was subtle poison deadly to freedom. Form and idea or form and function had become separated for the Greeks, the real separation fixed upon a helpless, unthinking people, whose tool was the chattel slave. By what power did such authority exist? In any case what could there be for democracy in this sophisticated abstraction, made by force, whether as intelligence or as power?

And then I thought of the beauty of Greek sculpture and the perfect *vase* of the Greeks . . . . Keats' *Ode to a Grecian Urn* came to mind. How different the sculpture and the vase were from their architecture—and yet the same. But Phidias fortunately had the living human body for his tradition. He was modern and his works eternal. The vase was sculpture too, pure and simple, so it could be perfected by them. It would live and represent them at their best. And their great stone architecture—it, too, was beautiful "sculpture"—but it had for its architectural *tradition* only a wooden temple!

It should die: here today in our new freedom, with the machine as liberator of the human mind, quickener of the artist-conscience—it is for us to bury Greek architecture deep. For us it is pagan poison. We have greater buildings to build upon a more substantial base—an ideal of organic architecture, complying with the ideal of true democracy.

Democracy is an expression of the dignity and worth of the individual; that ideal of democracy is essentially the thought of the man of Galilee, himself a humble architect, the architect in those days called carpenter. When this *unfolding* architecture as distinguised from *enfolding* architecture comes to America there will be truth of feature, to truth of being: individuality realized as a noble attribute of *being*. *That* is the character the architecture of democracy will take and probably that architecture will be an expression of the highest form of aristocracy the world has conceived, when we analyze it. Now what architecture? Clearly this new conception will realize architecture as no longer the sculptured block of some building material or as any *en*folding imitation. Architecture must now *un*fold an inner content—express "life" from the "*within*." Only a development according to nature, an intelligently aimed at purpose, will materialize this ideal, so there is very little to help us in the old sculptural ideals of the architecture Victor Hugo wrote about, so splendidly prophetic. And what little there is, is confined within the carved and colored corners of the world where and when it was allowed to be itself—and is underneath the surface, in far out-of-the-way places, hard to find.

But I imagine the great romantic poet himself would be first to subscribe to this modern ideal of an organic architecture, a *creation* of industry wherein power unlimited lies ready for use by the *modern mind,* instead of the *creature* of chisel and hammer once held ready in the hands of the chattel slave. An architecture no longer composed or arranged or pieced together as symbolic, but living as upstanding expression of reality. This organic architecture, too, would be so intimately a *growth,* all the while, as to make barbarous the continual destruction of the old by the new. American architecture, though both little and young, therefore conceives something deeper and at the same time more vital than the great Parthenon or even the beautiful Greek vase: an architecture no longer symbolic sculpture but a true culture that will *grow* greater buildings and *grow* more beautiful belongings true to the nature of the thing and more at one with the nature of man. Radical, its roots where they belong—in the soil—this architecture would be likely to live where all else has had to die or is dying.

Being integral this art will not know contrasted and separate existence as art, but will be as much "nature" as we are ourselves natural. This should be the expression of any true democracy. Such an ideal is nowise pagan, more nearly of the Crusades maybe—but racial or national no longer except in superficial sense. It is only the method, the proper technique in which to use our resources with new sense of materials, that remains to be realized. This realization may truly be said to be modern: New in the thought of the coming world, in which the new and the old shall be as one.

Now comes the usual feeling that this discourse has all been too free in idealization, not intimate enough realization of a very simple matter. The discourse simply means that "make-believe" is played out; that it has no longer nor ever had genuine significance as art; that we are in a hard but hopeful case where any pretence fails to satisfy us. Something has happened in this new ideal of freedom we call America that is contagious and goes around the world. I don't even know that it belongs to us as a nation particularly, because we, being the thing itself, seem to realize it least. It is often so. Of that which a man is most, he usually speaks least unless he has to speak, and then he will tell you less than someone who is not so much the thing himself, but can see it a little apart, in perspective. We see then that in us is a deeper hunger —a hunger for integrity. For some such reason as this we are waking to see ourselves as the provincial dumping-ground for the cast-off regalia of civilization entire. We have been the village aristocracy of the great art world—"putting on" the style we took "by taste" from the pattern-books, or saw at the movies, or admired on postcards sent home by those who have "been abroad"—don't you know? It never occurred to us that we had greater and more coming to us *as our own* than any of the aristocracy of art we aped and imitated ever had. But now we are beginning to see that even Colonial was a "hangover," was a cornice, a nice, neat one, but the machine soon made it nasty-nice. *Ad libitum,* intoxicated by facility of "reproduction," we ran the gamut of all the "styles," the machine right after us to spoil the party. What, I ask you, in all history haven't we as a "free" people made free with in the name of art and architecture? We have acted like hungry orphans turned loose in a bake-shop.

And like the poor orphans, too, we have a bad case of indigestion now that would kill a less young and robust adventurer in that tasty, pasty, sugary realm we have known as art and decoration. The confectionery we have consumed—yes, but not digested, mind you—would have mussed up the sources from which it came beyond hope of any mortal recovery.

We are sick with it and we are sick of it. Some of us for that reason, and some of us because we are growing up. It was all bad for us—the machine made such "good taste" as we had, poisonous. Spanish was the latest acquired taste until "modernistic" got itself here by way of the Paris market with Madame. We will soon be no better satisfied eating that layer-cake than with the other cake-eating. It is all too modish, too thin, too soon empty—too illiberal, too mean. Our dyspeptic American souls hunger for realization, for a substantial "inner experience." Something more than a mere matter of taste, a taste for cake! All we've had has been predilection in this matter of taste, and we've tasted until we're so taste full that it is only a question of "where do we go from here?"

No wonder sensible Henry says "art is the bunk." He is right; all that *he* has known by that name is no more than what he says it is. And pretty much all that all America knows, too, is likewise. The corruption of our own sources of power and inspiration shames or amuses us when we try to go deeper. But we are going deeper now, just the same. When we get the *meaning* of our shame we are disgusted—likely we turn from it all, but we come back to it again.

We have realized that life without beauty accomplished is no life; we grasp at anything that promises beauty and are somehow punished. We find that like the rose it has thorns; like the thistle, it has defenses not to be grasped that way. The old canons have lost fire and force. They no longer apply. We are lost in the face of a great adversary whose lineaments we begin to see. Destruction of the old standards we see on every side. This new thing becomes hateful—but fascinates us. As we struggle, we begin to realize that we live on it, and with it, but still we despise and fear it—nevertheless and all the more because it fascinates us.

Well—we begin to glimpse this great adversary as the instrument of a new order. We are willing to believe there is a common sense. . . . A sense common to our time directed toward specific purpose. We see an aeroplane clean and light-winged—the lines expressing power and purpose; we see the ocean liner, streamlined, clean and swift—expressing power and purpose. The locomotive, too—power and purpose. Some automobiles begin to look the part. Why are not buildings, too, indicative of their special purpose? The forms of things that are perfectly adapted to their function, we now observe, seem to have a superior beauty of their own. We like to look at them. Then, as it begins to dawn on us that form follows function—why not so in architecture especially? We see that all features in a good building, too, should correspond to some necessity for being—the reason for them, as well as for other shapes, being found in their very purpose. Buildings are made of materials, too. Materials have a life of their own that may enter into the building to give it more life. Here certain principles show counte-

128

nance. It is the countenance of organic simplicity. Order is coming out of chaos. The word organic now has a new meaning, a spiritual one! Here is hope.

With this principle in mind we see new value in freedom because we see new value in individuality: And there is no individuality without freedom. The plane is a plane; the steamship is a steamship; the motor-car is a motor-car, and the more they are and *look* just that thing the more beautiful we find them. Buildings, too—why not? Men too? Why not? And now we see democracy itself in this fresh light from within as an ideal that is consistent with all these new expressions of this new power in freedom. We see this adversary to the old order, the machine, as—at last—a sword to cut old bonds and provide escape to freedom; we see it as the servant and savior of the new order—if only it be creatively used by man!

Now, how to use it?

Then—what architecture?

4: THE CARDBOARD HOUSE

"Inasmuch as the rivalry of intelligences is the life of the beautiful —O poet!—the first rank is ever free. Let us remove everything which may disconcert daring minds and break their wings! Art is a species of valor. To deny that men of genius to come may be the peers of the men of genius of the past would be to deny the everworking power of God!" . . .

Now what architecture for America?

Any house is a far too complicated, clumsy, fussy, mechanical counterfeit of the human body. Electric wiring for nervous system, plumbing for bowels, heating system and fireplaces for arteries and heart, and windows for eyes, nose and lungs generally. The structure of the house, too, is a kind of cellular tissue stuck full of bones, complex now, as the confusion of bedlam and all beside. The whole interior is a kind of stomach that attempts to digest objects—objects, "objets d'art" maybe, but objects always. There the affected affliction sits, ever hungry—for ever more objects—or plethoric with over plenty. The whole life of the average house, it seems, is a sort of indigestion. A body in ill repair, suffering indisposition—constant tinkering and doctoring to keep alive. It is a marvel, we its infestors do not go insane in it and with it. Perhaps it is a form of insanity we have put into it. Lucky we are able to get something else out of it, though we do seldom get out of it alive ourselves.

But the passing of the cornice with its enormous "baggage" from foreign parts in its train clears the way for American homes that may be modern biography and poems instead of slanderous liars and poetry-crushers.

A house, we like to believe, is *in statu quo* a noble consort to man and the trees; therefore the house should have repose and such texture as will quiet the whole and make it graciously at one with external nature.

Human houses should not be like boxes, blazing in the sun, nor should we outrage the machine by trying to make dwelling-places too complementary to machinery. Any building for humane purposes should be an elemental, sympathetic feature of the ground, complementary to its nature-environment, belonging by kinship to the terrain. A house is not going anywhere, if we can help it. We hope it is going to stay right where it is for a long, long time. It is not yet anyway even a moving-van. Certain houses for Los Angeles may yet become vans and roll off most anywhere or everywhere, which is something else again and far from a bad idea for certain classes of our population.

But most new "modernistic" houses manage to look as though cut from cardboard with scissors, the sheets of cardboard folded or bent in rectangles with an occasional curved cardboard surface added to get relief. The cardboard forms thus made are glued together in box-like forms—in a childish attempt to make buildings resemble steamships, flying machines or locomotives. By way of a new sense of the character and power of this machine age, this house strips and stoops to conquer by emulating, if not imitating, machinery. But so far, I see in most of the cardboard houses of the "modernistic" movement small evidence that their designers have mastered either the machinery or the mechanical processes that build the house. I can find no evidence of integral method in their making. Of late, they are the superficial, badly built product of this superficial, new "surface-and-mass" aesthetic falsely claiming French painting as a parent. And the houses themselves are not the new working of a fundamental architectural principle in any sense.

They are little less reactionary than was the cornice—unfortunately for Americans, looking forward, lest again they fall victim to the mode. There is, however, this much to be said for this house—by means of it imported art and decoration may, for a time, completely triumph over "architecture." And such architecture as it may triumph over—well, enough has already been said here, to show how infinitely the cardboard house is to be preferred to that form of bad surface-decoration. The simplicity of nature is not something which may easily be read—but is inexhaustible. Unfortunately the simplicity of these houses is too easily read—visibly an attitude, strained or forced. They are therefore decoration too. If we look into their construction we may see how construction itself has been complicated or confused, merely to arrive at exterior simplicity. Most of these houses at home and abroad are more or less badly built complements to the machine age, of whose principles or possibilities they show no understanding, or, if they do show such understanding to the degree of assimilating an aspect thereof, they utterly fail to make its virtues honorably or humanly effective in any final result. Forcing surface-effects upon mass-effects which try hard to resemble running or steaming or flying or fighting machines, is no radical effort in any direction. It is only more scene-painting and just another picture to prove Victor Hugo's thesis of renaissance architecture as the setting sun—eventually passing with the cornice.

The machine—we are now agreed, are we not—should build the building, if the building is such that the machine may build it naturally and therefore build it supremely well. But it is not necessary for that reason to build as though the building, too, were a machine—because, except in a very low sense, indeed, it is not a machine, nor at all like one. Nor in that sense of being a machine, could it be architecture at all! It would be difficult to make it even good decoration for any length of time. But I propose, for the purposes of popular negation of the cornice-days that are passed and as their final kick into oblivion, we might now, for a time, make buildings resemble modern bathtubs and aluminum kitchen utensils, or copy pieces of well designed machinery to live in, particularly the liner, the aeroplane, the street-car, and the motor-bus. We could trim up the trees, too, shape them into boxes—cheese or cracker—cut them to cubes and triangles or tetrahedron them and so make all kinds alike suitable consorts for such houses. And we are afraid we are eventually going to have as citizens machine-made men, corollary to machines, if we don't "look out?" They might be face-masked, head-shaved, hypodermically rendered even less emotional than they are, with patent-leather put over their hair and aluminum clothes cast on their bodies, and Madam herself altogether stripped and decoratively painted to suit. This delicate harmony, characteristic of machinery, ultimately achieved, however, could not be truly affirmative, except insofar as the negation, attempted to be performed therein, is itself affirmative. It seems to me that while the engaging cardboard houses may be appropriate gestures in connection with "Now What Architecture," they are merely a negation, so not yet truly conservative in the great cause which already runs well beyond them.

Organic simplicity is the only simplicity that can answer for us here in America that pressing, perplexing question—now what architecture? This I firmly believe. It is vitally necessary to make the countenance of simplicity the affirmation of reality, lest any affectation of simplicity, should it become a mode or fashion, may only leave this heady country refreshed for another foolish orgy in surface decoration of the sort lasting thirty years "by authority and by order," and by means of which democracy has already nearly ruined the look of itself for posterity, for a half-century to come, at least.

Well then and again—"what architecture?"

Let us take for text on this, our fourth afternoon, the greatest of all references to simplicity, the inspired admonition: *"Consider the lilies*

HOWARD ANTHONY HOUSE, BENTON HARBOR, MICHIGAN

INA HARPER HOUSE, INTERIOR, ST. JOSEPH, MICHIGAN

of the field—they toil not, neither do they spin, yet verily I say unto thee—Solomon in all his glory was not arrayed like one of these." An inspired saying—attributed to an humble architect in ancient times, called carpenter, who gave up architecture nearly two thousand years ago to go to work upon its source.

And if the text should seem to you too far away from our subject this afternoon—

"The Cardboard House"

—consider that for that very reason the text has been chosen. The cardboard house needs an antidote. The antidote is far more important than the house. As antidote—and as practical example, too, of the working out of an ideal of organic simplicity that has taken place here on American soil, step by step, under conditions that are your own—could I do better than to take apart for your benefit the buildings I have tried to build, to show you how they were, long ago, dedicated to the ideal of organic simplicity? It seems to me that while another might do better than that, I certainly could not—for that is, truest and best, what I know about the subject. What a man *does, that* he has.

When, "in the cause of architecture," in 1893, I first began to build the houses, sometimes referred to by the thoughtless as "The New School of the Middle West" (some advertiser's slogan comes along to label everything in this our busy woman's country), the only way to simplify the awful building in vogue at the time was to conceive a finer entity—a better building—and get it built. The buildings standing then were all tall and all tight. Chimneys were lean and taller still, sooty fingers threatening the sky. And beside them, sticking up by way of dormers through the cruelly sharp, saw-tooth roofs, were the attics for "help" to swelter in. Dormers were elaborate devices, cunning little buildings complete in themselves, stuck to the main roof slopes to let "help" poke heads out of the attic for air.

Invariably the damp sticky clay of the prairie was dug out for a basement under the whole house, and the rubble-stone walls of this dank basement always stuck up above the ground a foot or more and blinked, with half-windows. So the universal "cellar" showed itself as a bank of some kind of masonry running around the whole house, for the house to sit up on—like a chair. The lean, upper house walls of the usual two floors above this stone or brick basement were wood, set on top of this masonry-chair, clapboarded and painted, or else shingled and stained, preferably shingled and mixed, up and down, all together with moldings crosswise. These overdressed wood house walls had, cut in them—or cut out of them, to be precise—big holes for the big cat and little holes for the little cat to get in and out or for ulterior purposes of light and air. The house walls were be-corniced or bracketed up at the top into the tall, purposely profusely complicated roof, dormers plus. The whole roof, as well as the roof as a whole, was scalloped and ridged and tipped and swanked and gabled to madness before they would allow it to be either shingled or slated. The whole exterior was be-deviled—that is to say, mixed to puzzle-pieces, with corner-boards, panel-boards, window-frames, corner-blocks, plinth-blocks, rosettes, fantails, ingenious and jigger work in general. This was the only way they seemed to have, then, of "putting on style." The scroll-saw and turning-lathe were at the moment the honest means of this fashionable mongering by the wood-butcher and to this entirely "moral" end. Unless the householder of the period were poor indeed, usually an ingenious corner-tower on his house eventuated into a candle-snuffer dome, a spire, an inverted rutabaga or radish or onion or—what is your favorite vegetable? Always elaborate bay-windows and fancy porches played "ring around a rosy" on this "imaginative" corner feature. And all this the building of the period could do equally well in brick or stone. It was an impartial society. All material looked pretty much alike in that day.

Simplicity was as far from all this scrap pile as the pandemonium of the barnyard is far from music. But it was easy for the architect. All he had to do was to call: "Boy, take down No. 37, and put a bay-window on it for the lady!"

So—the first thing to do was to get rid of the attic and, therefore, of the dormer and of the useless "heights" below it. And next, get rid of the unwholesome basement, entirely—yes, absolutely—in any house built on the prairie. Instead of lean, brick chimneys, bristling up from steep roofs to hint at "judgment" everywhere, I could see necessity for one only, a broad generous one, or at most, for two, these kept low down on gently sloping roofs or perhaps flat roofs. The big fireplace below, inside, became now a place for a real fire, justified the great size of this chimney outside. A real fireplace at that time was extraordinary. There were then "mantels" instead. A mantel was a marble frame for a few coals, or a piece of wooden furniture with tiles stuck in it and a "grate," the whole set slam up against the wall. The "mantel" was an insult to comfort, but the *integral* fireplace became an important part of the building itself in the houses I was allowed to build out there on the prairie. It refreshed me to see the fire burning deep in the masonry of the house itself.

Taking a human being for my scale, I brought the whole house down in height to fit a normal man; believing in no other scale, I broadened the mass out, all I possibly could, as I brought it down into spaciousness. It has been said that were I three inches taller (I am 5′ 8½″ tall), all my houses would have been quite different in proportion. Perhaps.

House walls were now to be started at the ground on a cement or stone water table that looked like a low platform under the building, which it usually was, but the house walls were stopped at the second story window-sill level, to let the rooms above come through in a continuous window-series, under the broad eaves of a gently sloping, overhanging roof. This made enclosing screens out of the lower walls as well as light screens out of the second story walls. Here was true *enclosure of interior space*. A new sense of building, it seems.

The climate, being what it was, a matter of violent extremes of heat and cold, damp and dry, dark and bright, I gave broad protecting roof-shelter to the whole, getting back to the original purpose of the "cornice." The undersides of the roof projections were flat and light in color to create a glow of reflected light that made the upper rooms not dark, but delightful. The overhangs had double value, shelter and preservation for the walls of the house as well as diffusion of reflected light for the upper story, through the "light screens" that took the place of the walls and were the windows.

At this time, a house to me was obvious primarily as interior space under fine *shelter.* I liked the sense of shelter in the "look of the build-ing." I achieved it, I believe. I then went after the variegate bands of material in the old walls to eliminate odds and ends in favor of one material and a single surface from grade to eaves, or grade to second story sill-cope, treated as simple enclosing screens—or else made a plain screen band around the second story above the window-sills, turned up over on to the ceiling beneath the eaves. This screen band was of the same material as the under side of the eaves themselves, or what architects call the "soffit." The planes of the building parallel to the ground were all stressed, to grip the whole to earth. Sometimes it was possible to make the enclosing wall below this upper band of the second story, from the second story window-sill clear down to the ground, a heavy "wainscot" of fine masonry material resting on the cement or stone platform laid on the foundation. I liked that wainscot to be of masonry material when my clients felt they could afford it.

As a matter of form, too, I liked to see the projecting base, or water table, set out over the foundation walls themselves—as a sub-stantial preparation for the building. This was managed by setting the studs of the walls to the inside of the foundation walls, instead of to the outside. All door and window tops were now brought into line with each other with only comfortable head-clearance for the average hu-man being. Eliminating the sufferers from the "attic" enabled the roofs to lie low. The house began to associate with the ground and become natural to its prairie site. And would the young man in architecture ever believe that this was all "new" then? Not only new, but destructive heresy—or ridiculous eccentricity. So new that what little prospect I had of ever earning a livelihood by making houses was nearly wrecked. At first, "they" called the houses "dress-reform" houses, because society was just then excited about that particular "reform." This simplifica-tion looked like some kind of "reform" to them. Oh, they called them all sorts of names that cannot be repeated, but "they" never found a better term for the work unless it was "horizontal Gothic," "temperance archi-tecture" (with a sneer), etc., etc. I don't know how I escaped the accu-sation of another "renaissance."

What I have just described was all on the *outside* of the house and was there chiefly because of what had happened *inside*. Dwellings of that period were "cut-up," advisedly and completely, with the grim determination that should go with any cutting process. The "interiors" consisted of boxes beside or inside other boxes, called *rooms*. All boxes inside a complicated boxing. Each domestic "function" was properly box to box. I could see little sense in this inhibition, this cellular sequestration that implied ancestors familiar with the cells of penal institutions, except for the privacy of bedrooms on the upper floor. They were perhaps all right as "sleeping boxes." So I declared the whole lower floor as one room, cutting off the kitchen as a laboratory, putting servants' sleeping and living quarters next to it, semi-detached, on the ground floor, screening various portions in the big room, for certain domestic purposes—like dining or reading, or receiving a formal caller. There were no plans like these in existence at the time and my clients were pushed toward these ideas as helpful to a solution of the vexed servant-problem. Scores of doors disappeared and no end of partition. They liked it, both clients and servants. The house became more free as "space" and more livable, too. Interior spaciousness began to dawn.

Having got what windows and doors there were left lined up and lowered to convenient human height, the ceilings of the rooms, too, could be brought over on to the walls, by way of the horizontal, broad bands of plaster on the walls above the windows, the plaster colored the same as the room ceilings. This would bring the ceiling-surface down to the very window tops. The ceilings thus expanded, by extending them downward as the wall band above the windows, gave a generous overhead to even small rooms. The sense of the whole was broadened and made plastic, too, by this expedient. The enclosing walls and ceilings were thus made to flow together.

Here entered the important element of plasticity—indispensable to successful use of the machine, the true expression of modernity. The outswinging windows were fought for because the casement window associated the house with out-of-doors—gave free openings, outward. In other words the so-called "casement" was simple and more human. In use and effect, more natural. If it had not existed I should have invented it. It was not used at that time in America, so I lost many clients because I insisted upon it when they wanted the "guillotine" or "double-hung" window then in use. The guillotine was not simple nor human. It was only expedient. I used it once in the Winslow House—my first house—and rejected it thereafter—forever. Nor at that time did I entirely eliminate the wooden trim. I did make it "plastic," that is, light and continuously flowing instead of the heavy "cut and butt" of the usual carpenter work. No longer did the "trim," so called, look like carpenter work. The machine could do it perfectly well as I laid it out. It was all after "quiet."

This plastic trim, too, with its running "back-hand" enabled poor workmanship to be concealed. It was necessary with the field resources at hand at that time to conceal much. Machinery versus the union had already demoralized the workmen. The machine resources were so little understood that extensive drawings had to be made merely to show the "mill-man" what to leave off. But the "trim" finally became only a single, flat, narrow, horizontal wood band running around the room, one at the top of the windows and doors and another next to the floors, both connected with narrow, vertical, thin wood bands that were used to divide the wall surfaces of the whole room smoothly and flatly into folded color planes. The trim merely completed the window and door openings in this same plastic sense. When the interior had thus become wholly plastic, instead of structural, a new element, as I have said, had entered architecture. Strangely enough an element that had not existed in architectural history before. Not alone in the trim, but in numerous ways too tedious to describe in words, this revolutionary sense of the plastic whole, an instinct with me at first, began to work more and more intelligently and have fascinating, unforeseen consequences. Here was something that began to organize itself. When several houses had been finished and compared with the house of the period, there was very little of that house left standing. Nearly every one had stood the house of the period as long as he could stand it, judging by appreciation of the change. Now all this probably tedious description is intended to indicate directly in bare outline how thus early there *was* an ideal of organic simplicity put to work, with historical consequences,

140

here in your own country. The main motives and indications were (and I enjoyed them all):

First— To reduce the number of necessary parts of the house and the separate rooms to a minimum, and make all come together as enclosed space—so divided that light, air and vista permeated the whole with a sense of unity.

Second— To associate the building as a whole with its site by extension and emphasis of the planes parallel to the ground, but keeping the floors off the best part of the site, thus leaving that better part for use in connection with the life of the house. Extended level planes were found useful in this connection.

Third— To eliminate the room as a box and the house as another by making all walls enclosing screens—the ceilings and floors and enclosing screens to flow into each other as one large enclosure of space, with minor subdivisions only.

Make all house proportions more liberally human, with less wasted space in structure, and structure more appropriate to material, and so the whole more livable. *Liberal* is the best word. Extended straight lines or streamlines were useful in this.

Fourth— To get the unwholesome basement up out of the ground, entirely above it, as a low pedestal for the living portion of the home, making the foundation itself visible as a low masonry platform on which the building should stand.

Fifth— To harmonize all necessary openings to "outside" or to "inside" with good human proportions and make them occur naturally—singly or as a series in the scheme of the whole building. Usually they appeared as "light-screens" instead of walls, because all the "architecture" of the house was chiefly the way these openings came in such walls as were grouped about the rooms as enclosing screens. The *room* as such was now the essential architectural expression, and there were to be no holes cut in walls as holes are cut in a box, because this was not in keeping with the ideal of "plastic." Cutting holes was violent.

Sixth— To eliminate combinations of different materials in favor of mono-material so far as possible; to use no ornament that did not come out of the nature of materials to make the whole building clearer and more expressive as a place to live in, and give the conception of the building appropriate revealing emphasis. Geometrical or straight lines were natural to the machinery at work in the building trades then, so the interiors took on this character naturally.

Seventh—To incorporate all heating, lighting, plumbing so that these systems became constituent parts of the building itself. These service features became architectural and in this attempt the ideal of an organic architecture was at work.

Eighth— To incorporate as organic architecture—so far as possible—furnishings, making them all one with the building and designing them in simple terms for machine work. Again straight lines and rectilinear forms.

Ninth— Eliminate the decorator. He was all curves and all efflorescence, if not all "period."

This was all rational enough so far as the thought of an organic architecture went. The particular forms this thought took in the feeling of it all could only be personal. There was nothing whatever at this time to help make them what they were. All seemed to be the most natural thing in the world and grew up out of the circumstances of the moment. Whatever they may be worth in the long run is all they are worth.

Now *simplicity* being the point in question in this early constructive effort, organic simplicity I soon found to be a matter of true coordination. And beauty I soon felt to be a matter of the sympathy with which such coordination was effected. Plainness was not necessarily símplicity. Crude furniture of the Roycroft-Stickley-Mission Style, which came along later, was offensively plain, plain as a barn door—but never was simple in any true sense. Nor, I found, were merely machine-made things in themselves simple. To think "in simple," is to deal in simples, and that means with an eye single to the altogether. This, I believe, is the secret of simplicity. Perhaps we may truly regard nothing at all as simple in itself. I believe that no one thing in itself is ever so, but must achieve simplicity (as an artist should use the term) as a perfectly realized part of some organic whole. Only as a feature or any part becomes an harmonious element in the harmonious whole does it arrive at the estate of simplicity. Any wild flower is truly simple, but double the same wild flower by cultivation, it ceases to be so. The *scheme* of the original is no longer clear. Clarity of design and perfect significance both are first essentials of the spontaneously born simplicity of the lilies of the field who neither toil nor spin, as contrasted with Solomon who had "toiled and spun"—that is to say, no doubt had put on himself and had put on his temple, properly "composed," everything in the category of good things but the cook-stove.

Five lines where three are enough is stupidity. Nine pounds where three are sufficient is stupidity. But to eliminate expressive words that intensity or vivify meaning in speaking or writing is not simplicity; nor is similar elimination in architecture simplicity—it, too, may be stupidity. In architecture, expressive changes of surface, emphasis of line and especially textures of material, may go to make facts eloquent, forms more significant. Elimination, therefore, may be just as meaningless as elaboration, perhaps more often is so. I offer any fool, for an example.

To know what to leave out and what to put in, just where and just how—ah, *that* is to have been educated in knowledge of simplicity.

As for objects of art in the house even in that early day they were the "bête noir" of the new simplicity. If well chosen, well enough in the house, but only if each was properly digested by the whole. Antique or modern sculpture, paintings, pottery, might become objectives in the architectural scheme and I accepted them, aimed at them, and assimilated them. Such things may take their places as elements in the design of any house. They are then precious things, gracious and good to live with. But it is difficult to do this well. Better, if it may be done, to design all features together. At that time, too, I tried to make my clients see that furniture and furnishings, not built in as integral features of the building, should be designed as attributes of whatever furniture was built in and should be seen as minor parts of the building itself, even if detached or kept aside to be employed on occasion. But when the building itself was finished, the old furniture the clients already possessed went in with them to await the time when the interior might be completed. Very few of the houses were, therefore, anything but painful to me after the clients moved in and, helplessly, dragged the horrors of the old order along after them.

But I soon found it difficult, anyway, to make some of the furniture in the "abstract"; that is, to design it as architecture and make it "human" at the same time—fit for human use. I have been black and blue in some spot, somewhere, almost all my life from too intimate contacts with my own furniture. Human beings must group, sit or recline—confound them—and they must dine, but dining is much easier to manage and always was a great artistic opportunity. Arrangements for the informality of sitting comfortably, singly or in groups, where it is desirable or natural to sit, and still to belong in disarray to the scheme as a whole—that is a matter difficult to accomplish. But it can be done now, and should be done, because only those attributes of human comfort and convenience, made to belong in this digested or integrated sense to the architecture of the home as a whole, should be there at all, in modern architecture. For that matter about four-fifths of the contents of nearly every home could be given away with good effect to that home. But the things given away might go on to poison some other home. So why not at once destroy undesirable things . . . make an end of them?

Here then, in foregoing outline, is the gist of America's contribution to modern American architecture as it was already under way in 1893. But the gospel of elimination is one never preached enough. No matter how much preached, simplicity is a spiritual ideal seldom organically reached. Nevertheless, by assuming the virtue by imitation —or by increasing structural makeshifts to get superficial simplicity—

the effects may cultivate a taste that will demand the reality in course of time, but it may also destroy all hope of the real thing.

Standing here, with the perspective of long persistent effort in the direction of an organic architecture in view, I can again assure you out of this initial experience that repose is the reward of true simplicity and that organic simplicity is sure of repose. Repose is the highest quality in the art of architecture, next to integrity, and a reward for integrity. Simplicity may well be held to the fore as a spiritual ideal, but when actually achieved, as in the "lilies of the field," it is something that comes of itself, something spontaneously born out of the nature of the doing whatever it is that is to be done. Simplicity, too, is a reward for fine feeling and straight thinking in working a principle, well in hand, to a consistent end. Solomon knew nothing about it, for he was only wise. And this, I think, is what Jesus meant by the text we have chosen for this discourse—"Consider the lilies of the field," as contrasted, for beauty, with Solomon.

Now, a chair *is* a machine to sit in.

A home *is* a machine to live in.

The human body *is* a machine to be worked by will.

A tree *is* a machine to bear fruit.

A plant *is* a machine to bear flowers and seeds.

And, as I've admitted before somewhere, a heart *is* a suction pump. Does that idea thrill you?

Trite as it is, it may be as well to think it over because the *least* any of these things may be, *is* just that. All of them are that before they are anything else. And to violate that mechanical requirement in any of them is to finish before anything of higher purpose can happen. To ignore the fact is either sentimentality or the prevalent insanity. Let us acknowledge in this respect, that this matter of mechanics is just as true of the work of art as it is true of anything else. But, were we to stop with that trite acknowledgment, we should only be living in a low, rudimentary sense. This skeleton rudiment accepted, *understood,* is the first condition of any fruit or flower we may hope to get from ourselves. Let us continue to call this flower and fruit of ourselves, even in this machine age, art. Some architects, as we may see, now consciously acknowledge this "machine" rudiment. Some will eventually get to it by circuitous mental labor. Some *are* the thing itself without question and already in need of "treatment." But "Americans" (I prefer to be more specific and say "Usonians") have been educated "blind" to the higher human uses of it all—while actually in sight of this higher human use all the while.

Therefore, now let the declaration that "all is machinery" stand nobly forth for what it is worth. But why not more profoundly declare that "form follows function" and let it go at that? Saying, "form follows function," is not only deeper, it is clearer, and it goes further in a more comprehensive way to say the thing to be said, because the implication of this saying includes the heart of the whole matter. It may be that function follows form, as, or if, you prefer, but it is easier thinking with the first proposition just as it is easier to stand on your feet and nod your head than it would be to stand on your head and nod your feet. Let us not forget that the simplicity of the universe is very different from the simplicity of a machine.

New significance in architecture implies new materials qualifying form and textures, requires fresh feeling, which will eventually qualify both as "ornament." But "decoration" must be sent on its way or now be given the meaning that it has lost, if it is to stay. Since "decoration" became acknowledged as such, and ambitiously set up for itself as decoration, it has been a makeshift, in the light of this ideal of organic architecture. Any house decoration, as such, is an architectural make-shift, however well it may be done, unless the decoration, so-called, is part of the architect's design in both concept and execution.

Since architecture in the old sense died and decoration has had to shift for itself more and more, all so-called decoration is become *ornamental*, therefore no longer *integral*. There can be no true simplicity in either architecture or decoration under any such condition. Let decoration, therefore, die for architecture, and the decorator become an architect, but not an "interior architect."

Ornament can never be applied to architecture any more than architecture should ever be applied to decoration. All ornament, if not developed within the nature of architecture and as organic part of such

146

expression, vitiates the whole fabric no matter how clever or beautiful it may be as something in itself.

Yes—for a century or more decoration has been setting up for itself, and in our prosperous country has come pretty near to doing very well, thank you. I think we may say that it is pretty much all we have now to show as domestic architecture, as domestic architecture still goes with us at the present time. But we may as well face it. The interior decorator thrives with us because we have no architecture. Any decorator is the natural enemy of organic simplicity in architecture. He, persuasive doctor-of-appearances that he *must* be when he becomes architectural substitute, will give you an imitation of anything, even an imitation of imitative simplicity. Just at the moment, he is expert in this imitation. France, the born decorator, is now engaged with Madame, owing to the good fortune of the French market, in selling us this ready-made or made-to-order simplicity. Yes, imitation simplicity is the latest addition to imported "stock." The decorators of America are now equipped to furnish *especially* this. Observe. And how very charming the suggestions conveyed by these imitations sometimes are!

Would you have again the general principles of the spiritual ideal of organic simplicity at work in our culture? If so, then let us reiterate: first, simplicity is constitutional order. And it is worthy of note in this connection that 9 x 9 equals 81 is just as simple as $2 + 2$ equals 4. Nor is the obvious more simple necessarily than the occult. The obvious is obvious simply because it falls within our special horizon, is therefore easier for us to *see;* that is all. Yet all simplicity near or far has a countenance, a visage, that is characteristic. But this countenance is visible only to those who can grasp the whole and enjoy the significance of the minor part, as such, in relation to the whole when in flower. This is for the critics.

This characteristic visage may be simulated—the real complication glossed over, the internal conflict hidden by surface and belied by mass. The internal complication may be and usually is increased to create the semblance of and get credit for—simplicity. This is the simplicity-lie usually achieved by most of the "surface and mass" architects. This is for the young architect.

Truly ordered simplicity in the hands of the great artist may flower into a bewildering profusion, exquisitely exuberant, and render all more clear than ever. Good William Blake says exuberance is *beauty*, meaning that it is so in this very sense. This is for the modern artist with the machine in his hands. False simplicity—simplicity as an affectation, that is, simplicity constructed as a decorator's *outside* put upon a complicated, wasteful engineer's or carpenter's "structure," outside or inside— is not good enough simplicity. It cannot be simple at all. But that is what passes for simplicity, now that startling simplicity-effects are becoming the *fashion*. That kind of simplicity is *violent*. This is for "art and decoration."

Soon we shall want simplicity inviolate. There is one way to get that simplicity. My guess is, there is *only* one way really to get it. And that way is, on principle, by way of *construction* developed as architecture. That is for us, one and all.

5: THE TYRANNY OF THE SKYSCRAPER

Michelangelo built the first skyscraper, I suppose, when he hurled the Pantheon on top of the Parthenon. The Pope named it St. Peter's and the world called it a day, celebrating the great act ever since in the sincerest form of human flattery possible. As is well known, that form is imitation.

Buonarrotti, being a sculptor himself (he was painter also but, unluckily, painted pictures of sculpture), probably thought architecture, too, ought to be sculpture. So he made the grandest statue he could conceive out of Italian Renaissance architecture. The new church dome that was the consequence was empty of meaning or of any significance whatever except as the Pope's mitre has it. But, in fact, the great dome was just the sort of thing authority had been looking for as a symbol. The world saw it, accepted and adopted it as the great symbol of great authority. And so it has flourished as this symbol ever since, not only in the great capitals of the great countries of the world, but, alas, in every division of *this* country, in every state, in every county, in every municipality thereof.

From general to particular the imitation proceeds, from the dome of the national Capitol itself to the dome of the state capitol. From the state capitol to the dome of the county court house, and then from the county court house on down to the dome of the city hall. Everywhere the symbol leaves us, for our authority, in debt to Michelangelo for life. Great success the world calls this and Arthur Brisbane called it great art. Many institutions of learning also adopted the dome. Universities themselves affected it until they preferred Gothic. Big business, I suspect, covets it and would like to take it. But to its honor be it said that it has not yet done so. Yes—this is success. Probably every other sculptor who ever lived would like to have done or to do the thing that Michelangelo did.

Yet, as consequence of a great sculptor's sense of grandeur in an art that was not quite his own, we may see a tyranny that might well make the tyrannical skyscraper of the present day sway in its socket sick with envy, although the tyrannical dome is by no means so cruel as the tyrannical skyscraper. But the tyrannical dome *is* more magniloquent waste. How tragic it all is! It is not only as though Buonarrotti himself had never seen the Grand Canyon, which of course he never could have seen, but it is as though no one else had ever seen it either, and monumental buildings therefore kept right on being domeous, domicular or dome-istic—on stilts because they knew no better.

Domed or damned was and is the status of official buildings in all countries, especially in ours, as a consequence of the great Italian's impulsive indiscretion. But no other individual sculptor, painter or architect, let us hope, may ever achieve such success again, or architecture at the end of its resources may pass out in favor of something else.

It would be interesting to me to know what Buonarrotti would think of it now. But it is too late. We shall never know except as we imagine it for ourselves.

We should have to ignore the cradle-of-the-race, Persia, even Rome itself, to say that the sculptor did more than appropriate the dome. The earlier Romans had already made flat ones thrusting against the building walls, and the domes of Persia, relatively modest, though seated deep in the building, were tall and very beautiful. Stamboul and Hagia Sophia of course make St. Peter's look like the scrap-pile of reborn posts, pilasters and moldings of the Graeco-Roman sort that it is.

But Buonarrotti got his dome up higher than all others—got it out of the building itself up onto stilts! Ah! that was better. History relates, however, that a hurry-up call had to be sent in at the last moment for the blacksmith. A grand chain was needed, and needed in a hurry, too, to keep this monumental grandeur, up there where it was, long enough for it to do its deadly work. While they were getting this grand chain fastened around the haunches of the grand dome, in jeopardy on its stilts, our hero, the truly great sculptor, deeply, or rather highly, in trouble with architecture, must have known some hours of anguish such as only architects can ever know.

I can imagine the relief with which he crawled into bed when all was secure, and slept for thirty-six hours without turning over. This contribution "by the greatest artist who ever lived"—Arthur Brisbane said that is what he is—was our grandest heritage from the rebirth of architecture in Italy, called the Renaissance, and countless billions it has cost us to brag like that.

But all triumph, humanly speaking, is short-lived and we ourselves have found a new way to play hobby-horse with the Renaissance—a way particularly our own, and now we, in our time, astonish the world similarly. We are not putting a dome up on stilts—no, but we are carrying the stilts themselves on up higher than the dome ever stood and hanging reborn architecture, or architecture-soon-to-be-born, all over the steel, chasing up and down between the steel-stilts in automatic machines at the rate of a mile a minute; until the world gasps, votes our innovation a success, and imitates. Another worldly success, but not this time empty in the name of grandeur. By no means; we are no longer like that. We are doing it for money, mind you—charging off whatever deficit may arise in connection therewith to advertising account.

150

We are now, ourselves, running races up into the sky for advertis-ing purposes, not necessarily advertising authority now but still nobly experimenting with human lives, meantime carrying the herd-instinct to its logical conclusion. Eventually, I fervently hope, carrying the aforesaid instinct to its destruction by giving it all that is coming to it so that it will have to get out into the country where it belongs—and stay there, for the city will be no more, having been "done to death."

Our peculiar invention, the skyscraper, began on our soil when Louis H. Sullivan came through the door that connected my little cubi-cle with his room in the Auditorium Tower, pushed a drawing board with a stretch of manila paper upon it over onto my table.

There it was, in delicately pencilled elevation. I stared at it and sensed what had happened. It was the Wainwright Building—and there was the very first human expression of a tall steel office building as architecture. It was tall and consistently so—a unit, where all before had been one cornice building on top of another cornice building. This was a greater achievement than the Papal dome, I believe, because here was utility become beauty by sheer triumph of imaginative vision.

Here out of chaos came one harmonious thing in service of human need where artist-ingenuity had struggled with discord in vain. The vertical walls were vertical screens, the whole emphatically topped by a broad band of ornament fencing the top story, resting above the screens and thrown into shade by an extension of the roof-slab that said, em-phatically, "*finished*." The extension of the slab had no business to say "finished," or anything else, so emphatically above the city streets, but that was a minor matter soon corrected. The skyscraper as a piece of architecture had arrived.

About the same time John Wellborn Root conceived a tall build-ing that was a unit—The Monadnock. But it was a solid-walled brick building with openings cut out of the walls. The brick, however, was carried across openings on concealed steel angles and the flowing con-tours, or profile, unnatural to brick work was got by forcing the mate-rial—hundreds of special molds for special bricks being made—to work out the curves and slopes. Both these buildings therefore had their faults. But the Wainwright Building has characterized all skyscrapers since, as St. Peter's characterized all domes, with this difference: there was synthetic architectural stuff in the Wainwright Building, it was in the line of organic architecture—St. Peter's was only grandiose sculpture.

A man in a congested downtown New York street, not long ago, pointed to a vacant city lot where steam shovels were excavating. "I own it," he said, in answer to a question from a man next to him (the man happened to be me), "and I own it clear all the way up," making an upward gesture with his hand. Yes—he did own it, "all the way up," and he might have added, too, "all the way down through to the other side of the world." But then he might have thoughtfully qualified it by, "at least through to the center of the earth." Yes, there stood His Majesty, legal ownership. Not only was he legally free to sell his lucky lot in the landlord lottery to increase this congestion of his neighbors "all the way up," but he was blindly encouraged by the great city itself to do so, in favor of super-concentration. The city, then, gets a thrill out of "going tall?" Architects, advertising as wholesale "manufacturers of space for rent," are advocating tall, taller and tallest, in behalf of their hardy clients. Inventive genius, too, properly invited, aids and abets them all together, until this glorious patriotic enterprise, space-making for rent, is looked upon as bona-fide proof of American progress and greatness. The space-makers-for-rent say skyscrapers solve the problem of congestion, and might honestly add, create congestion, in order to solve it some more some other day, until it will all probably dissolve out into the country, as inevitable reaction. Meantime, these machine-made solutions with an ancient architectural look about them all, like the Buonarrotti dome, are foolishly imitated out on the western prairies and in the desolate mountain states. In large or even in smaller and perhaps even in very small towns, you may now see both together.

Our modern steel Goliath has strayed as far away from native moorings as Tokyo, Japan, where it is almost as appropriate to that country as the cornice is appropriate to Abraham Lincoln, in our own.

This apotheosis of the landlord may be seen now as another tyranny —the tyranny of the skyscraper. It is true, so it seems, that "it is only on extremes that the indolent popular mind can rest."

152

Having established an approximate form for these lectures—a preliminary amble in the direction of the subject, then a reference to authority as text, then the discourse and a conclusion to lay it finally before you, all in the good old manner of my father's sermons—let us keep the form, choosing as text this time: "Do unto others as ye would that others should do unto you." The attribution is universally known. But not so well known perhaps is the command by Moti, the Chinese sage: "Do yourselves that which you would have others do themselves."

The Tyranny of the Skyscraper

It has only just begun, but we may observe that Father Knickerbocker's village, to choose our most conspicuous instance, is already gone so far out of drawing, beyond human scale, that—become the great metropolis—it is no good place in which to live, to do good work in, or wherein even to go to market. This, notwithstanding the stimulus or excitation of the herd-instinct that curses the whole performance.

None the less—in fact just because of this—the price of ground that happens to be caught in the urban drift as it runs uptown in a narrow streak—no doubt to rush back again—soars just because the lucky areas may be multiplied by as many times as it is possible to sell over and over again the original ground area—thanks to the mechanical device of the skyscraper. The ground area used to be multiplied by ten, it was soon multiplied by fifty, and it may now be multiplied by one hundred or more. Meantime, we patiently pass over wide, relatively empty spaces in the city to get from one such congested area to another such congested area, waiting patiently, I suppose, until the very congestion, which is the source of inflated values, overreaches itself by solution and the very congestion it was built to serve severely interferes with and finally curses its own sacred sales-privilege. New York, even at this very early stage of the high and narrow, speaks of the traffic problem, openly confessing such congestion—though guardedly. And as congestion must rapidly increase, metropolitan misery has merely begun. Yes—merely begun—for should every owner of a lot contiguous to or even already within the commercially exploited areas, not to mention those hopefully lying empty in between, actually take advantage of this opportunity to

153

soar, all upward flights of ownership would soon become useless and worthless. This must be obvious to anyone. Moreover the occupants of the tall buildings are yet only about one-third the motor-car men that all will eventually emerge if their devotion to machine-made concentration means anything profitable to them.

So only those congestion-promoters with their space-manufacturers and congestion-solvers who came first, or who will now make haste, with their extended telescopes, uplifted elephant trunks, Bedford-stone rockets, Gothic toothpicks, modern fountain pens, shrieking verticality, selling perpendicularity to the earthworms in the village lane below, can ever be served. Nevertheless property owners lost between the luck, continue to capitalize their undeveloped ground on the same basis as the man lucky enough to have got up first into the air. So fictitious land-values are created on paper. Owing to the vogue of the skyscraper, real estate values boom on a false basis, and to hold and handle these unreal values, now aggravated by the machine-made, standard solution, subways—sub-subways—are proposed, and super sidewalks, or super, super sidewalks or double-decked or triple-decked streets. Proposals are made to set all the fair forest of buildings up out of reach of the traffic on their own fair stilts as a concession to the crowd. The human life flowing in and out of all this crowded perpendicularity is to accommodate itself to growth as of potato sprouts in a cellar. Yes—these super-most solutions are seriously proposed to hold and handle landlord *profits* in a dull craze for verticality and vertigo that concentrates the citizen in an exaggerated super-concentration that would have shocked Babylon—and have made the tower of Babel itself fall down to the ground and worship.

"To have and to hold," that is now the dire problem of the skyscraper minded. Just why it should be unethical or a weakness to allow this terrific concentration to relieve itself by spreading out is quite clear. Anyone can see why. And to show to what lengths the landlord is willing and prepared to go to prevent it: as superior and philanthropic a landlord as Gordon Strong of Chicago recently argued—as the Germans originally suggested—the uselessness of the freedom of sun and air, claiming artificial ventilation and lighting now preferable, demanding that walls be built without windows, rooms be hermetically sealed, distribution and communication be had by artificially lighted and ventilated tunnels, subways and super-ways. Here, on behalf of the landlord, by way of the time-serving space-maker-for-rent, we arrive at the "City of Night": Man at last and all so soon enslaved by, and his very life at the mercy of, his own appliances.

A logical conclusion, this one of Gordon Strong's, too, with its strong points—if the profits of exciting and encouraging the concentration of citizens are to be kept up to profitable pitch and the citizen be further educated and reconciled to such increased congestion as this would eventually put up to him. This patient citizen—*so much more valuable, it seems, if and when congested*! Must the patient animal be further congested or further trained to congest himself until he has utterly relinquished his birthright? Congested yet some more and taught—he can learn—to take his time (his *own* time especially, mind you), and watch his step more carefully than ever? Is he, the pickle in this brine, to be further reconciled or harder pushed to keep on insanely crowding himself into vertical grooves in order that he may be stalled in horizontal ones?

Probably—but in the name of common sense and an organic architecture, why should the attempt be made to so reconcile him, by the architects themselves, at least? Architects are yet something more than hired men, I hope. Else why should they not quit and get an honest living by honest labor in the country, preparing for the eventual urban exodus?

May we rightfully assume architecture to be in the service of humanity?

Do we not know that if architecture is not reared and maintained in such service it will eventually be damned?

The city, too, for another century, may we not still believe, was intended to add to the happiness, security and beauty of the life of the individual considered as a human being? Both assumptions, however, are denied by the un-American false premium put upon congestion by the skyscraper minded: un-American, I say, because for many years past rapid mobilizing, flying, motoring, teletransmission, steadily proceeding, have given back to man the sense of space, free space, in the sense that a great, free, new country ought to know it—given it back again to a free people. Steam took it away. Electricity and the machine are giving it back again to man and have not only made super-concentration in a tight, narrow tallness unnecessary, but vicious, as the human motions of the city-habitant became daily more and more compact and violent. All appropriate sense of the space-values the American citizen is entitled to now in environment are gone in the great American city, as freedom is gone in a collision. Why are we as architects, as citizens, and as a nation, so slow to grasp the nature of this thing? Why do we continue to allow a blind instinct driven by greed to make the fashion and kill, for a free people in a new land, so many fine possibilities in spacious city planning? The human benefits of modern automobilization and teletransmission—where are they? Here we may see them all going by default, going by the board, betrayed—to preserve a stupid, selfish tradition of proprietorship. Is it because we are all, more or less, by nature and opportunity, proprietors? Are we proprietors first and free men afterward—if there is any afterward? At any rate, all these lately increased capacities of men for a wide range of lateral movement due to mechanicization are becoming useless to the citizen, because we happen to be sympathetic to the cupidity of proprietorship and see it not only as commercially profitable but as sensational.

Now, as a matter of course and in common with all Usonian villages that grow up into great cities and then grow on into the great metropolis, Father Knickerbocker's village grew up to its present jammed estate; the great metropolis grew up on the original village-gridiron. New York, even without skyscrapers and automobiles, would have been crucified long ago by the gridiron. Barely tolerable for a village, the grid becomes a dangerous crisscross check to all forward movements even in a large town where horses are motive power. But with the automobile and skyscraper that opposes and kills the automobile's contribution to the city, stop-and-go attempts to get across to somewhere or to anywhere, for that matter, in the great metropolis, are inevitable waste—dangerous and maddening to a degree where sacrificial loss, in every sense but one, is for everyone.

156

Erstwhile village streets become grinding pits of metropolitan misery. Frustration of all life, in the-village-that-became-a-city, is imminent in this, the great unforeseen metropolis; the machine that built it and furnishes it forth also was equally unforeseen. Therefore it may not be due, alone, to this ever-to-be-regretted but inherited animal tendency of his race to herd, that the citizen has landed in all this urban jam. But that animal tendency to herd is all that keeps him jammed now against his larger and more important interests as a thinking being. He is tragically, sometimes comically, jammed. True, properly fenced, he jams himself. Properly fenced he may continue to jam himself for another decade or so, and cheerfully take the consequences. Strangely helpless for long periods of time is this Usonian, human social unit! But let us try to believe that—as Lincoln observed—not all of him for all of the time.

Now what does the human unit, so far in contempt in all this commercial Bedlam, receive as recompense for the pains of stricture and demoralizing loss of freedom, for the insulting degradation of his appropriate sense of space? What does he receive beside a foolish pride in the loss of himself to his time, increase in his taxes and increase in the number of handsome policemen at crossings?

A little study shows that the skyscraper in the rank and file of the "big show" is becoming something more than the rank abuse of a commercial expedient. *I see it as really a mechanical conflict of machine resources. An internal collision!* Even the landlord must soon realize that, as profitable landlordism, the success of verticality is but temporary, both in kind and character, because the citizen of the near future preferring horizontality—the gift of his motorcar, and telephonic or telegraphic inventions—will turn and reject verticality as the body of any American city. The citizen himself will turn upon it in self-defense. He will gradually abandon the city. It is now quite easy and safe for him to do so. Already the better part of him can do better than remain.

The landlord knows to his dismay that to sell the first ten floors of New York City is his new problem. The city fathers, too, now see that, except on certain open spaces, and under changed conditions where beautiful tall buildings might well rise as high as the city liked, the haphazard skyscraper in the rank and file of city streets is doomed—doomed by its own competition. In certain strategic locations in every village, town or city, tall buildings, and as tall as may be, should be permissible. But even in such locations very tall buildings should be restricted to only such area of the lot on which they stand as can be lighted from the outside and be directly reached from a single interior vertical groove of direct entrance to such space. Normal freedom of movement may thus be obtained below on the lot-area that is proprietary to the building itself. Thus all tall building would be restricted to the central portion thus usable of each private lot area, adding the balance of that area, as park space, to the city streets. There would then be no longer interior courts in any building.

All real estate in the rank and file and upon which the tall buildings will cast their shadows, and from which they must partly borrow their light, should in building stay down to the point where the streets will be relieved of motorcar congestion, whether that point be three, five, seven or nine stories, this to be determined according to the width of the streets on which the buildings stand.

As for the widening of streets, the present sidewalk and curb might be thrown into the street as transportation area, and the future sidewalks raised to headroom above the present street level, becoming in skillful hands well designed architectural features of the city. And these elevated sidewalks should be connected across, each way, at the street intersections and down, by incline, to the streets below at the same four points of street intersections. This would make all pedestrian movement free of automobilization and—crossing in any direction above the traffic—safe. Motorcars might be temporarily parked just beneath these elevated sidewalks, the sidewalks, perhaps, cantilevered from the buildings.

Parking space in front of all present shop windows would thus be provided and protected overhead by the elevated sidewalks. Show windows would become double-decked by this scheme. Show windows above for the sidewalks and show windows below for the roadbed. This practical expedient, for of course it is no more than an expedient—only expedients are possible—would put a show-window emphasis on the second-story sidewalk level, which might become a mezzanine for entrances to the different shops also.

Entrances could be had to stores from the roadbed by recessions built in the lower store front or by loggias that might be cut back into them. Such restraint and ordered release for tall buildings as here proposed might enhance the aspect of picturesque tallness and not leave further chaotic unfinished masses jamming into the blue. Such well designed separation of transportation and pedestrians as this might save the wear and tear of citizens doing daily the stations of the cross on their way to work.

Since in the metropolis the gridiron is organic disaster, and to modify it much is impossible, why not, therefore, accept and respect it as definite limitation and ease it by some such practical expedient? Working toward such modifications as suggested would vastly benefit all concerned:

> First—By limiting construction.
> Second—By taking pedestrians off the roadbed and so widening it.

The upper sidewalks might be made sightly architectural features of the city. While all this means millions expended, it might be done; whereas to abandon the old cities may be done but to build new ones will not be done.

Various other expedients are now practicable, too, if they were to be insisted upon, as they might well be, in the public welfare—such as allowing no coal to be burned in the city, all being converted into electricity outside at the mines, and cutting down the now absurd automobile sizes of distinctly city carriers. All these things would palliate the evil of the skyscraper situation. But the danger of the city to humanity lies deeper, in the fact that human sensibilities naturally become callous or utterly damned by the constantly increasing futile sacrifices of time and space and patience, when condemned by stricture to their narrow grooves and crucified by their painful mechanical privileges. Condemned by their own senseless excess? Yes, and worse soon.

It seems that it has always been impossible to foresee the great city; not until it has grown up and won an individuality of its own is it aware of its needs. Its greatest asset is this individuality so hard won. The city begins as a village, is sometimes soon a town and then a city. Finally, perhaps, it becomes a metropolis; more often the city remains just another hamlet. But every village could start out with the plans and specifications for a metropolis, I suppose. Some few, Washington among them, did so and partially arrived after exciting misadventures.

But the necessity for the city wanes because of the larger human interest. That larger human interest? Is it not always on the side of *being,* considering the individual as related, even in his work—why not especially in his work?—to health and to the freedom in spacing, mobile in a free new country; living in and related to sun and air; living in and related to growing greenery about him as he moves and has his little being here in his brief sojourn on an earth that should be inexpressibly beautiful to him!

What is he here for anyway? *Life* is the one thing of value to him, is it not? But the machine-made in a machine age, here in the greatest of machines, a great city, conspires to take that freedom away from him before he can fairly start to civilize himself. We know why it does. And let us at this moment try to be honest with ourselves on another point, this "thrill"—the vaunted *beauty* of the skyscraper as an individual performance. At first, as we have seen, the skyscraper was a pile of cornice-buildings in reborn style, one cornice-building riding the top of another cornice-building. Then a great architect saw it as a unit, and as beautiful architecture. Pretty soon, certain other architects, so educated—probably by the Beaux-Arts—as to see that way, *saw it as a column,* with base, shaft and capital. Then other architects with other tastes seemed to see it as Gothic—commercial competitor to the cathedral. Now the wholesale manufacturers of space-for-rent are seeing it as a commercial tower-building with plain masonry surfaces and restrained ornament upon which New York's set-back laws have forced a certain picturesque outline, an outline pretty much all alike. A picturesqueness at first welcome as a superficial relief, but already visible as the same monotony-in-variety that has been the fate of all such attempts to beautify our country. Standardization defeats these attempts—the

160

machine triumphs over them all, because they are all false. Principle is not at work in them.

The skyscraper of today is only the prostitute semblance of the architecture it professes to be. The heavy brick and stone that falsely represents walls is, by the very set-back laws, unnaturally forced onto the interior steel stilts to be carried down by them through twenty, fifty or more stories to the ground. The picture is improved, but the picturesque element in it all is false work built over a hollow box. These new tops are shams, too—box-balloons. The usual service of the doctor-of-appearances has here again been rendered to modern society.

New York, so far as material wealth goes, piled high and piling higher into the air, is a commercial machine falsely qualified by a thin disguise. The disguise is a collection of brick and masonry façades, glaring signs and staring dead walls, peak beside peak, rising from canyon cutting across canyon. Everything in the narrowing lanes below is "on the hard," groaning, rattling, shrieking! In reality the great machine-made machine is a forest of riveted steel posts, riveted girder-beams, riveted brackets and concrete slabs, steel reinforced, closed in by heavy brick and stone walls, all carried by the steel framing itself—finally topped by water tanks, set-backs, and spires, dead walls decorated by exaggerated advertising or chastely painted in panels with colored brickwork.

What beauty the whole has is haphazard, notwithstanding the book-architecture which space-makers-for-rent have ingeniously tied onto the splendid steel sinews that strain from story to story beneath all this weight of make-believe. But the lintels, architraves, pilasters and cornices of the pseudo-classicist are now giving way to the better plainness of surface-and-mass effects. This is making, now, the picturesque external New York, while the steel, behind it all, still nobly stands up to its more serious responsibilities. Some of the more recent skyscraper decoration may be said to be very handsomely suggestive of an architecture to come. But how far away, yet, are appearances from reality!

The true nature of this thing is prostitute to the shallow picturesque, in attempt to render a wholly insignificant, therefore inconsequential, beauty. In any depth of human experience it is an ignoble sacrifice. No factitious sham like this should be accepted as "culture."

As seen in "THE PASSING OF THE CORNICE," we are the modern Romans.

Reflect that the ancient Romans at the height of their prosperity lied likewise to themselves no less shamefully, when they pasted Greek architecture onto their magnificent engineering invention of the masonry arch to cover it decently. The Romans, too, were trying to make the kind of picture or the grand gesture demanded by culture. The Roman arch was, in that age, comparable to the greatest of all scientific or engineering inventions in our own machine age, comparable especially to our invention of steel. So likewise, what integrity any solution of the skyscraper problem might have in itself as good steel-and-glass construction has been stupidly thrown away. The native forests of steel, concrete and glass, the new materials of our time, have great possibilities. But in the hands of the modern doctor-of-appearances they have been made to *seem* rather than allowed to *be*. Sophisticated polishing by the accredited doctor only puts a glare upon its shame. It cannot be possible that sham like this is really our own civilized choice?

But owing to the neglect of any noble standard, such as that of an organic architecture, it is all going by default. All—sold.

Were it only strictly business there would be hope. But even that is not the case except as competitive advertising in any form is good business. Business ethics make a good platform for true aesthetics in this machine age or in any other.

No—what makes this pretentious ignorance so tragic is that there is a conscious yearn, a generosity, a prodigality in the name of taste and refinement in nearly all of it. Were only mummery dropped, temporary expedient though it may be in itself, space-manufacturing-for-rent, so far as that goes in the skyscraper, might become genuine architecture and be beautiful as standardization in steel, metals and glass.

We now have reasonably safe mechanical means to build buildings as tall as we want to see them, and there are many places and uses for them in any village, town, or city, but especially in the country. Were we to learn to limit such buildings to their proper places and give them the integrity as standardized steel and glass and copper they deserve,

162

we would be justly entitled to a spiritual pride in them; our submission to them would not then be servile in any sense. We might take genuine pride in them with civic integrity. The skyscraper might find infinite expression in variety—as beauty.

But today the great city as an edifice mocks any such integrity. Artists idealize the edifice in graphic dreams of gigantic tombs into which all life has fled—or must flee—or in which humanity remains to perish. Uninhabitable monstrosities? An insanity we are invited to admire?

From any humane standpoint the super-concentration of the sky-scraper is super-imposition not worth its human price.

It is impossible not to believe that, of necessity, horizontality and the freedom of new beauty will eventually take the place of opportune verticality and senseless stricture. And if these desiderata cannot be realized *in* the city, if they have no place there, they will take *the place of the city*. Breadth is now possible and preferable to verticality and vertigo, from any sensible human standpoint. Transportation and electrical transmission have made breadth of space more a human asset than ever, else what does our great machine-power mean to human beings? In all the history of human life upon earth, breadth, the consciousness of freedom, the sense of space appropriate to freedom, is more desirable than height to live with in the use and beauty that it yields mankind.

Why then, has commerce, the soul of this great, crude and youthful nation, any pressing need further to capitalize and exploit the rudimentary animal instincts of the race it thrives on, or need to masquerade in the path picturesque, like the proverbial wolf in sheep's clothing, in New York City or anywhere else?

As for beauty—standardization and its cruel but honest tool, the machine, given understanding and accomplished technique, might make our own civilization beautiful in a new and noble sense. These inept, impotent, mechanistic elements, so cruel in themselves, have untold possibilities of beauty. In spite of prevalent and profitable abuses standardization and the machine are here to serve humanity. However much they may be out of drawing, human imagination may use them as a means to more life, and greater life, for the commonwealth. So why should the architect as artist shirk or ignore humane possibilities to become anybody's hired man—for profit? Or if he is on his own why should he be willing to pay tribute to false gods merely to please the unsure taste of a transitory period, or even his own "superior" taste?

Today all skyscrapers have been whittled to a point, and a smoking chimney is usually the point. They whistle, they steam, they moor dirigibles, they wave flags, or they merely aspire, and nevertheless very much resemble each other at all points. They compete—they pictorialize—and are all the same.

But they do not materialize as architecture. Empty of all other significance, seen from a distance something like paralysis seems to stultify them. They are monotonous. They no longer startle or amuse. Verticality is already stale; vertigo has given way to nausea; perpendicularity is changed by corrugation of various sorts, some wholly crosswise, some crosswise at the sides with perpendicularity at the center, yet all remaining "envelopes." The types of envelope wearily reiterate the artificial set-back, or are forced back for effect, with only now and then a flight that has no meaning, like the Chrysler Building.

The light that shone in the Wainwright Building as a promise, flickered feebly and is fading away. Skyscraper architecture is a mere matter of a clumsy imitation masonry envelope for a steel skeleton. They have no life of their own—no life to give, receiving none from the nature of construction. No, none. And they have no relation to their surroundings. Utterly barbaric, they rise regardless of special consideration for environment or for each other, except to win the race or get the tenant. Space as a becoming psychic element of the American city is gone. Instead of this fine sense is come the tall and narrow stricture. The skyscraper envelope is not ethical, beautiful, or permanent. It is a commercial exploit or a mere expedient. It has no higher ideal of unity than commercial success.

6: THE CITY

Is the city a natural triumph of the herd instinct over humanity, and therefore a temporal necessity as a hang-over from the infancy of the race, to be outgrown as humanity grows?

Or is the city only a persistent form of social disease eventuating in the fate all cities have met?

Civilization always seemed to need the city. The city expressed, contained, and tried to conserve what the flower of the civilization that built it most cherished, although it was always infested with the worst elements of society as a wharf is infested with rats. So the city may be said to have served civilization. But the civilizations that built the city invariably died with it. Did the civilizations themselves die *of it*?

Acceleration invariably preceded such decay.

Acceleration in some form usually occurs just before decline and while this acceleration may not be the cause of death it is a dangerous symptom. A temperature of 104 in the veins and arteries of any human being would be regarded as acceleration dangerous to life.

In the streets and avenues of the city acceleration due to the sky-scraper is similarly dangerous to any life the city may have left, even though we yet fail to see the danger.

I believe the city, as we know it today, is to die.

We are witnessing the acceleration that precedes dissolution.

Our modern civilization, however, may not only survive the city but may profit by it; probably the death of the city is to be the greatest service the machine will ultimately render the human being if, by means of it, man conquers. If the machine conquers, it is conceivable that man will again remain to perish with his city, because the city, like all minions of the machine, has grown up in man's image—minus only the living impetus that is man. The city is itself only man-the-machine—the deadly shadow of sentient man.

But now comes a shallow philosophy accepting machinery, in it-self, as prophetic. Philosophers draw plans, picture, and prophesy a future city, more desirable, they say, than the pig-pile now in travail, their pictures reducing everything to a mean height—geometrically spaced.

In order to preserve air and passage, this future city relegates the human individual as a unit or factor to pigeonhole 337611, block F, avenue A, street No. 127. And there is nothing at which to wink an eye that could distinguish No. 337611 from No. 337610 or 27643, bureau D, intersection 118 and 119.

Thus is the sentient individual factor—the citizen—appropriately disposed of in the cavernous recesses of a mechanistic system appropriate to man's ultimate extinction.

This future city may be valuable and utilitarian along a line of march toward the ultimate triumph of the machine over man and may be accomplished before the turn finally comes.

To me it is dire prophecy. Skull and crossbones symbolize a similar fate. Let us prefer to prophesy, finally, the triumph of man over the machine.

For final text, then, for our final discourse:
"Except as you, sons-of-earth, honor your birthright, and cherish it well by human endeavor, you shall be cut down, and perish in darkness, or go up in high towers—a sacrifice to the most high God. Look you well, therefore, to yourselves in your posterity. Keep all close to earth, your feet upon the earth, your hands employed in the fruitfulness thereof be your vision never so far, and on high."
—*Attributed to some unheeded Babylonian prophet.*

What built the cities that, invariably, have died? Necessity.

With that necessity gone, only dogged tradition that is another name for *habit* can keep the city alive, tradition that has the vitality of inertia and the power of the ball and chain.

Necessity built the city when we had no swift, universal means of transportation and had no means of communication except by various

166

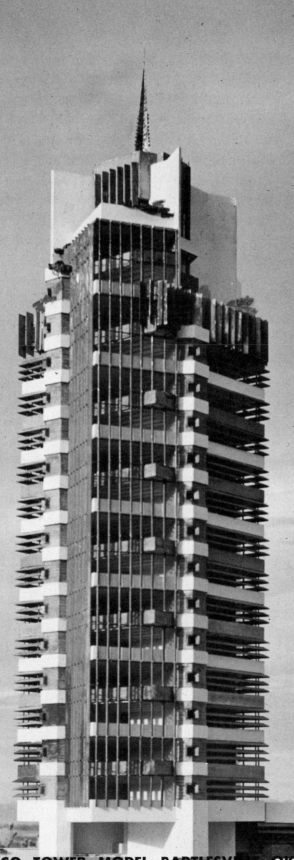

H. C. PRICE CO. TOWER, MODEL, BARTLESVILLE, OKLAHOMA

H. C. PRICE CO. TOWER, MODEL, BARTLESVILLE, OKLAHOMA

direct personal contacts. Then the city became naturally the great meeting-place, the grand concourse, the immediate source of wealth and power in human intercourse. Only by congregating thus, the vaster the congregation the better, could the better fruits of human living then be had.

In that day the real life of the city lay in the stress of individual ties and the variety of contacts. The electric spark of curiosity and surprise was alive in the street, in public buildings, in the home.

Government the city had—fashions and fads. But the salt and savor of individual wit, taste and character made the city a festival of life: a carnival as compared with any city today.

And architecture then reflected this livelier human condition as it now reflects the machine. Nor had the common denominator then arrived in the reckoning.

The common denominator has arrived with the machine in Usonia. Machine prophecy such as we have just referred to shows, if nothing else, that we are to deal with machinery considered as common-denominator salvation and in its most dangerous form here among us and deal with it soon, before it has finally to deal with our posterity as dominator. To deny virtue to the common denominator or to deny virtue to its eventual emancipator the machine would be absurd. But the eventual city the common denominator will build with its machines will not only be greatly different from the olden city or the city of today; it will be vastly different from the new machine-city of machine-prophecy as we see it outlined by Le Corbusier and his school.

What once made the city the great and powerful human interest that it was is now preparing the reaction that will drive the city somewhere, into something else. The human element in the civic equation may already be seen drifting or pushed—going in several different directions.

Congestion was no unmixed human evil until electricity, electrical intercommunication, motorcars, the telephone and publicity came; add to these the airship when it lays away its wings and becomes a self-contained mechanical unit.

Accepting all these, everything changes.

Organic consequences of these changes, unperceived at first, now appear. Freedom of human reach and movement, therefore the human *horizon* as a sphere of *action* is, in a single decade, immeasurably widened by new service rendered by the machine. Horizontality has received an impetus that widens human activities immeasurably.

Therefore such need for concentration as originally built the city is really nearing an end. But these new facilities—of movement—gifts to us of the machine, have, for a time, only intensified the old activity.

We are really witnessing an inevitable collision between mechanistic factors. The struggle is on. Additional human pressure, thus caused, thoughtlessly finds release by piling high into the air. The thoughtless human tendency in any emergency is to stand still, or to run away. We do—stay right there and pile up, or run away from the collision, to live to fight again some other day. To meet this human trait of staying right where we are, the skyscraper was born and, as we have seen, has become a tyranny. But the skyscraper will serve, equally well, those who are to run away, because probably the tall building has its real future in the country. But the skyscraper is now the landlord's ruse to hold the profits not only of concentration but of super-concentration: in the skyscraper itself we see the commercial expedient that enables the landlord to exploit the city to the limit, and exploit it by ordinance.

So greater freedom to spread out without inconvenience, the most valuable gift brought by these new servants—electrical intercommunication, the automobile, telephone, airship and radio—has been perverted for the moment into the skyscraper, and the gifts of the machine diverted to profit lucky realty.

Let us admit popular thrill in the acceleration, the excitement, directly due to these *new* mechanistic facilities. Temperatures run high. No one seems to know whether the excess is healthy excitement of growth or the fever of disease; whether it means progress or is only some new form of exploitation.

Forces are themselves blind. In all history we may see that the human beings involved with elemental forces remain blind also for long periods of time. But—saving clause—along with the forces released by our new mechanistic servants, there comes in our day an *ubiquitous publicity,* a valuable publicity that often succeeds in getting done in a month what formerly may have drifted a decade. We have already cut elapsed time in all forms of human intercommunication, a hundred to one. To be conservative, what took a century in human affairs now takes ten years.

Fifteen years, an epoch.

Thirty years, an age.

So the reactions to any human activity, idea or movement may control this great agency, and even in one lifetime show the people the wisdom or folly of the nature of any particular activity and call for correction before the affair is too far gone. Thus the fate of earlier civilization may be avoided by the dissemination of knowledge in ours. Educational influences thus brought to bear may avert disaster.

The traffic problem, as we have already seen in "THE TYRANNY OF THE SKYSCRAPER," forces attention to tyrannical verticality. The traffic problem is new but increasingly difficult—if not impossible—of solution.

Other problems will call soon and call louder.

As we have seen, the gridiron, originally laid out for the village now grown to the metropolis, already is cause for sufficient economic waste and human pain to wreck the structure of the city. High blood pressure, in the congested veins and arteries that were once the peaceful village gridiron, is becoming intolerable.

The pretended means of relief provided by space-makers-for-rent —the skyscraper itself—is now rendering distress more acute. The same means of relief carried somewhat further, and long before the solution reaches its logical conclusion, will have killed the patient—the overgrown city. Witness the splitting up of Los Angeles and Chicago into several centers, again to be split into many more.

And yet in new machine-prophecy, the tyranny of the skyscraper now finds a philosophy to fortify itself as an *ideal!*

We see, by the prophetic pictures of the city of the future, how the humanity involved therein is to be dealt with in order to render the human benefits of electricity, the automobile, the telephone, the airship and radio into herd-exploitation instead of into individual human lives.

And alongside these specific skyscraper solutions-by-picture of downtown difficulties there usually goes the problem of the tenement, the none-too-pretty picture of wholesale housing of the poor.

The poor, it seems, are still to be with us and multiplied, in this grand new era of the machine. At any rate they are to be accepted, confirmed and especially provided for therein as we may see in the plans.

Catastrophe is to be made organic—built in.

That the poor will benefit by increased sanitation may be seen and granted at first glance. But not only are the living quarters of the poor to be made germproof, but life itself, wherever individual choice is concerned, is to be made just as antiseptic, if we trust our own eyes.

The poor man is to become just as is the rich man—No. 367222, block 99, shelf 17, entrance K.

But the surface-and-mass architecture that now proposes to extinguish the poor man as human, has already proposed to do the same for his landlord. Therefore why should the poor man complain? Has he not, still, his labor for his pains?

There he is, the poor man! No longer in a rubbish heap. No. He is a mechanized unit in a mechanical system, but, so far as he goes, he still is but two by twice. He has been cleaned up but toned down.

Nor can the poor in the modernistic picture choose anything aesthetically alive to live with, at least so far as neighbors or landlord can see it. Dirty rags have been covered with a clean cardboard smock.

The poor man is exhibit C—cog 309,761,128 in the machine, in this new model for the greater machine the city is to become.

Observe the simplified aspect!

This indeed, is the *ne plus ultra* of the *e pluribus unum* of machinery. This new scheme for the city is delightfully impartial, extinguishes everyone, distinguishes nothing except by way of the upper stories, unless it be certain routine economies sacred to a business man's civilization, certain routine economies to be shared by the innovators with the ubiquitous numericals who are the "common denominator," shared with them by the nominators of the system as seen perfected in the picture. Shared fifty-fifty? Half to the initial nominator, half to the numericals? Fair enough—or—who can say?

The indistinguishable division of the benefits must in any case be left to the generosity of the initial nominators themselves, whoever they are. And who may say who they are?

But Humanity here is orderly. Human beings are again rank and file in the great war—this time industrial—a peaceful war. The rank and file of the common denominator this time is gratuitously officered by architecture, standardized like any army, marched not only to and fro but up and down. Up and down—even more—much more and more to come. The common denominator on these up-and-down terms would be no more alive without the initial nominator than the machine will be without the human brain. The common denominator itself has become the machine, come into its very own at last before the war is fairly begun.

"The Noble Duke of York, he had ten thousand men"—he made them all go ten floors up and ten floors up again. And none may know just why they now go narrowly up, up, up, to come narrowly down, down, down—instead of freely going in and out and comfortably around about among the beautiful things to which their lives are related on this earth. Is this not to reduce everyone but the mechanistic devisors and those who may secure the privileges of the top stories, to the ranks —of the poor?

Well—the poor?

Why are they the poor? Is there mechanical cure, then, for shiftlessness—machine-made? Or are the thriftless those whom the machine age is to herd beneficially in the mass and cover becomingly with a semblance of decency in a machine-made utopia? Or are the poor now to be the thrifty—themselves thus turned poor in all senses but one?

The lame, halt, blind and the sick are the only poor. As for the other poor—the discouraged, the unhappy—fresh air, free space, green grass growing all around, fruits, flowers, vegetables in return for the little work on the ground they require, would do more to abolish their poverty than any benefice mechanistic devisors can ever confer.

At present the urban whirl *is* common-denominator recreation; the urban crowd *is* common-denominator consolation; the dark corners of movie halls *are* the common-denominator retreats for recreation when those retreats are not far worse.

And the herd instinct that moves in the crowd and curses it is only the more developed by the mechanistic conditions in which the crowd swarms and lives. Millions are already sunk so low as to know no other preferment, to desire none. The common denominator—so profitable when congested—being further educated to congest, *taught* to be lost when not excited by the pressure and warmth of the crowd, turns argus-eyed toward what—more whirl?

Yet many of the individuals composing the crowd, the best among them, know well that an ounce of independence and freedom in spacing under natural circumstances, is worth a ton of machine patronage, however disguised or distributed as sanitation or as "art."

A free America, democratic in the sense that our forefathers intended it to be, means just this *individual* freedom for all, rich or poor, or else this system of government we call democracy is only an expedient to enslave man to the machine and make him like it.

But democracy will, by means of the machine, demonstrate that the city is no place for the poor, because even the poor are human.

The machine, once our formidable adversary, is ready and competent to undertake the drudgeries of living on this earth. The margin of leisure even now widens as the machine succeeds. This margin of leisure should be spent, with the fields, in the gardens and in travel. The margin should be expanded and devoted to making beautiful the environment in which human beings are born to live—into which one brings the children who will be the Usonia of tomorrow.

And the machine, I believe—absurd as it may seem now, absurd even to those who are to be the first to leave—will enable all that was human in the city to go to the country and grow up with it: enable human life to be based squarely and fairly on the ground. The sense

174

of freedom in space is an abiding human desire, because the horizontal line is the line of domesticity—the earthline of human life. The city has taken this freedom away.

A market, a counting-house and a factory is what the city has already become: the personal element in it all—the individual—withdrawing more and more as time goes on.

Only when the city becomes purely and simply utilitarian, will it have the order that is beauty, and the simplicity which the machine, in competent hands, may very well render as human benefit. That event may well be left to the machine.

This, *the only possible ideal machine* seen as a *city,* will be invaded at ten o'clock, abandoned at four, for three days of the week. The other four days of the week will be devoted to the more or less joyful matter of living elsewhere under conditions natural to man. The dividing lines between town and country are even now gradually disappearing as conditions are reversing themselves. The country absorbs the life of the city as the city shrinks to the utilitarian purpose that now alone justifies its existence. Even that concentration for utilitarian purposes we have just admitted may be first to go, as the result of impending decentralization of industry. It will soon become unnecessary to concentrate in masses for any purpose whatsoever. The individual unit, in more sympathetic grouping on the ground, will grow stronger in the hard-earned freedom gained at first by that element of the city not prostitute to the machine. Henry Ford stated this idea in his plan for the development of Muscle Shoals.

Even the small town is too large. It will gradually merge into the general non-urban development. Ruralism as distinguished from urbanism is American, and truly democratic.

The country already affords great road systems—splendid highways. They, too, leading toward the city at first, will eventually hasten reaction away from it. Natural parks in our country are becoming everywhere available. And millions of individual building sites, large and small, good for little else, are everywhere neglected. Why, where there is so much idle land, should it be parceled out by realtors to families, in strips 25', 50' or even 100' wide? This imposition is a sur-

175

vival of feudal thinking, of the social economies practiced by and upon the serf. An acre to the family should be the democratic minimum if this machine of ours *is a success*!

What stands in the way?

It is only necessary to compact the standardized efficiency of the machine, confine the concentration of its operation to where it belongs and distribute the benefits at large. The benefits are human benefits or they are bitter fruit. Much bitter fruit already hangs on the city-tree beside the good, to rot the whole.

An important feature of the coming disintegration of the Usonian city may be seen in any and every service station along the highway. The service station is future city service in embryo. Each station that happens to be naturally located will as naturally grow into a neighborhood distribution center, meeting-place, restaurant, rest room or whatever else is needed. A thousand centers as city equivalents to every town or city center we now have, will be the result of this advance agent of decentralization.

To many such traffic stations, destined to become neighborhood centers, will be added, perhaps, features for special entertainment not yet available by a man's own fireside. But soon there will be little not reaching him at his own fireside by broadcasting, television and publication. In cultural means, the machine is improving rapidly and constantly.

Perfect distribution like ubiquitous publicity is a common capacity of the machine. This single capacity, when it really begins to operate, will revolutionize our present arrangement for concentration in cities. Stores, linked to decentralized chain service stations, will give more perfect machinery of distribution than could ever be had by centralization in cities.

Complete mobilization of the people is another result fast approaching. Therefore the opportunity will come soon for the individual to pick up by the wayside anything in the way of food and supplies he may require, as well as to find a satisfactory temporary lodging.

The great highways are in process of becoming the decentralized metropolis. Wayside interests of all kinds will be commonplace. The luxurious motorbus, traveling over magnificent road systems, will make intercommunication universal and interesting. The railway is already only for the "long haul" in many parts of the country.

A day's journey anywhere will soon be something to be enjoyed in itself, enlivened, serviced and perfectly accommodated anywhere en route. No need to tangle up in spasmodic stop-and-go traffic in a trip to town or to any city at all.

Cities are great mouths. New York the greatest mouth in the world. With generally perfect distribution of food and supplies over the entire area of the countryside, one of the vital elements helping to build the city has left it forever, to spread out on the soil from which it came: local products finding a short haul direct, where an expensive long haul and then back again was once necessary.

Within easy distance of any man's dwelling will be everything needed in the category of foodstuffs or supplies which the city itself can now supply. The "movies," through television, will soon be seen and heard better at home than in any hall. Symphony concerts, operas and lectures will eventually be taken more easily to the home than the people there can be taken to the great halls in old style, and be heard more satisfactorily in congenial company. The home of the individual social unit will contain in itself in this respect all the city heretofore could afford, plus intimate comfort and free individual choice.

Schools will be made delightful, beautiful places, much smaller, and more specialized. Of various types, they will be enlivening, charming features along the byways of every *countryside*. Our popular games will be features in the school parks, which will be really sylvan parks available far and near to everyone.

To gratify what is natural and desirable in the get-together instinct of the community natural places of great beauty—in our mountains, seasides, prairies and forests—will be developed as automobile objectives, and at such recreation grounds would center the planetarium, the race-track, the great concert hall, the various units of the national theater, museums, and art galleries. Similar common interests of the many will be centered there naturally, ten such places to one we have now.

There will be no privately owned theaters. although there will be places for them along the highways. But good plays and other entertainments might be seen at these automobile objectives from end to end of the country in various national circuits—wherever a play showed itself popular or desired.

Such objectives would naturally compete with each other in interest and beauty, stimulate travel, and make mobilization a pleasure, not a nuisance—affording somewhere worth while to go. The entire countryside would then be a well developed park—buildings standing in it, tall or wide, with beauty and privacy for everyone.

There will soon remain the necessity for only shorter and shorter periods of concentration in the offices directly concerned with invention, standardization and production. The *city of the near future* will be a depot for the factory—perhaps. Whatever it is, it will be only a degraded mechanistic servant of the machine, because man himself will have escaped to find all the city ever offered him, plus the privacy the city never had and is trying to teach him that he does not want. Man will find the *manlike freedom* for himself and his that democracy must mean.

Very well—how to mitigate, meantime, the horror of human life caught helpless or unaware in the machinery that is the city? How easiest and soonest to assist the social unit in escaping the gradual paralysis of individual independence that is characteristic of the machine-made moron, a paralysis of the emotional nature necessary to the triumph of the machine over man, instead of the quickening of his humanity necessary to man's triumph over the machine?

That is the architect's immediate problem, as I see it.

Measured over great free areas, the living interest should be educated to lie in the contact of free individualities in the freedom of sun, light and air, breadth of spacing—*with* the ground. Again we need the stress of encountering varieties on a scale and in circumstances worthy the ideal of democracy and more a part of external nature than ever before seen—more so because of internal harmony. We want the electric spark of popular curiosity and surprise to come to life again, along the highways and byways and over every acre of the land. In charming homes and schools and significant public gathering places . . . architectural beauty related to natural beauty. Art should be natural and be itself the joy of creating perfect harmony between ourselves and the birthright we have all but sold.

We may now dream of the time when there will be less government, yet more ordered freedom. More generous human spacing, we may be sure, will see to that.

When the salt and savor of individual wit, taste and character in modern life will have come into its own and the countryside far and near will be a festival of life—great life—then only will man have succeeded with his machine. The machine will then have become the liberator of human life.

And our architecture will reflect this.

Shirking this reality, vaunted "modernity" is still making another "picture," everywhere clinging to the pictorial—missing joy in merely seeking pleasure. "Modernistic" is attempting by fresh attitudinizing to improve the "picture." The "new movement" still seeks to recreate joy by making shift to improve the imitation, neglectful of all but appropriate gestures.

But even an improved imitation as a picture will soon be trampled down and out—because of the machine. No amount of picture making will ever save America now!

The artifex alone in search of beauty can give back the significance we have lost—and enable the republic to arrive at that great art, in the inevitably man-made concerns of life, which will be to the human spirit what clear springs of water, blue sky, green grass and noble trees are to parched animal senses. For where the work of the artificer is a necessity, there the artist must be creatively at work on *significance* as a higher *form* of life, or the life of the human spirit will perish in this fresh endeavor that as yet is only a promise in this twentieth century.

The necessity for artistry, that is laid upon us by the desire to be civilized, is not a matter only of appearances. Human *necessity*, however machine-made or mechanically met, carries within itself the secret of the beauty we must have to keep us fit to live or to live with. We need it to live in or to live on. That new beauty should be something to live *for*. The "picture," never fear, will take care of itself. In any organic architecture the picture will be a natural result, a significant consequence, not a perverse *cause* of pose and sham.

Eventually we must live for the beautiful whether we want to or not. Our industrial champion, Henry Ford, was forced to recognize this—probably not connecting the beautiful with art, "the bunk." Just as he did in his industry, so America will be compelled to allow necessity its own honest beauty, or die a death nowise different from those nations whose traditions we accepted and idolized.

Unless what we now miscall culture becomes natively fit and is no longer allowed to remain superficial, this picture, which America is so extravagantly busy "pictorializing," can only hasten the end. The buttons, stuffs, dictums, wheels and things we are now using for the purpose of the picture will smother the essential—the life they were falsely made to falsely conceal instead of to express. And this experiment in civilization we call democracy will find its way to a scrap heap into which no subsequent race may paw with much success for proofs of quality.

Suppose some catastrophe suddenly wiped out what we have done to these United States at this moment. And suppose, ten centuries thereafter, antiquarians came to seek the significance of what *we* were in the veins of us—in the ruins that remained, what would they find? Just what would they find to be the nature of this picture-minded "pictorialization" of life and its contribution to the wisdom or the beauty of the ages past or to come?

Would the future find we were a jackdaw-people with a monkey-psychology given over to the vice of devices—looking to devices for salvation—and discovering this very salvation to be only another and final device?

No? Just the same, they *would* find broken bits of every civilization that ever took its place in the sun hoarded in all sorts of irrelevant places in ours.

They would dig up traces of sacred Greek monuments for banking houses. The papal dome in cast iron fragments would litter the ancient site of every seat of authority, together with fragments in stone and terra-cotta of twelfth century cathedrals where offices and shops were indicated by mangled machinery—relics of dwellings in fifty-seven varieties and fragments of stone in heaps, none genuine in character, all absurdly mixed. They would find the toilet appurtenances of former ages preserved as classic parlor ornaments in ours. They would find a wilderness of wiring, wheels and complex devices of curious ingenuity, and—ye gods—what a collection of buttons! They might unearth traces of devices that enabled men to take to the air like birds or to go into the water like fishes, and they might find relics of our competent schemes of transportation and a network or web of tangled wires stringing across the country, the relic of all our remarkable teletransmissions. But I think the most characteristic relic of all would be our plumbing. Everywhere a vast collection of enameled or porcelain waterclosets, baths and washbowls, white tiles and brass piping. Next would be the vast confusion of riveted steelwork in various states of collapse and disintegration where it had been imbedded in concrete. Where the steel was not so buried all would be gone except here and there where whole machines—a loom, a linotype, a cash register, a tractor, a dynamo, a passenger elevator—might be entombed in concrete chambers and so preserved to arouse speculation and curiosity, or to cause amusement as they were taken for relics of a faith in devices—a faith that failed! Of the cherished PICTURE we are making nothing of any significance would remain. The ruin would defy restoration by the historian; it would represent a total loss in human culture, except as a possible warning. A few books might be preserved to assist restoration, although the chemicalized paper now in use would probably have destroyed most of them utterly. Such glass and pottery as we make could tell but little except curious falsehoods. Certain fragments of stone building on the city sites would remain to puzzle the savant, for they would be quite Greek or quite Roman or quite Medieval Gothic, unless they were Egyptian or Byzantine. But mainly they would find heaps of a pseudo-renaissance,—something that never told, nor ever could tell, anything at all. Only our industrial buildings could tell anything worth knowing about us. But few of these buildings would survive that long

—electrolysis and rust would have eaten them utterly, excepting those where steel was buried in concrete. Glass fragments would be found in great quantity, but the frames, unless they happened to be bronze, and all else would be gone. They would have no skyscraper to gauge us by. Not one of those we have built would be there.

How and where, then, were it suddenly interrupted, would our progressive democratizing based upon picturizing the appliance, take its place in the procession of civilizations that rose and fell at appointed times and places? What architecture would appear in the ruins?

And yet—in all this attempt behind the significantly insignificant picture, may we not see culture itself becoming year by year more plastic? Are not some of our modern ideas less obviously constructed and more potent from within wherever we are beginning to emerge from the first intoxication of liberty? The eventual consequence of individual freedom is surely the elimination by free thought of the insignificant and false. Imprisoning forms and fascinating philosophic abstractions grow weaker as character grows stronger and more enlightened according to nature; this they will do in freedom such as we profess—*if only we will practice* that freedom. And, in spite of our small hypocrisy and adventitious reactions, let no one doubt that we really do yearn to practice genuine freedom to a far greater extent than we do, all inhibitions and prohibitions notwithstanding. Yes, we may see a new sense of manlike freedom growing up to end all this cruel make-believe. Freedom, in reality, is already impatient of pseudo-classic posture and will soon be sick of all picturizing whatsoever.

A common sense is on the rise that will sweep our borrowed finery, and the scene-painting that always goes with it, to the museums, and encourage good life so to live that America may honorably pay her debt to manhood by keeping her promises to her own ideal.

TWO LECTURES ON ARCHITECTURE

IN THE REALM OF IDEAS

THE idealist has always been under suspicion as performer,—perhaps justly. The explorer Stanley wrote of a monkey caught and tied up overnight by a rope around his neck. The monkey gnawed the rope in two and departed, the knot still tied about his neck. Next morning found the monkey with the strange "necktie" trying to go home, but each approach to rejoin the tribe would bring wild cries from his fellows and such commotion,—no doubt inspired by the Scribes,—that the monkey "with something about him" now,—would stop, dazed, pull at his "experience" a little, and think it over. Then he would move toward his fellows again, but such commotion would result that he would have to give it up. The Scribes had succeeded with the Pharisees. This kept up all day because the poor monkey kept on trying to come home, (to "tell the truth"?). Finally just before dark, the whole tribe, exasperated, rushed upon the suspected monkey . . . tore him limb from limb.

Monkey psychology? Of course; but our own tribe too, often destroys on similar suspicion the man who might impart something of tremendous importance and value to his tribe . . . such ideas as this poor "suspect" might have imparted, concerning how to avoid being caught and tied up, say—or if tied up,—how to escape.

In our own tribe we have another tendency, the reverse side of this same shield, and that tendency, no doubt *inherited* too, hails the mon-

184

key with delight, puts on rope-ends likewise, makes them the fashion, soon ostracizing any monkey without the fashionable necktie.

And yet as similar experience ideas are not bad in their way, nor are ideas troublesome necessarily, unless they are great and useful ideas. Then, in earnest, the chattering, warning, prophesizing and crucifying begin with the Scribes. Some form of murder is usually the result. In America we are now perfectly well used to ideas in the mechanical-industrial world. An inventor on that plane is practically immune, and may safely come in with almost anything about him or on him, and be acclaimed. We will try the thing though we are killed by thousands; we will scrap millions in the way of paper currency to put a shiny new dime in our pockets: as a result we get somewhere along commercial and mechanical lines.

But the absorbed idealist, egocentric-inventor in the realm of the thought-built, has a hard time with us socially, financially, and with peculiar force, morally. In addition to the instinctive fear for the safety of the tribe, in our form of social contract the man with an idea seems to have become an invidious reflection upon his many fellows who have none. And certain effects belonging naturally to the idealist,—such as belief in himself as having caught sight of something deeper, wider, higher or more important just beyond, mark him. He, all unsuspecting, will appear soon on the "path" as peculiar to his own individuality in ways the poor fool, less absorbed, would have realized as unimportant if true, and have kept under cover. Ridicule from his many fellows, safely in the middle of the road, is always ready. And now it is only the incurably *young* person, in our country, who ever attempts to break through all down the line—and is laughed out of countenance, laughed out of a job, and eventually out of house and home.

But at the absorbed idealist the tribe has laughed wrong so many times that the prevailing "middle of the road egotists" are getting sensitive on the subject. They should realize, as Carlyle reminded us;—himself a perfectly good specimen of the absorbed egocentric,—"Great thoughts, great hearts once broke for, we breathe cheaply as the common air." History will continue to repeat itself: the "middle of the road egotist" will keep on breathing "cheaply," and egocentric hearts will keep on breaking in the cause of ideas.

But our "middle of the road egotist" is not so safe as he imagines. He may as well face the fact that just as commerce has no soul, and therefore cannot produce as life,—so no inventive genius on the commercial or the mechanical plane can preserve him now. In a flood of carbon-monoxide he is hell-bound for somewhere and he does not know where. Ask him! He is trapped by the device, soon to be victimized, no doubt, by a *faith* in devices, now become a device in itself, and soon seen as a fool's faith that failed. Meantime machine-overproduction has made the statesman a propagandist for the poor, the banker a bulkhead, the salesman a divinity. Around each revolves a group of white-collar satellites as parasites while the workman himself continues to trip the lever or press the button of the automaton that is substitute for hundreds of workmen like him. Yes, for many reasons America, herself the great "middle of the road egotist," should be kind to her absorbed egocentrics. Russia killed off hers, and was compelled to import many before her tragic experiment could turn a wheel forward. America may also bankrupt herself, but America is likely to bankrupt life by commercial, political and utensil machinery. No. No political device, no device of organization, no device of salesmanship, no mechanical device can help our country much further on beyond. Only ideas can help her now. Unhappily the word "ideas" and the word "egocentric" come naturally together in human affairs, and go together. Never mind; patience now with the "Nut"; toleration and a turn for the "Crank!"

Although egocentricity may develop egomania all too often and be only a folly, egotism, like other qualities of human nature, is bad only when it is poor and mean in quality, that is to say, pretentious, vain and selfish; in a word dishonest. We should realize, too, that *optimism* to the *idealist,* to the *realist pessimism,* are but the two sides of the same shield, . . . both extremes of egotism.

But however all this by way of "setting the stage" may be, I am going to be direct and personal with you now in this matter of ideas.

What a man *does,* that he *has;* and I shall best show you respect by the self-respect that means hereafter talking out of my own experience. Nevertheless I shall try not to sing "but of myself," and so fail, and, like Pei-Woh, Prince of Chinese harpists, I shall leave the harp to choose and, as he said, "know not whether the harp be I or I the harp. . . ."

An idea is a glimpse of the nature of the thing as more workable or "practical" as we say (we like that word "practical," but abuse it) than found in current practice or custom. An idea, therefore, is an act expressing in terms of human thought implicit faith in the character of nature, something for lesser men to build and improve upon.

A fancy or conceit trifles with appearances as they are. An idea searches the *sources* of appearances, comes out as a form of inner experiences, to give fresh proof of higher and better order in the life we live. Finally . . . AN IDEA IS SALVATION BY IMAGINATION.

Such ideas as I shall rehearse for you now belong to your immediate present, but instead of saying the "present," to be truthful, we should say, with Laotze, your infinite. Laotze said two thousand five hundred years ago that the present was "the ever-moving *infinite* that divides Yesterday from Tomorrow. . . ."

Suppose something you always took for granted as made up of various things, "composed" as artists say, suddenly appeared to you as organic growth. Suppose you caught a glimpse of that "something" as a living entity and saw it as no creature of fallible expediency at all but really a creation living with integrity of its own in the realm of the mind. Suppose too you saw this something only awaiting necessary means to be born as living creation instead of existing as you saw it all about you as miserable makeshift or sentimental, false appliance.

Well, something like this is what happened to Louis Sullivan when he *saw* the first skyscraper, and something like that, in architecture, has been happening to me ever since in various forms of experience.

Thus a single glimpse of reality may change the *world* for any of us if, from the fancies and conceits of mere appearances, we get within the source of appearances. By means of human imagination at work upon this source untold new life may find expression, for, with new force, ideas do actually fashion our visible world. A new order emerges to deepen life that we may become less wasted in anxious endeavor to

187

go from here to somewhere else in order to hurry on somewhere from there. Any true conception as an idea, derived from any *original* source, has similar consequences in all the fields of our common endeavor to build a civilization.

As it worked with Louis Sullivan in designing the skyscraper—thus did going to the source work with me in building houses as the subsequent, consequent, flock of ideas that take flight from any constructive ideal put to work.

Here at hand was the typical American dwelling of 1893 standing about on the Chicago prairies. (I used to go home to Oak Park, a Chicago suburb, which denies Chicago.) That dwelling there became somehow typical, but, by any faith in nature implicit or explicit, it did not belong there. I longed for a chance to build a house, and soon got the chance because I was not the only one then sick of hypocrisy and hungry for reality. And I will venture to say, at this moment ninety out of a hundred of you are similarly sick.

What was the matter with the house? Well, just for a beginning, it lied about everything. It had no sense of unity at all nor any such sense of space as should belong to a free people. It was stuck up in any fashion. It was stuck on wherever it happened to be. To take any one of those so-called "homes" away would have improved the landscape and cleared the atmosphere.

This *typical* had no sense of proportion where the human being was concerned. It began somewhere in the wet, and ended as high up as it could get in the blue. All materials looked alike to it or to anybody in it. Essentially this "house" was a bedeviled box with a fussy lid: a box that had to be cut full of holes to let in light and air, with an especially ugly hole to go in and come out of. The holes were all trimmed, the doors trimmed, the roofs trimmed, the walls trimmed. "Joinery," everywhere, reigned supreme. Floors were the only part of the house left plain. The housewife and her "decorator" covered those with a tangled rug collection, because otherwise the floors were "bare,"—"bare" only because one could not very well walk on jig-sawing or turned spindles or plaster ornament.

It is not too much to say that as architect my lot was cast with an inebriate lot of criminals, sinners hardened by habit against every human significance, except one. (Why mention "the one touch of nature that makes the whole world kin"?) And I will venture to say too that the aggregation was at the lowest aesthetic level in all history:—steam heat, plumbing, and electric light its only redeeming features.

The first feeling therefore was for a new simplicity, a new idea of simplicity as organic. Organic simplicity might be seen producing significant character in the harmonious order we call nature:—all around, beauty in growing things. None insignificant. I loved the prairie by instinct as a great simplicity, the trees and flowers, the sky itself, thrilling by contrast. I saw that a little of height on the prairie was enough to look like much more. Notice how every detail as to height becomes intensely significant and how breadths all fall short! Here was a tremendous spaciousness sacrificed needlessly,—all cut up crosswise and lengthwise into fifty-foot lots, or would you have twenty-five feet? Salesmanship parceled it out and sold it without restrictions. In a great new free country, everywhere, I could see only a mean tendency to tip up everything in the way of human habitation edgewise instead of letting it lie comfortably flatwise with the ground. Nor has this changed much today since automobilization made it a far less genuine economic issue and a social crime.

I had an idea that the planes parallel to earth in buildings identify themselves with the ground,—make the building belong to the ground. At any rate I perceived it and put it to work. I had an idea that every house in that low region should begin *on* the ground,—not *in* it,—as they then began, with damp cellars. This idea put the house up on the "prairie basement" I devised, entirely above the ground. And an idea that the house should *look* as though it began there *at* the ground, put a projecting base-course as a visible edge to this foundation, where as a platform it was seen as evident preparation for the building itself.

An idea that shelter should be the essential look of any dwelling put the spreading roof with generously projecting eaves over the whole: —I saw a building primarily not as a cave, but as shelter in the open.

But, before this, had come the idea that the size of the human figure should fix every proportion of a dwelling,—and later—why not

189

the proportions of all buildings whatsoever? What other scale could I use? So I accommodated heights in the new buildings to no exaggerated established order but to the human being. I knew the dweller could not afford too much freedom to move about in space at best, so, perceiving the horizontal line as the earthline of human life, I extended horizontal spacing by cutting out all the room partitions that did not serve the kitchen or give privacy for sleeping apartments or (it was the day of the parlor) prevent some formal intrusion into the family circle, like the small social office set aside as a necessary evil to receive callers. Even this concession soon disappeared as a relic of barbarism.

To get the house down in the horizontal to appropriate proportion with the prairie, the servants had to come down out of the complicated attic and go into a separate unit of their own attached to the kitchen on the ground floor. Closets disappeared as unsanitary boxes wasteful of floorspace: built-in wardrobes took their places.

Freedom of floorspace and elimination of useless heights worked a miracle in the new dwelling place. A sense of appropriate freedom changed its whole aspect. The whole became more fit for human habitation and more natural to its site. An entirely new sense of space values in architecture came home. It now appears it came into the architecture of the modern world. It was due. A new sense of repose in quiet streamline effects had then and there found its way into building as we now see it in steamships, aeroplanes and motorcars. The "age" came into its own.

But more important than all, rising to greater dignity as an idea was the ideal of plasticity as now emphasized in the treatment of the whole building. (Plasticity may be seen in the expressive lines and surfaces of your hand as contrasted with the articulation of the skeleton itself.) This ideal in the form of continuity has appeared as a natural means to achieve truly organic architecture. Here was direct expression, the only true means I could see, or can now see to that end. Here, by instinct at first (all ideas germinate), principle had entered into building as continuity that has since gone abroad and come home again to go to work as it will continue to work to revolutionize the use and custom of our machine-age. This means an architecture that can live and let live.

The word "plastic" was a word Louis Sullivan himself was fond of using in reference to his scheme of ornamentation, as distinguished from all other or any applied ornament. But now, and not merely as form following function, why not a larger application of this element of plasticity considered as *continuity* in the building itself?—why any principle working in the part if not working in the whole? If form really followed function (it might be seen that it did by means of this concrete ideal of plasticity as continuity), why not throw away entirely the implications of post and beam? Have *no* beams, *no* columns, *no* cornices nor any fixtures, nor pilasters or entablatures as such. Instead of two things, *one* thing. Let walls, ceilings, floors become part of each other, flowing into one another, getting continuity out of it all or into it all, eliminating any constructed feature such as any fixture or appliance whatsoever as Louis Sullivan eliminated background in his ornament in favor of an integral sense of the whole. Conceive now that here the idea was a new sense of building that could *grow* forms not only true to function but expressive beyond any architecture known. Yes, architectural forms by this means might now "grow up."

Grow up—in what image? Here was concentrated appeal to pure imagination. Gradually proceeding from generals to particulars "plasticity," now "*continuity*," as a large means in architecture began to grip and work its own will. I would watch sequences fascinated, seeing other sequences in those consequences already in evidence. The old architecture, as far as its grammar went, began literally to disappear: as if by magic new effects came to life.

Vistas of a simplicity would open to me and harmonies so beautiful that I was not only delighted but often startled, sometimes amazed. I concentrated with all my energy on the principle of plasticity as continuity and a practical working principle within the building construction itself to accomplish the thing we call architecture.

Some years later I took "continuity" as a practical working principle of construction into the actual method of constructing the building. But to eliminate the *post* and *beam,* as such, I could get no help from the engineer. By habit, engineers reduced everything in the field of calculation to the post and the girder before they could calculate anything and tell you where and just how much. Walls that were part of floors and ceilings all merging together and reacting upon each other the engineer had never met, and the engineer has not yet enough scientific formulæ to enable him to calculate for such continuity. Slabs stiffened and used over supports as cantilevers to get planes parallel to the earth, such as were now necessary to develop emphasis of the third dimension, were new. But the engineer soon mastered this element of continuity in these floor slabs. The cantilever became a new feature in architecture. As used in the Imperial Hotel in Tokyo it was one of the features that insured the life of that building in the terrific temblor. After that demonstration not only a new aesthetic, but (proving the aesthetic as sound), a great new *economic stability* had entered building construction. And, as further sequence of this idea that plasticity should be at work as continuity in actual construction, from laboratory experiments made at Princeton by Professor Beggs it appears that the principle of continuity actually works in physical structure as specific proof of the soundness of the aesthetic ideal. So the ideal of "continuity" in designing architectural forms will soon be available as structural formulæ. Thus "continuity" will become a new and invaluable economy in building construction itself. Welding instead of riveting steel is a new means to the same end, but that is ahead of the story.

An idea soon came from this stimulating, simplifying ideal that, to be consistent in practice or, indeed, if it was at all to be put to work successfully, this new element of plasticity must have a new sense as well as a science of materials. It may interest you to know, as it astonished me,—there is nothing in the literature of the civilized world on that subject.

I began to study the nature of materials. I learned to see brick as brick, learned to see wood as wood and to see concrete or glass or metal each for itself and all as themselves. Strange to say this required concentration of imagination; each required a different handling and each had possibilities of use peculiar to the nature of each. Appropriate designs for one material would not be appropriate at all for any other material in the light of this ideal of simplicity as organic.

Had our new materials—steel, concrete and glass,—existed in the ancient order, we would have had nothing at all like ponderous "classic" architecture. No,—nothing. Nor can there now be an organic architecture where the nature of these materials is ignored or misunderstood. How can there be? Perfect correlation is the first principle of growth. Integration means that nothing is of any great value except as naturally related to the whole. Even my great old master designed for materials all alike: all were grist for his rich imagination with his sentient ornamentation. All materials were only one material to him in which to weave the stuff of his dreams. I still remember being ashamed of the delight I at first took in so plainly "seeing around" the beloved master. But acting upon this new train of ideas soon brought work sharply and immediately up against the tools that could be found to get these ideas put into form. What were the tools in use everywhere? *Machines!*—automatic many of them, stone or wood planers, stone or wood molding-shapers, various lathes, presses and power saws—all in commercially organized mills: sheet-metal breakers, presses, shears, cutting-, molding- and stamping-machines in foundries and rolling mills,—commercialized in the "shops": concrete-mixers, clay-bakers, casters, glass-makers and the trades union,—all laborers, units in a more or less highly commercialized greater union in which craftsmanship only had place as survival for burial. Standardization was already inflexible necessity, either enemy or friend—you might choose. And as you chose you became either master and useful or a luxury,—and eventually a parasite.

Already machine-standardization had taken the life of handicraft in all its expressions. But the outworn handicraft as seen in the forms of the old architecture never troubled me. The new forms as expression of the new order of the machine did trouble me. If I wanted to realize new forms I should have to make them not only appropriate to old and new materials, but so design them that the machines that would have to make them could and would make them well. But now with this ideal of internal order as integral in architecture supreme in my

193

mind, I would have done nothing less even could I have commanded armies of craftsmen. By now had come the discipline of a great ideal. There is no discipline, architectural or otherwise, so severe, but there is no discipline that yields such rich rewards in work, nor is there any discipline so safe and sure of results as this ideal of "internal order," the integration that is organic. Lesser ideas took flight, like birds, from this exacting, informing ideal, always in the same direction, but further on each occasion for flight until great goals were in sight. You may see the "signs and portents" gathered together in the exhibition gallery.

But, before trying to tell you about the goals in sight, popular reactions to this new endeavor might be interesting. After the first house was built—(it was the Winslow house in 1893)—my next client did not want a house so different that he would have to go down the back way to his morning train to avoid being laughed at. Bankers at first refused to loan money on the houses and friends had to be found to finance the early buildings. Mill-men would soon look for the name on the plans when they were presented for estimates, read the name and roll the drawings up again, handing them back to the contractor, with the remark "they were not hunting for trouble." Contractors often failed to read the plans correctly,—the plans were so radically different, —so much had to be "left off" the building.

Clients usually "stood by," often interested and excited beyond their means. So, when they "moved in," quite frequently they had to take in their old furniture. The ideal of "organic simplicity," seen as the countenance of perfect integration, abolished all fixtures, rejected all superficial decoration, made all electric lighting and heating features an integral part of the architecture. So far as possible all furniture was to be designed in place as part of the architecture. Hangings, rugs, carpets—all came into the same category, so any failure of this particular feature of the original scheme often crippled results,—made trouble in this plan of constructive elimination.

Nor was there any planting done about the house without cooperating with the architect. No sculpture, no painting unless cooperating with the architect. This made trouble. No decoration, as such, anywhere;—decorators hunting a job would visit the owners, learn the

194

name of the architect, lift their hats, and turning on their heels leave with a curt and sarcastic "Good day"—meaning really what the slang "Good night" meant, later. The owners of the houses were all subjected to curiosity, sometimes to admiration, but they submitted, most often, to the ridicule of the "middle of the road egotist." There was "something about them too," now, when they had a house like that,—"the rope-tie?"

A different choice of materials would mean a different scheme altogether. Concrete was coming into use and Unity Temple became the first concrete monolith in the world—that is to say—the first building complete as monolithic architecture in the wooden forms in which it was cast.

Plastered houses were then new. Casement windows were new. So many things were new. Nearly everything was new but the law of gravitation and the idiosyncrasy of the client.

But, as reward for independent thinking in building, first plainly shown in the constitution and profiles of Unity Temple at Oak Park, more clearly emerging from previous practice, now came clear *an entirely new sense of architecture*, a higher conception of architecture: architecture not alone as form following function, but conceived as space enclosed. The enclosed space itself might now be seen as the reality of the building. This sense of the "within" or the room itself, or the rooms themselves, I now saw as the great thing to be expressed as *architecture*. This sense of interior space made exterior as architecture transcended all that had gone before, made all the previous ideas only useful now as means to the realization of a far greater ideal. Hitherto all classical or ancient buildings had been great masses or blocks of building material, sculptured into shape outside and hollowed out to live in. At least that was the sense of it all. But here coming to light was a sense of building as an organism that had new release for the opportunities of the machine age. This interior conception took architecture entirely away from sculpture, away from painting and entirely away from architecture as it had been known in the antique. The building now became a creation of interior-space in light. And as this sense of the interior space as the reality of the building began to work walls as walls fell away. The vanishing wall joined the disappearing cave. Enclosing screens and protecting features of architectural character took the place of the solid wall.

More and more light began to become the beautifier of the building—the blessing of the occupants. Our arboreal ancestors in their trees are more likely precedent for us than the savage animals that "holed in for protection." Yes, in a spiritual sense, a higher *order* is the sense of sunlit space and the lightness of the structure of the spider spinning as John Roebling saw it and realized it in his Brooklyn Bridge.

Inevitably, it seems to me, this sense of building is to construct the physical body of our machine-age.

Our civilization is emerging from the cave. We are through with the fortification as a dwelling place. Feudal society, if not feudal thinking, is disappearing. With its disappearance will disappear the massive building that protected the might of its estate. With our new materials, steel, glass, and ferro-concrete with the steel always in tension, lightness and strength become more and more obvious as directly related to each other in modern building. The resources of the machine-age confirm the new materials in this space-conception of architecture at every point. Steel-in-tension brings entirely new possibilities of spanning spaces and new aid in creating a more livable world.

Yes, already a sense of cleanliness directly related to living in sunlight is at work in us and working not only to emancipate us from the cavern but waking in us a desire for the substance of a new and more appropriate simplicity as the countenance of building construction:—simplicity appearing now as a youthful clear countenance of truth. This reality is new. This sense of the reality as "within" and with no exterior pretensions of architecture as something applied to construction makes all the heavy pretentious masonry masses ornamented by brick or stone walls seem heavy, monstrous and wrong, as in matter of fact they are utterly false in this age, as is, no less, the little decorated cavern for a house.

Modern architecture is weary of academic make-believe. Architecture sees the aeroplane fly overhead, emancipated from make-believe, soon, when it lays its wings aside, free to be itself and true to itself. It sees the steamship ride the seas, triumphant as the thing it is, for what it is. It sees the motorcar becoming more the machine it should be, becoming daily less like a coach, more a freedom to be itself for what it is. In them all and in all utensils whatsoever, the machine age is seen more and more freely declaring for freedom to express the truths of being instead of remaining satisfied to be a false seeming. Modern architecture is profiting by what it sees and in five years' time you may look upon any sham-boxes with holes or slots cut in them for light and air as senile, undesirable.

A new sense of beauty seen in the machine-age, characteristic of direct simplicity of expression, is awakening in art to create a new world, or better said, to create the world anew. No mind that is a mind considers that world inferior to the antique. We may confidently see it as superior. And, within the vision of this conception of architecture, see the very city itself, as a *necessity*, dying. The acceleration we are witnessing in the tyranny of the skyscraper is no more than the hang-over of a habit. The very acceleration we mistake for growth heralds and precedes decay!

Decentralization not only of industry, but of the city itself is desirable and imminent. Necessity built the city, but the great service rendered to man as a luxury by the machine as seen in automobiliza-tion and electrification will destroy that necessity. Already internal collision of the mechanistic device of the skyscraper and of these more beneficent automobilization and electrical factors may be seen win-ning in the struggle between the greedy skyscraper and the fleet auto-mobile,—the city splitting up in consequence. This is only one of the more obvious evidences of disintegration.

In the growth of the great highways, natural, state and county, and in the gradually extending servicing of the ubiquitous gasoline station, we see in embryo other advance agents of decentralization! Such new avenues and spreading centers of distribution and servicing mean eventually the disintegration and subordination of the centraliza-tion now seen in the city. The greatest service sentient man is to receive from the machine he has built in his own image, if he conquers the machine and makes the machine serve him, will be the death of urbanism! Hectic urbanism will be submerged in natural ruralism. And we shall see soon that the natural place for the beautiful tall building,—not in its present form but in this new sense,—is in the country, not in the city.

If the machine conquers man, man will remain to perish with his city, as he has before perished in all the cities the great nations of the world have ever built.

Mankind is only now waking to any vision of the machine as the true emancipator of the individual as an individual. Therefore we may yet see the machine-age as the age of a true democracy, wherein human life is based squarely on and in the beauty and fruitfulness of the ground: life lived in the full enjoyment of the earthline of human life, —the line of freedom for man, whereby man's horizon may be immeasurably extended by the machine, the creature of his brain in service of his heart and mind.

So, we may see, even now, taking shape in the realm of ideas in architecture to express all this—a new significance, or we might fairly enough say: *significance as new*. Significance as new because in architecture for five centuries at least "significance" has been lost, except as an outworn symbolism was feebly significant, or except as a tawdry sentimentality had specious significance. This new significance repudiates the sentimentality of any symbol; looks the philosophic abstraction full in the eye for the impostor it usually is; reads its lessons direct in the book of creation itself, and despises all that lives either ashamed or afraid to live as itself, for what it is or may become because of *its own nature*.

A new integrity then? Yes, integrity new to us in America,—and yet so ancient! A new integrity, alive and working with new means, —greater means than ever worked before. A new integrity working for freedom,—yours and mine and our children's freedom,—in this realm, we have called, for the purpose of this hour together, *THE REALM OF IDEAS*.

TO THE YOUNG MAN
IN ARCHITECTURE

Today the young man I have in mind hears much, too much about new and old. Sporadic critics of the "new" take their little camera-minds about—(snapshot emulation by the halfbaked architect)—and wail, or hail the dawn. If by chance the novice builds a building the cackling, if not the crowing, outdoes the egg. Propagandists, pro and con, classify old as new and new as old. Historians tabulate their own oblique inferences as fact. The "ites" of transient "ists" and "isms" proclaim the modern as new. And yet architecture was never old and will ever be new. From architecture the main current, little streams detach themselves, run a muddy course to be regathered and clarified by the great waters as though the little rills and rivulets had never been. All art in our time is like that and we witness only the prodigal waste Nature sponsors when she flings away a million seeds to get a single plant,—seeming in the meantime to enjoy her extravagance. Nature's real issue, no doubt, in the life of the mind is no less wasteful, and she may enjoy her extravagance in the million fancies for one idea: millions of cerebrations for one thought: a million buildings for even one small piece of genuine architecture. Yes, she gives gladly a million for one now, because the species has declined five hundred years to the level of a commercially expedient *appliance*. The species itself, you see, is in danger. So be glad to see as evidence of life the babel of personal books, the dereliction of aesthetic movements,—especially be glad to see the halfbaked buildings by the novitiate.

But confusion of ideas is unnatural waste of purpose. Such confusion as we see means a scattering of aim nature herself would never tolerate. The confusion arises because there is doubt in some minds and fear in some minds and hope in other minds that architecture is shifting its circumference. As the hod of mortar and some bricks give way to sheet-metal, the lockseam, and the breaker,—as the workman gives way to the automatic machine,—so the architect seems to be giving way either to the engineer, the salesman or the propagandist.

I am here to assure you that the circumference of architecture *is* changing with astonishing rapidity, but that its *center* remains unchanged. Or am I here only to reassure you that architecture eternally returns upon itself to produce new forms that it may live on forever? In the light of the new and with pain of loss, only now does America waken to see why and how "art" conceived as a commercial expedient, or degraded to the level of a sentimental appliance, has betrayed American life. Yes, that is one reason why the circumference of art, as a whole, is rapidly shifting. The circumference is shifting because hunger for reality is not yet dead and because human vision widens with science as human nature deepens with inner experience.

The center of architecture remains unchanged because,—though all unconfessed or ill-concealed,—beauty is no less the true purpose of rational modern architectural endeavor than ever, just as beauty remains the essential characteristic of architecture itself. But today because of scientific attainment the modern more clearly perceives beauty as integral order; order divined as an image by human sensibility; order apprehended by reason, executed by science. Yes, by means of a greater science, a more integral order may now be executed than any existing. With integral order once established you may perceive the rhythm of consequent harmony. To be harmonious is to be beautiful in a rudimentary sense: a good platform from which to spring toward the moving infinity that is the present. It is in architecture in this sense that "God meets with nature in the sphere of the relative." Therefore the first great necessity of a modern architecture is this keen sense of order as integral. That is to say the *form* itself in orderly relationship with purpose or function: the *parts* themselves in order with the form: the materials and methods of work in order with both: a kind of natural integrity,—the integrity of each in all and of all in each. This is the exacting new order.

Wherein, then, does the new order differ from the ancient? Merely

FLORIDA SOUTHERN COLLEGE, ADMINISTRATION BUILDING, LAKELAND, FLORIDA

FLORIDA SOUTHERN COLLEGE, CHAPEL INTERIOR, LAKELAND, FLORIDA

in this—the ancient order had gone astray, betrayed by "culture," misled by the historian. But the organic simplicity to be thus achieved as new is the simplicity of the universe which is quite different from the simplicity of any machine, just as the art of being in the world is not the same thing as making shift to get about in it.

Internal disorder is architectural disease if not the death of architecture. Needed then, young man, by you who would become an architect, and needed as a very beginning, is some intellectual grasp, the more direct the better, of this radical order of your universe. You will see your universe as architecture.

An inspired sense of order you may have received as a gift—certainly the schools cannot give it to you. Therefore, to the young man in architecture, the word *radical* should be a beautiful word. Radical means "of the root" or "to the root"—begins at the beginning and the word stands up straight. Any architect should be radical by nature because it is not enough for him to begin where others have left off.

Traditions in architecture have proved unsafe. The propaganda of the dead which you now see in a land strewn with the corpses of opportunity, is no more trustworthy than the propaganda of the living. Neither can have much to do with organic architecture. No, the working of principle in the direction of integral order is your only safe precedent. So the actual business of your architectural schools should be to assist you in the perception of such order in the study of the various architectures of the world—otherwise schools exist only to hinder and deform the young. Merely to enable you, young man, to make a living by making plans for buildings is not good enough work for any school. Thus you may see by this definition of order that the "orders" as such have less than nothing at all to do with modern, that is to say organic, architecture. And too, you may see how little any of the great buildings of the ages can help you to become an architect *except as you look within them* for such working of principle as made them new in the order of their own day. As a matter of course, the particular forms and details appropriate to them become eccentricities to you,—fatalities, should you attempt to copy them for yourselves when you attempt to build. This much at least, I say, is obvious to all minds as the machine-age emerges into human view, with more severe limitations than have ever been imposed upon architecture in the past, but these very limitations are your great, fresh opportunity.

Now, even the scribes are forced by inexorable circumstances to see old materials give way to new materials,—new industrial systems taking the place of old ones,—just as all see the American concepts of social liberty replace the feudal systems, oligarchies and hereditary aristocracies: and by force of circumstances too, all are now inexorably compelled to see that we have nothing, or have very little, which expresses, as architecture, any of these great changes.

Due to the very principles at work as limitations in our mechanical or mechanized products, today, you may see coming into the best of them a new order of beauty that, in a sense, *is* negation of the old order. In a deeper sense, a little later, you may be able to see it, too, as scientific affirmation of ancient order. But you, young man, begin anew, limited, though I hope no less inspired, by this sense of the new order that has only just begun to have results. Only a horizon widened by science, only a human sensibility quickened by the sense of the dignity and worth of the individual as an individual, only this new and finer sense of internal order, *inherent* as the spirit of architecture, can make you an architect now. Your buildings *must* be new because the law was old before the existence of heaven and earth.

You may see on every side of you that principle works in this spirit of cosmic change today just as it worked since the beginning. Lawless you cannot be in architecture, if you are for nature. And do not be afraid, you may disregard the laws, but you are never lawless if you are for nature.

Would you be modern? Then it is the nature of the thing which you now must intelligently approach and to which you must reverently appeal. Out of communion with nature, no less now than ever, you will perceive the order that is new and learn to understand that it is old because it was new in the old. Again I say be sure as sure may be that a clearer perception of principle has to be "on straight" in your mind today before any architectural ways or any technical means can accomplish anything for you at all.

As to these technical ways and means, there are as many paths as there are individuals with capacity for taking infinite pains, to use Carlyle's phrase. All are found in the field itself, the field where all that makes the America of today is active commercial issue. An architect's office may be a near corner of that field. A school in which modern machinery and processes were seen at actual work would be your true corner of that field. If only we had such schools one such school would be worth all the others put together. But only a radical and rebellious spirit is safe in the schools we now have, and time spent there is time lost for such spirits. Feeling for the arts in our country, unfortunately for you, is generally a self-conscious attitude, an attitude similar to the attitude of the provincial in society. The provincial will not act upon innate kindness and good sense, and so tries to observe the other guests to do as they do. Fear of being found ridiculous is his waking nightmare. Innate good sense, in the same way, forsakes the provincial in the realm of ideas in art. By keeping in what seems to him good company, the company of the "higher-ups," he thinks himself safe. This self-conscious fear of being oneself, this cowardly capitulation to what is "being done," yes, the architectural increment *servility* deserves,—this is your inheritance, young man!—your inheritance from the time when the architect's lot was cast "in between," neither old nor new, neither alive nor quite dead. Were this not so it would not be so hard for you to emerge, for you to be born alive. But as a consequence of the little modern architecture we already have, young architects, whatever their years, will emerge with less and less punishment, emerge with far less anguish, because the third generation is with us. That generation will be less likely to advertise to posterity by its copied mannerisms or borrowed "styles" that it was neither scholar nor gentleman in the light of any ideal of spiritual integrity.

It would be unfair to let those architects "in between" who served as your attitudinized or commercialized progenitors go free of blame for your devastating architectural inheritance. Where they should have led they followed by the nose. Instead of being arbiters of principle as a blessed privilege, they became arbiters or victims of the taste that is usually a matter of ignorance. When leisure and money came these progenitors of yours became connoisseurs of the antique, patrons and peddlers of the imitation. So with few exceptions it was with these sentimentalized or stylized architects: "Boy, take down Tudor No. 37 and put a bay window on it for the lady"; or, solicitous, "Madam, what style will you have?" A few held out, all honor to them. A tale told of Louis Sullivan has the lady come in and ask for a Colonial house— "Madam" said he, "you will take what we give you."

Except in a few instances (the result of some such attitude as this) the only buildings we have today approaching architecture are the industrial buildings built upon the basis of common sense: buildings built for the manufacturer who possessed common sense or buildings for residence built to meet actual needs without abject reference to the "higher-ups"—nor with foolish, feathered hat in hand to "culture." These sensible works we possess and the world admires, envies and emulates. This American of common sense, is today the only "way out" for America. He is still the only architectural asset America ever had or has. Give him what he needs when he needs it.

To find out what he needs go whenever and wherever you can to the factories to study the processes in relation to the product and go to the markets to study the reactions. Study the machines that make the product what it is. To acquire technique study the materials of which the product is made, study the purpose for which it is produced, study the manhood *in* it, the manhood *of* it. Keep all this present in your mind in all you do, because ideas with bad technique are abortions.

In connection with this matter of "technique" you may be interested to know that the Beaux Arts that made most of your American progenitors is itself confused, now likely to reinterpret its precepts, disown its previous progeny and disinherit its favorite sons or be itself dethroned, since posterity is already declining the sons as inheritance: the sons who enabled the plan-factory to thrive, the "attitude" to survive in a sentimental attempt to revive the dead. Yes, it is becoming day by day more evident to the mind that is a mind how shamefully the product of this culture betrayed America. It is beginning to show and it shames America. At our architecture as "culture" quite good-naturedly the Old World laughs. Coming here expecting to see our ideals becomingly attired, they see us fashionably and officially ridiculous, by way of assumption of customs and manners belonging by force of nature and circumstances to something entirely different. They see us betraying not only ourselves but our country itself. But now by grace of freedom we have a little otherwise to show to command dawning respect. No, young man, I do not refer to the skyscraper in the rank and file as that something nor does the world refer to it, except as a stupendous adventure in the business of space-making for rent,—a monstrosity. I again refer you to those simple, sincere attempts to be ourselves and make the most of our own opportunities which are tucked away in out-of-the-way places or found in industrial life as homes or workshops. Our rich people do not own them. Great business on a large scale does not invest in them unless as straightforward business buildings where "culture" is no consideration and columns can give no credit.

American great wealth has yet given nothing to the future worth having as architecture or that the future will accept as such unless as an apology. In building for such uses as she had, America has made shift with frightful waste.

Though half the cost of her buildings was devoted to making them beautiful as architecture, not one thought-built structure synthetic in design has American great-wealth, and even less American factotumized "learning," yet succeeded in giving to the modern world. American wealth has been "sold" as it has, itself, bought and sold and been delivered over by professions, or the Scribes, to the Pharisees. So, young man, expect nothing from the man of great wealth in the United States for another decade. Expect nothing from your government for another quarter of a century! Our government, too (helpless instrument of a majority hapless in art), has been delivered over to architecture as the sterile hang-over of feudal thought, or the thought that served the sophist with the slave. That is why the future of architecture in America really lies with the well-to-do man of business,—the man of independent judgment and character of his own, unspoiled by great

207

financial success,—that is to say the man not persuaded, by winning his own game, that he knows all about everything else.

Opportunity to develop an architecture today lies with those sincere and direct people, who, loving America for its own sake, live their own lives quietly in touch with its manifold beauties,—*blessed by comprehension of the ideal of freedom that founded this country.* In our great United States notwithstanding alleged "rulers" or any "benign" imported cultural influences, these spontaneous sons and daughters are the soul of our country; they are fresh unspoiled life and therefore they are your opportunity in art, just as you, the artist are their opportunity. You will be their means to emerge from the conglomerate "in between."

And this brings us to the American "ideal." This American ideal must be in architecture what it is in life. Why obscure the issue by any sophisticated aesthetics or involution with academic formulæ? The arts are only such media as we have for the direct expression of life reacting in turn with joy-giving force upon that life itself—enriching all human experience to come. The arts in America are on free soil, and therefore all-imperatively call for the creative artist.

The soul of that new life we are fond of calling American is liberty: liberty tolerant and so sincere that it must see all free or itself suffer. This freedom is the highest American ideal. To attain it, then, is innerexperience, because there is no "exterior" freedom. Freedom develops from within and is another expression of an integral order of the mind in high estate. Freedom is impossible where discord exists either within or without. So, perfect freedom no one has though all may aspire. But, to the degree freedom is attained, the by-product called "happiness," meaning, I suppose, innocent life, will be the consequence.

Very well,—take the American ideal of freedom from the realm of human consciousness to our specific expression of that consciousness we call architecture. Could any decorator's shop, even were it called a "studio," sell anything ready-made out of the world's stock of "styles" to do more than bedizen or bedevil this essential sentiment?—artificially dress it up for artificiality-making social occasion? No, it would be im-

208

possible to do more,—architecture like freedom *cannot be put on*, it must be worked out from within.

Could any school of architecture inculcating the culture of Greece or Rome fit the case any better with current abstractions of ancient culture as dedicated to the sophist and the slave? No, ancient culture produced nothing to fit the case of an individual freedom evolved by the individual from within. And this is justification,—(is it?) . . . for evolving nothing and going on with make-believe just because make-believe is organized and therefore the decorator has it in stock, the plan-factory sells it, and the schools provide it. The present tendency in architecture which we style modern says emphatically "NO" to this betrayal.

If we are determining ourselves as a free people (and we are), by what you build you will now say proudly "NO" to further menial treason of this academic type.

Are we a free people? Of course not. The question that is important however, is—do we have it in our hearts as it is written in our constitutional charter to be free? Is it sincerely and passionately our ideal to be free? Notwithstanding so much cowardly popular evidence to the contrary, I say it is our ideal. Those highest in the realm of freedom should build suitable buildings and build them now, for that spirit, first—and for America to ponder. There is no longer any doubt in the mind that eventually America will have a truly characteristic architecture,—that much is already written for you on the vanishing wall and the disappearing cave.

Young man in architecture, wherever you are and whatever your age, or whatever our job, we—the youth of America—should be the psychological shock-troops thrown into action against corruption of this supreme American ideal. It will be for youth, in this sense, to win the day for freedom in architecture.

That American architecture cannot be imitative architecture is self-evident in spite of false standards. It is self-evident that neither architect who imitates nor architecture imitative can be free,—the one is a slave, the other forever in bondage. It is as evident that free architecture must develop from within,—an integral, or as we now say in architecture, an "organic" affair. For this reason if for no other reason modern architecture can be no "mode" nor can it ever again be any "style." You must defend it against both or senility will again set in for another cycle of thirty years.

Specifically then, you may ask, what is truly "modern" in architecture? . . . The answer is *power*,—that is to say material resources,—*directly applied to purpose.* Yes, modern architecture is power directly applied to purpose in buildings in the same sense that we see it so applied in the airship, ocean liner or motor car. Therefore it is natural enough perhaps for newly awakened architects to make the error of assuming that, beyond accepting the consequences of directness and integral character, the building itself must resemble utensil-machines or flying-, fighting- or steaming-machines, or any other appliances. But there is this essential difference (it makes all the difference) between a machine and a building. A building is not an appliance nor a mobilization. The building as architecture is born out of the heart of man, permanent consort to the ground, comrade to the trees, true reflection of man in the realm of his own spirit. His building is therefore consecrated space wherein he seeks refuge, recreation and repose for body but especially for mind. So our machine-age building need no more look like machinery than machinery need look like buildings.

Certain qualities, humanly desirable qualities, I am sure you may obtain by means of machinery or by intelligent use of our mechanized systems without selling your souls to factotums by way of a factorialized aesthetic. There is rather more serious occasion for becoming ourselves in our environment, our architecture becoming more human, our dwelling-places becoming more imaginatively fresh and original in order to overcome not only the "cultured tag" but the deadly drag of mechanical monotony and the purely mechanical insignificance that otherwise characterizes us and that will eventually destroy us. But the "ites" of the "ism" and "ist" give signs of being so engrossed in a new machine-aesthetic that they will be unable to rise above themselves—sunk, and so soon, in the struggle for machine-technique. Already hectic architects' "modernistic" and the decorators' "modernism" obscure the simple issue. I would have you believe that to be genuinely new, the man must begin to win over the machine, and not the machine win over the man by way of the man.

We have already observed that whenever architecture was great it was modern, and whenever architecture was modern human values were the only values preserved. And I reiterate that modern architecture in this deeper sense is novelty only to novitiates, that the principles moving us to be modern now are those that moved the Frank and Goth, the Indian, the Maya and the Moor. They are the same principles that will move Atlantis recreated. If there is architecture in Mars or Venus, and there is, at least there is the architecture of Mars and Venus themselves,—the same principles are at work there too.

Principles are universal.

If you approach principles from within you will see that many of the traditions we flattered to extinction by emulation never were even on speaking terms with principle, but were bound up with education by way of impotence or deadly force of habit, or what not? Modern architecture knows them now for impositions, and is gaining courage to cast them out, together with those who insist upon their use and administer them. This in itself you should gratefully recognize as no small value of "the modern-movement," so-called.

Goethe observed that death was nature's ruse in order that she might have more life. Therein you may see the reason why there must be a new, and why the new must ever be the death of the old, but this tragedy need occur only where "forms" are concerned, if you will stick to principle. It is because we have not relied on principle that the genius of the *genus homo* is now to be taxed anew to find an entirely new kind of building that will be a more direct application of power to purpose than ever before has existed in history. But again let us repeat that to secure beauty of the kind we perceive in external nature in the inflexible standardization that characterizes that "power" today, we must not dramatize the machine but dramatize the man. You must work, young man in architecture, to lift the curse of the "appliance" either mechanical or sentimental from the life of today.

But this modern constructive endeavor is being victimized at the start by a certain new aesthetic wherein appearance is made an aim instead of character made a purpose. The "new" aesthetic thus becomes at the very beginning "old" because it is only another "appliance." The French with all the delicacy and charm they seem to possess as substitute for soul, and with French flair for the appropriate gesture at the opportune moment, have contributed most to this affix or suffix of the appliance. Initiators of so many "art movements" that prove ephemera, they recognize the opportunity for another "movement." The new world and the old world too had both already recognized a certain new order that is beauty in the clean-stripped, hard look of machines,—had admired an exterior simplicity due to the direct construction by which automatons were made to operate, move and stop. But certain aesthetes, —French by sympathy or association,—are trying to persuade us that this exterior simplicity *as a new kind of decoration,* is the appropriate "look" of everything in our machine age. French painting foolishly claims to have seen it first,—foolishly because we saw it first ourselves. But French Modernism proceeds to set it up flatwise in architecture in two dimensions,—that is to say to survey it in length and breadth. Although these effects of surface and mass were already well along in our own country (two dimensions, completed by surfaces parallel to the earth, as a third dimension to grip the whole building to the ground)—Paris nevertheless ignores this, with characteristic desire for "movement," and sets up characteristic machine-appearance in two dimensions (that is to say in the surface and mass effects with which Paris is familiar), and architecture thus becomes decoration. You may see it in the fashionable shops while France contemplates a fifty-four million dollar building to propagandize her arts and crafts in the American field while America is busy making enough motorcars to go around.

A certain inspiration characterized the first French recognition but uninspired emulation has become reiteration and in the end nothing will have happened unless another "mode," another aesthetic dictum gone forth to languish as superficial fashion. Another "istic," another "ism" comes to town to pass away,—this time not in a hansom cab but in a flying machine!

Yes, America is young, so healthy it soon wearies of negation. The negation we have here is stranger to mysterious depths of feeling. It is protestant. The protestant is useful but seldom beautiful. When he ceases to protest and becomes constructive himself,—some new protestant will arise to take his place and we may see this happening at the moment.

Yet for young America today a light too long diverted to base uses is shining again through all the propaganda and confusion. This light is the countenance of integral order, a more profound, consistent order than the world has fully realized before, wherein power is applied to purpose in construction just as mathematics is sublimated into music. By that light you may clearly see that, where there is no integral order, there is no beauty, though the order be no more obvious than mathematics in music is obvious.

Not so strange then that the novitiate takes the machine itself as the prophet of this new order, though you must not forget that although music is sublimated mathematics the professor of mathematics cannot make music. Nor can the doctor of philosophy nor the master of construction nor the enthusiastic antiquarian make architecture.

No rationalizing of the machine or factorializing of aesthetics can obscure the fact that architecture is born, not made,—must consistently grow from within to whatever it becomes. Such forms as it takes must be spontaneous generation of materials, building methods and purpose. The brain is a great tool with great craft; but in architecture you are concerned with our sense of the specific beauty of human lives as lived on earth in relation to each other. Organic architecture seeks superior sense of use and a finer sense of comfort, expressed in organic simplicity. That is what you, young man, should call *architecture*. Use and comfort in order to become architecture must become *spiritual satisfactions* wherein the soul insures a more subtle use, achieves a more constant repose. So, architecture speaks as poetry to the soul. In this machine age to utter this poetry that is architecture, as in all other ages, you must learn the organic language of the natural which is *ever the language of the new*. To know any language you must know the alphabet. The alphabet in architecture in our machine age is the nature of steel, glass and concrete construction,—the nature of the machines used as tools, and the nature of the new materials to be used.

Now what language?

Poverty in architecture,—architecture the language of the human heart,—has grown by unnatural appropriation of artificiality, has grown wretched and miserable by the fetish of the appliance, whether by the appliance as mechanical or sentimental. Prevailing historical sympathy administered as standardized learning has confused art with archaeology. In this academic confusion we have been unable to cultivate the principles that grow architecture as a flower of the mind out of our own nature as flowers grow out of earth.

To make architectural growth, you must now perceive that the essential power of our civilization can never be expressed or even capitalized for long in any shallow terms of any factorialized or merely mechanized art. If you would be true to the center of architecture wherever the circumference of architecture may be formed you will see the machine as a peerless tool but otherwise you will see any machine as sterility itself. Engrossed in the serious struggle for new technique, you may not override your love of romance, except such foolish abuse of romance as is our present sentimentality or senility,—our barren lot long since past.

I assure you that at least enough has appeared in my own experience to prove to me that the power of the man with the machine is really no bar at all to tremendously varied *imaginative* architecture.

Nor does any mind that is a mind doubt that the worthy product of our own industrialism should and would give us more digestible food for artistic enjoyment, than the early Italian, Italian pasticcio or the medieval ever gave us. But such artistic enjoyment should not, could not, mean that the machine-age commonplaces were accepted as worthy. It would mean these commonplaces transfigured and transformed by inner fire to take their places in the immense vista of the ages as human masterpieces. Such interpretation by inner fire as *character in the realm of nature* is the work of the young man in architecture.

Oh—America will have to go through a lot of amateurish experiments with you. We as Americans may have to submit to foolish experiments used in the American manner as "quick-turnover" propaganda. But we must be patient because architecture is profound.

Architecture is the very body of civilization itself. It takes time to grow,—begins to be architecture only when it is thought-built,—that is to say when it is a synthesis completed from a rational beginning and, naturally as breathing, genuinely *modern*.

America will factorialize and factotumize much more, and as many Americans will die of ornaphobia as of ornamentia by the wayside before any goal is reached. She will listen to much reasoning from all and sundry and will justly despise the poisonous fruits of most of the reasoning. She will see many little bands or cliques among you muddling about near-ideas, attempting to run with them and kick a goal for personal glory in what we already sufficiently know as "modern movements." And you yourselves will see exploitation of perfectly good ideals by every shade of every imported nationality on earth when the women's clubs of America wake to the great significance to the family of this rapidly changing order in which we live and which they are only now learning to call modern from the midst of antiques. And then in characteristic fashion America will be inclined to mistake abuse of the thing for the thing itself and kick the thing out. As a characteristic abuse we have already seen pseudo-classic architecture stripping off its enabling cornices, entablatures and columns, and fundamentally unchanged, hung up to us on a grand scale as "modern." We will soon see more of it on a grander scale. But washing pseudo-classic behind the ears cannot make architecture modern.

One abusive formula that enables the plan-factory to modernize overnight is that all architecture without ornament is modern. Another agonizing formula that gives the decorator "a break," is, that sharp angles cutting flat surfaces are modern. Never mind,—we will accept anything, just so recurrent senility does not again become a new aesthetic.

Yes, modern architecture is young architecture,—the joy of youth must bring it. The love of youth, eternal youth must develop and keep it. You must see this architecture as wise, but not so much wise as sensible and wistful,—nor any more scientific than sentient, nor so much resembling a flying machine as a masterpiece of the imagination.

Oh yes, young man; consider well that a house is a machine in which to live, but by the same token a heart is a suction-pump. Sentient man begins where that concept of the heart ends.

Consider well that a house is a machine in which to live but architecture begins where that concept of the house ends. All life is machinery in a rudimentary sense, and yet machinery is the life of nothing. Machinery is machinery only because of life. It is better for you to proceed from the generals to the particulars. So do not rationalize from machinery to life. Why not think from life to machines? The utensil, the weapon, the automaton—all are *appliances*. The song, the masterpiece, the edifice are a warm outpouring of the heart of man,—human delight in life triumphant: we glimpse the infinite.

That glimpse or vision is what makes art a matter of inner experience,—therefore sacred, and no less but rather more individual in this age, I assure you, than ever before.

Architecture expresses human life, machines do not, nor does any appliance whatsoever. Appliances only serve life.

Lack of appreciation of the difference between the appliance and life is to blame for the choicest pseudo-classic horrors in America. And yet our more successful "modern" architects are still busy applying brick or stone envelopes to steel frames in the great American cities. Instead of fundamentally correcting this error, shall any superficial aesthetic disguised as new enable this same lack of appreciation of the principles of architecture to punish us again this time with a machinery abstract which will be used as an appliance of the appliance of another cycle of thirty years? If so as between architecture as sentimental appliance and architecture as mechanical appliance or even the aesthetic abstract itself as an architectural appliance,—it would be better for America were you to choose architecture as the mechanical appliance. But, then, organic architecture would have to keep on in a little world of its own. In this world of its own the hard line and the bare upright plane in unimaginative contours of the box both have a place,—just as the carpet has a place on the floor, but the creed of the naked stilt, as a stilt, has no place. The horizontal plane gripping all to earth comes into organic architecture to complete the sense of forms that do not "box up" contents but imaginatively express space. This is modern.

In organic architecture the hard straight line breaks to the dotted line where stark necessity ends and thus allows appropriate rhythm to enter in order to leave suggestion its proper values. This is modern.

In organic architecture, any conception of any building as a building begins at the beginning and goes *forward* to incidental expression as a picture and does not begin with some incidental expression as a picture and go groping *backward*. This is modern.

Eye-weary of reiterated bald commonplaces wherein light is rejected from blank surfaces or fallen dismally into holes cut in them, organic architecture brings the man once more face to face with nature's play of shade and depth of shadow seeing fresh vistas of native creative human thought and native feeling presented to his imagination for consideration. This is modern.

The sense of interior space as reality in organic architecture coordinates with the enlarged means of modern materials. The building is now found in this sense of interior space; the enclosure is no longer found in terms of mere roof or walls but as "screened"—space. This reality is modern.

In true modern architecture, therefore, the sense of surface and mass disappears in light, or fabrications that combine it with strength. And this fabrication is no less the expression of principle as power-directed-toward-purpose than may be seen in any modern appliance or utensil machine. But modern architecture affirms the higher human sensibility of the sunlit space. Organic buildings are the strength and lightness of the spiders' spinning, buildings qualified by light, bred by native character to environment—married to the ground. That is modern!

Meanwhile by way of parting moment with the young man in architecture—this he should keep—concerning ways and means:

1. Forget the architectures of the world except as something good in their way and in their time.

2. Do none of you go into architecture to get a living unless you

love architecture as a principle at work, for its own sake—prepared to be as true to it as to your mother, your comrade, or yourself.

3. Beware of the architectural school except as the exponent of engineering.

4. Go into the field where you can see the machines and methods at work that make the modern buildings, or stay in construction direct and simple until you can work naturally into building-design from the nature of construction.

5. Immediately begin to form the habit of thinking "why" concerning any effects that please or displease you.

6. Take nothing for granted as beautiful or ugly, but take every building to pieces, and challenge every feature. Learn to distinguish the curious from the beautiful.

7. Get the habit of analysis,—analysis will in time enable synthesis to become your habit of mind.

8. "Think in simples" as my old master used to say,—meaning to reduce the whole to its parts in simplest terms, getting back to first principles. Do this in order to proceed from generals to particulars and never confuse or confound them or yourself be confounded by them.

9. Abandon as poison the American idea of the "quick turnover." To get into practice "halfbaked" is to sell out your birthright as an architect for a mess of pottage, or to die pretending to be an architect.

10. Take time to prepare. Ten years' preparation for preliminaries to architectural practice is little enough for any architect who would rise "above the belt" in true architectural appreciation or practice.

11. Then go as far away as possible from home to build your first buildings. The physician can bury his mistakes,—but the architect can only advise his client to plant vines.

12. Regard it as just as desirable to build a chicken-house as to build a cathedral. The size of the project means little in art, beyond the money-matter. It is the quality of character that really counts. Character may be large in the little or little in the large.

13. Enter no architectural competition under any circumstances except as a novice. No competition ever gave to the world anything worth having in architecture. The jury itself is a picked average. The

first thing done by the jury is to go through all the designs and throw out the best and the worst ones so, as an average, it can average upon an average. The net result of any competition is an average by the average of averages.

14. Beware of the shopper for plans. The man who will not grub-stake you in prospecting for ideas in his behalf will prove a faithless client.

It is undesirable to commercialize everything in life just because your lot happens to be cast in the machine-age. For instance, architecture is walking the streets today a prostitute because "to get the job" has become the first principle of architecture. In architecture the job should find the man and not the man the job. In art the job and the man are mates; neither can be bought or sold to the other. Meantime, since all we have been talking about is a higher and finer kind of integrity, keep your own ideal of honesty so high that your dearest ambition in life will be to call yourself an honest man, and look yourself square in the face. Keep your ideal of honesty so high that you will never be quite able to reach it.

Respect the masterpiece,—it is true reverence to man. There is no quality so great, none so much needed now.

AN ORGANIC ARCHITECTURE

FIRST EVENING

THANKING our Chairman for his warm welcome, I observe that "we, the British" do things with such imposing formality that already I feel, as I stand here I ought to be prepared to deliver a studied, formal lecture. Not knowing very well what formal lectures are, however, having attended none in my lifetime, I do not quite know how to give you one. At the outset I may as well confess that I have come here with a minority report: an informal Declaration of Independence. Great Britain had one from us, July 4, 1776: a formal Declaration of Independence which concerned taxes; this one concerns the spirit.

Am I, then, a rebel, too? Yes. But only a rebel as one who has in his actual work, for a lifetime—or is it more?—been carrying out in practice day by day, what he believes to be true. British myself—father Yorkshire, mother Carnarvon—fate took me out to the prairies of the Middle West of the United States of America—Usonia let us say—and there in the tall grass I grew up and learned to build, with due credit to a great master, Louis Sullivan.

We were doing fairly well in the States going on toward expression of ourselves as a people with an architecture of our own, when as luck would have it we got our first World's Fair, the World's Fair of 1893. And there, for the first time the United States of America saw architecture as a great orchestration, and loved it, without giving much consideration to its nature, not knowing that it all came to them on tracing paper from dry books, or that as "traditional" it all lay oblique against

222

the grain of our own integral indigenous effort. We had many too-well-educated architects at that time—you know their names, you who are familiar with architecture—and it became quite simple on their part, scholars—all—thus finding architecture ready-made, to sell it on a large scale, conveniently enough, to the American people. Architecture forthwith became a great business in the old forms of grandomania as architects themselves—scholars all—became active brokers. Our "great" architects were, what was not then known, "designing partners," in behind the scenes. Most architectural firms were composed of several men—"architects." There was the "designing" partner who *designed* the buildings, there was the man who was an engineer and managed somehow to get the imitative buildings—damned things—built by the aid of a contractor—the damn'd. And then there was the general salesman—the job-getter. I think it was our great architect Henry Richardson who said that "the first principle of architecture was to get the job"!

Therefore, most architecture in our Usonia, after this 1893 World's Fair disaster, was a kind of mongering of that sort. For myself I could never see that such ready-made architecture obtained any great results or had anything to do with our life as our life was lived. I felt sure, even then, that architecture which was really architecture proceeded from the ground and that somehow the terrain, the native industrial conditions, the nature of materials and the purpose of the building, must inevitably determine the form and character of any good building. All this crowding in on the scene, therefore, was a great distress to me. Louis Sullivan, my old master, with whom I had been growing up, had already demonstrated his thought as independent and worthy of the attention of his people but this world's-fair wave of pseudo "classic" now an 'ism, swept over and swept us all under. It was years and years before we began to emerge from the undertow of that tremendous backwash. Meantime, keeping on as I could, little by little, step by step, year by year an entirely new idea of building had taken hold of me. I am calling it new, but the idea dates back to at least five hundred years before Jesus. Although I did not know it then, the principle now at the center of our modern movement was very clearly stated as early as that by the Chinese philosopher Lao Tze. The first building which I

223

consciously built as an honest endeavor on my part to express this "new" idea of building was Unity Temple—Oak Park 1904.

What is that new idea of a building? Well—I have come over here to you hoping to show you something that may make it easier to get this ideal of modern architecture a little straighter in your minds than it seems to me to be. Because of this early endeavor a new countenance definitely showed itself on our Mid-western prairies—the unfamiliar countenance of principle. The countenance soon went abroad by way of Germany and Holland but the principle seems mostly to have stayed at home. You are all familiar now with that countenance as it appeared in several subsequent World's Fairs, Paris first. And in many other modern buildings you may see in every country such appearances as are called modernistic. But the principle is still, so I think, little understood or not at all practiced. In these conversations therefore I shall endeavor to state as clearly as I can, the center line of principle animating—originally—this ideal so that organic architecture may stand firm against this now world-wide wave of imitation of itself. Unhappily I feel that this great ideal which I so long ago, early in my life came to love and diligently practiced has been betrayed, unintentionally betrayed, but—nonetheless—betrayed by its would-be friends who fell to imitating it without understanding it.

Architecture in Usonia has always imported your traditional forms into our country. First and foremost we had with us (always) the old English Colonial tradition as a stumbling block; the tradition which was responsible for such cultural life as we knew; we had this Colonial tradition to fight then, and we still have to fight it because to this day many of our private and most of our public buildings in the United States try to express this early tradition of yours here in England. And when I come to you in London as I now do, I see nearly everything man-made we possess above our ground here with you in the original. But of course—let us admit it—it was never original with you . . . was it? With you at the time of its adoption it was an eclecticism, too, elected French, I believe. Our Colonial architecture was your Georgian? And your Georgian was French proceeding from Florence—Italy? It is this Italo-French-English architecture which is being largely reproduced in America today. The government is building Cape-cod ("cod-fish-colonial") houses on the prairies of the Middle West to this very day. In Kansas, the Dakotas, and Nebraska you may see these little "Colonial" hot-boxes recently put up by our government regardless, it seems, of nature or of the nature of architecture or of good sense: put up in the name of beneficent "housing."

If we are to live our own lives we must be true, but true to what? Seemingly in this matter of architecture true to the dwindling end of a culture arriving on our shores already degenerate, never having had in it at best more than the moot question of taste, little or no knowledge; no sense of the whole, nothing of real integrity of concept or structure by way of which a new nation might proceed to grow into its own way of life, and by ways of its own establish a culture belonging to itself instead of humbly accepting senility as the fashion.

Now, that old "Colonial" inheritance as we see it in the light of modern times—was tragic. Therefore the Declaration of Independence I bring you today is no mere negation. It is affirmative denial of the validity of any such thing as that servility on this earth and it is assertion of the right of life to live. In England you may proceed with the old traditional forms by which we were corrupted if you like. They are dead but more legitimate here; they are more or less yours, but they are not ours. I declare, the time is here for architecture to recognize its own nature, to realize the fact that it is out of life itself for life as it is now lived, a humane and therefore an intensely human thing; it must again become the most human of all the expressions of human nature. Architecture is a necessary interpretation of such human life as we now know if we ourselves are to live with individuality and beauty.

The "classic" of course made no such statement; the "classic" ideal can allow nothing of the kind to transpire. The "classic" was more a mask for life to wear than an expression of life itself. Then how much more so was pseudo-classic? So modern architecture rejects the major-axis and the minor-axis of classic architecture. It rejects all grando-mania, every building that would stand in military fashion heels together, eyes front, something on the right hand and something on the left hand. Architecture already favors the reflex, the natural easy atti-

225

tude, the occult symmetry of grace and rhythm affirming the ease, grace, and naturalness of natural life. Modern architecture—let us now say *organic* architecture—is a natural architecture—the architecture of nature, for nature.

To go back now for a moment to the central thought of organic architecture, it was Lao Tze, five hundred years before Jesus, who, so far as I know, first declared that the reality of the building consisted not in the four walls and the roof but inhered in the space within, the space to be lived in. That idea is entire reversal of all pagan—"classic"—ideals of building whatsoever. If you accept that concept of building classical architecture falls dead to the ground. An entirely new concept has entered the mind of the architect and the life of his people. My own recognition of this concept has been instinctive; I did not know of Lao Tze when I began to build with it in my mind; I discovered him much later. I came across Lao Tze quite by accident. One day I came in from the garden where I had been working and picked up a little book the Japanese Ambassador to America had sent me and in it I came upon the concept of building I have just mentioned to you. It expressed precisely what had been in my mind and what I had myself been trying to do with a building: "The reality of the building does not consist of walls and roof but in the space within to be lived in." There it was! At first I was inclined to dissemble a little; I had thought myself somewhat a prophet and felt I was charged with a great message which humanity needed, only to find after all, that I was an "Also Ran." The message had been given to the world thousands of years ago. . . . So what? I could not hide the book nor could I conceal the fact. For some time I felt as a punctured balloon looks. But then I began to see that, after all, I had not derived that idea from Lao Tze; it was a deeper, profound something that survived in the world, something probably eternal therefore universal, something that persisted and will persist for ever. Then I began to feel that I ought to be proud to have perceived it as Lao Tze had perceived it and to have tried to *build* it! I need not be too disappointed.

As I found, so you may find, that that concept of architecture alive today as *modern,* is first of all, *organic.* "Organic" is the word which we should apply to this new architecture. So here I stand before you preaching *organic* architecture; declaring organic architecture to be the modern ideal and the teaching so much needed if we are to see the whole of life, and to now serve the whole of life, holding no "traditions" essential to the great TRADITION. Nor cherishing any preconceived form fixing upon us either past, present or future, but—instead—exalting the simple laws of common sense—or of super-sense if you prefer—determining form by way of the nature of materials, the nature of purpose so well understood that a bank will not look like a Greek temple, a university will not look like a cathedral, nor a fire-engine house resemble a French château, or what have you? Form follows function? Yes, but more important now *form and function are one.* When this deeper concept enters the mind it all means this—that imposition upon our life of what we have come to call the "57 varieties" is dead wrong; that classicism, and all ism, is really imposition upon life itself by way of previous education. So I became rebellious where education is concerned, particularly the education of an architect. I believe that architects are born. I much doubt whether they can really be made. I think that if an architect is born and you try to *make* him you are going to ruin him at the present juncture because there is not enough data upon the tables with which you can indoctrinate him and let him live and work. If you are going to teach him, if you are going to tell him, what are you going to tell him and who is going to teach him? What have you in the universities, the academies and the schools—yet—to give to the young architect that is really out of life in this deeper, more valid sense, as he should himself be? What experience have you in architectural schools that is not something *on* life: some armchair theory or an aesthetic pattern of some kind? What I have now said and am going to say of this concept inevitably means the end of architecture and of all art as some fashionable *aesthetic.* Just *that* is our trouble now with the modern movement itself. Instead of taking these principles, following them faithfully and endeavoring to interpret life according to them, it is only the new countenance that is seen, and having been and being bred as eclectics, young architects take the new countenance by selection and election, giving us, by way of it (if they have their

227

way), another style, the 58th variety. Just too bad, because it is no better than before except for novelty and a certain superficial simplicity making plain surfaces and flat roofs an aesthetic.

So far as this 58th variety is concerned, you have some fresh examples in London. You have felt its impact here, and I think that while some of the motives and a certain devotion to the new ideal are there, and the courage and self-sacrifice of the effort therefore to be commended, the principle being absent results are likely to be, for the moment only, disastrous. What they do to London is—well, perhaps London deserves it; I do not know!

Seriously . . . going back again into the nature of this thing that I would champion, getting back to the minority report—the "Declaration of Independence," we may now ask, independence of what? Well, let me say again, independence of all imposition from without, from whatever sources not in touch with life; independence of classicism—new or old—and of any devotion to the "classics" so-called; independence of further crucifixion of life by current commercialized or academic standards and, more than that, a rejection of all imposition whatsoever upon life; a declaration of independence not only where the cultural lag of our own "old-colonial" traditions is concerned, but also where our educational eclecticism still stands. I am declaring resolute independence of any academic aesthetic, as such, whatsoever—however and wherever hallowed.

We used to guess, to "feel," to predicate and predict, but now we know somewhat. Strange as the assertion may seem, unbecoming and egotistic as it may seem, we do *know*. We now know that we can trust life in this deeper sense. We *know* that life is to be trusted. We *know* that the *interpretation* of life is the true function of the architect because we know that buildings are made for life, to be lived in and to be lived in happily, designed to contribute to that living, joy and living beauty. But, as a matter of fact, all these words—truth, beauty, love—have been so badly oversold by our advertising agents in Usonia (I imagine the same thing applies to England, because I am beginning to see, as I go about among you, that almost everything we do and have, is just about a little England, somehow, somewhere) that I have

228

avoided using the noble words as "suspect" until this moment. Were we to enquire seriously and deeply into the English practice, too, in these verbal matters we should find you guilty not only in much the same sense as ourselves but in many other directions where culture is concerned, I am sure . . . my lords, ladies and gentlemen!

Now, looking backward at the old order it comes to this . . . does it not . . . that instead of going to the fountain-head for inspiration, instead of going to the nature-principle by way of our trust in life and love of life, going there for inspiration and for knowledge, where have we been going? Going to the armchairs of universities, going to their hallowed musty books, going to the famous armchair men who were tutored by armchair men, themselves famous offspring of the armchair. We have been getting mere instruction and dubious formation in this vicarious, left-handed way until the whole social fabric, educated as it is far beyond its capacity, is unable to bear up, longer, under the strain of reality. *"Lieber Meister's"* * definition of a "highbrow" was "a man educated far beyond his capacity," and I can assure you that Usonia *is* educated far beyond capacity, and that education is not even on speaking terms with true culture at the present time. How much better off you are at the moment remains to be seen by yourselves, my lords, ladies and gentlemen.

And so comes this open challenge to England, no less a challenge to our own nation, yes . . . a challenge to the world at large: this new reality to face and to work out to larger purpose and a better end.

Now, reality is not new except as we are new to reality.

How new we are to reality I think you can all see by looking about you in city streets, in town suburbs or country. And you can see this not only in architecture; you can see it in dress, customs—utilities confused; you can see it just as well in the state of the world at the moment—hysterical, uneasy, an unhappy sense of impending danger and total loss. Everything material is at sixes and sevens with anything spiritual. In short, life itself is at a loss, not at a premium. Glance at yourselves with your "conscription." What does that indicate? What does the whole condition of this world at the moment indicate but the need for some

* *Louis Sullivan.*

trust in life; for some sense of direction such as our ideal of an organic architecture can give. It is a great peacemaker as well as a great pacemaker because it is constructive.

Out of the ground into the light—yes! Not only must the building so proceed, but we cannot have an organic architecture unless we achieve an organic society! We may build some buildings for a few people knowing the significance or value of that sense-of-the-whole which we are learning to call "organic," but we cannot have an architecture for a society. We who love architecture and recognize it as the great sense of structure in whatever is—music, painting, sculpture, or life itself—we must somehow act as intermediaries—maybe missionaries. But I know well how dangerous the missionary spirit is; I myself come of a long line of preachers going back to the days of the Reformation. I have seen missionaries miscarry in Japan and I have seen the harm others like them are doing round the world; but for an architecture to come to social being in this sense of an organic architecture we who practice it must inevitably become missionaries to a certain extent. Architects, however, would do better and well enough were they to stick to their own last and do their own work quietly in their own way. I do not suppose that I myself have much right to be standing here preaching and talking to you of all this except as I have done this thing for a lifetime and swear never to try to tell you of something that I myself have not practiced and so do not really know. This talk to you this afternoon, therefore, is not in the least academic. Like many another personal adventure story it will bristle with the personal singular. Never mind. I know of no form of egotism quite so backhand as British humility in the second person plural. Notwithstanding the pain and quite infinite disgust I may occasion certain tenderly nurtured British scholars—these talks are for you for what they may be worth to you.

Language, of course, difficult as it is, is comparatively easy to use; it will always be easier to phrase an ideal than to build it. You will know, if you try it, how difficult it is to build form from the ground, independently, truthfully and sincerely. Until it is done, however, this whole mad world will be just as jittery, jealous, envious, mean and unsatisfactory to live in as it is now.

I do feel, standing here and talking to you from out the field, a busy practicing architect, that here . . . in this ideal of form as organic lies the true center line not only of architecture itself but of indigenous culture throughout the modern world. What we call America already goes round the world. It is a spirit no longer a matter of Usonia, only. I find it here among you and I find it wherever I go. I know it is abroad in the whole of the world and that it needs only the definite lines of actual principle to form this new life that we call modern but which after all is so old, old as life itself, into vital entity—the new integrity. Yes—*integral* is criterion now.

And I will try, in several subsequent lectures, to show how this simple principle of an organic architecture has already gone to work, try to indicate what it is doing and show—on the screen, at least—the difference between buildings informed by that spirit and such buildings as our great cities still put up by government or "by order" and which our great nations build to express the dignity of official authority.

For such an instance, a world-wide one, let us take Michelangelo's dome: the dome of St. Peter's at Rome. Michelangelo was no architect; he was a painter—not a very good one; he was a sculptor and a good one. But he would build buildings and concerning one building in particular he had a grand idea. Now, you must see a dome as an arch, and know, as you do, that an arch is always thrusting outward at the bottom. Any arch whatsoever, must find something to resist that thrust or it comes down. Michelangelo seemed not to care so much about that. Probably he did not know much about it anyway. But this form "the dome" intrigued the man. Originally a dome had haunches well down within the building itself and so was valid architectural structure. But Michelangelo thought it fine to put his grand arch up in the sky on the top of tall posts. He did it. The result was a fantastic, aesthetic sculptural effect, actually nonsensical; a ponderous anachronism. Before the dome had been completed, cracks appeared in its base, and chunks of masonry began to fall. There was a hurried call in Rome for blacksmiths and every one of them got quickly to work to forge a great chain to put round the Angelo dome. The chain got there just in time. It is there yet. Well, the moral is that this singularly bastardized expression of architecture, be-corniced and be-pilastered, false, untrue to itself, became the symbol of official authority the world over. We have it everywhere in Usonia. We have it for the nation's Capitol and for the state house and for the county court houses. Even the district likes a dome up on its pilastered offices and big business has tried to steal it although getting along very well, thank you, with medieval mass.

Now as unthinking as that, just as inorganic as that, is all this un-thought-out academic building in which we find life embedded today. We no longer think about it at all. Even these buildings we live in, or for, are no longer *thought-built*. In fact, they never were. They were merely *taste-built*. Take your great St. Paul's. Sir Christopher Wren, darling of England (certainly he had the adoration of the people of his day), has built a dome for you patterned after the Michelangelo dome. Sir Christopher had the hardihood to boast that his dome would have stood alone without the chain—but at the same time he used the chain. I mention this as one little minor incident which stands out to show the sort of thing against which organic architecture has had to fight and for no good honest reason must continue fighting.

You may well see that it is quite a "job," this one the young in spirit have on hand; quite a work they now have to do? Some fight this, to clear away our dead past by clear thinking to make way for direct and honest building out of what ground we have to what light there is. No, it is all not so simple, nor is it too difficult. But it cannot be done by the architect alone while our social structure itself is in the same senseless chaotic state. But our spirits are still alive in this rubbish heap profes-sional aestheticism has left to us. The old order passes and the new meantime is groping, growing, hoping to find some way through the heap to something more integral and consistent with the laws of nature; the love of human nature square with human life. We will see what can be done.

SECOND EVENING

As the first line of this, our second talk, and as you see from Jimmie Thompson's fine film, you have no lecturer before you tonight. A worker is in from the field. I could wish that workers came more often from the field to your platform to talk to you straight from experience; talk, first-hand straight from the shoulder—about what is actually happening out in the world. Over the entrance to the new drafting room we are building at Taliesin, which you have just glimpsed in winter and summer, we are to have the following words carved in the oak wood over the door-way: "What a man does, that he has," and I believe that statement is—not the starting point perhaps, but at least a proper profession of direction for what we call this new adventure into reality, an organic archi-tecture. As I explained in my last lecture, this new architecture is—in truth—an earnest search for reality. Men and all their things have be-come so encrusted, so disguised by the pseudo-classic mask which is being worn everywhere people are educated, that the search is ardu-ous.

I suppose essentially the wearing of the mask was and still is defensive tactics of a sort. Having for five hundred years, at least, really created nothing cultural of our own, we have expropriated what we thought was best to take or—more likely—merely what we admired most, and we did the best we could with it. We did very well indeed? England did very well? And France did very well because France sent to the Italians themselves for help to get her Renaissance all on straight! But the English, though less delicate and elegant, did very well with it in England by living in it in the English way and domesticating it. They gave this curious French renaissance of the Renaissance a very homely aspect indeed. What I like most and admire most in your coun-try today is that homeliness which you have known so well how to achieve—in spite of renaissance, mind you, not because of it. It is hard to achieve such homeliness with the new, until God has "made it click" as they say in Hollywood. But we are achieving it, surpassing it, I think, in the Usonian buildings we are now building. The first condition of homeliness, so it seems to me, is that any building which is built should love the ground on which it stands. Too much of the old traditional architecture, certainly the pseudo-classic architecture, and, I would say, what Georgio-colonial architecture we have—a Renaissance of the renaissance of the Renaissance—really hates the ground and looks as though it did so. The house just stands there that way, that's all, and it is the same stance whether it be on a slope or whether the ground be flat, wooded or bare rock. No matter what the topographical conditions are, there the outlines of the same tradition are observed, lengthwise, crosswise—up and down. Usually the entrance is in the center. There are rooms right and rooms left, a wing here and a wing there. You take it all that way or you leave it! If you adhere to that sacred but stupid "tradition" you are, if not admirable, certainly respectable. If you depart from it at all you are a danger, or in danger. But now that is no longer living as we understand living. The reflex of which I have spoken is coming in, and it appears in all the buildings you have just seen on the screen this evening. If major and minor axes show in such buildings today, it is because that sacrifice happens to be natural in the circumstances. Sometimes major and minor axes are natural, but major and minor axis architecture, as we know it and call it "classic," was never intended to serve life; it was mainly an imposition upon it. We know that now.

The imposition was not made consciously, but there it stood—monarchic and not democratic—not of the life within the building, which if natural would be in the reflex. To put it very simply, that natural reflex expresses very directly the feeling we now have at Taliesin about what constitutes the basis of our buildings. In buildings we are building there the movement has developed and grown up as the trunk of the tree sends out branches and foliage. We practice these principles and ideals every day grappling with life and with nature at first hand in every way possible to us. But nevertheless we have had a too far left wing or branch and we have had a too far right wing or branch. The

234

DAVID WRIGHT HOUSE, PHOENIX, ARIZONA

DAVID WRIGHT HOUSE, INTERIOR, PHOENIX, ARIZONA

left wing has taken the aspect of the thing that we loved to practice and with painter-like perspicacity has made of it a mere scene, a superficial style; in other words we have come, by the left, to another superficiality trying to escape reality by the same old practice of art as an aesthetic instead of the feeling that now that the time has come when buildings may be scientifically built, science and art and even religion must find expression, as one, in what we build. The right-wing sees the manner and knowing something of the means proceeds to exaggerate both. Education unfortunately for us now, in our need, has produced only those young men who can do things by election and selection, rather than from within by creative impulse and instinct guided by tested principles.

So, the left wing of this movement, as it has grown up, you may see in the States and every other nation today in the buildings called "modernistic." You have some of them in London, and we have re-marked upon what they have done to London. In Russia too there are some. You may see what they did to Russia. The Russians taking one good look at them promptly threw out or were not very kind to the men who built them because, after all, the Russian character being rather wild and romantic, she was impatient of any such importation. And yet, strange to say, having thrown out the one aesthetic aspect of the thing because they did not like it they are now subscribing to an old one, another and a worse. They have gone back to "classic" architecture because knowing nothing, yet, of *organic* architecture they thought these left-wing two-dimensional buildings were modern architecture. And there is danger that, in London, you are going on to think the same thing. We at Taliesin see these new buildings, hard, unsympathetic in aspect, thin, as useful negation in appearance but, essentially, merely the expression of another aesthetic, though a better one and not greatly nearer the truth of architecture and no nearer the heart of life than the ornamenta and grandomania that preceded the modernistic.

Inasmuch as modern architecture may be anything built today, and we are talking of organic architecture, let us always say organic architecture. Now let me reiterate—the word "organic" does not, can-not apply to so-called classic architecture in any form whatsoever, and it does not apply to any of the "period" buildings, even the "Georgian" in which we live today. The term does not apply to anything else we happen to have. It would apply however to the old Japanese buildings; Japanese domestic architecture was truly organic architecture. It would apply to certain other periods in the architectures of the world. Egyptian architecture was in a sense organic architecture, an expression of the feeling for human form. The Gothic cathedrals in the Middle Ages had much in them that was organic in character, and they became influential and beautiful, insofar as that quality lived in them which was *organic*, as did all other architectures possessing it. Greek architecture knew it—not at all! It was the supreme search for the elegant solution.

Working with apprentices as I do, I have observed that when this idea of architecture as organic begins to work in the young mind something happens: something definite happens to life. Something larger happens to one's outlook upon life. One becomes impatient of these unfounded restraints, these empirical impositions, these insignificant gestures as in grand opera, these posturings which all the buildings of the pseudo-classic and pseudo-renaissance assume to be art and architecture. One begins to want something a little nearer to the ground, more *of* life not so much *on* it. We begin to want to live like spirited human beings. So the first rejection in this new movement, which took place at the beginning, was "the styles," next came the obvious major and minor axis of "classic" architecture. Symmetry and rhythm we wanted, because both are life, but symmetry occult, graceful, rhythm throughout as gracious as may be, but never putting on airs for itself alone at any time anywhere. Always in human scale in all proportions. But the new movement—it is genuinely a "movement"—as an assertion of these principles starting as it did in the tall grass of the western prairies, has in the main become more or less abortive. I myself could be, as I stand here, a bitterly disappointed old man. I am not. I am quite happy and still interested in the thing that I love, because I recognize that any new movement concerning the philosophy of building or being, must because of the character of the education which still prevails amongst us, be exploited, and probably temporarily exploded. We cannot blame young architects brought up at the plan-factory drawing board or by book or become architects by armchair precepts, for getting no further than exterior precedent with new principles. There is very little precedent yet safe to go upon. If they can find a precedent at all they will soon though not intentionally exploit the precedent. So naturally enough we soon have only another drawing-board architecture of a slightly different type of fallacious façade. And, also, we have with us by emulation what, among ourselves, we have come to call the "reformed" or the "deflowered" classic. Today at least that has been our modern movement's influence on the ancient classic orders. The "classic" not yielding a jot where thought is concerned, but by scraping off exterior detail simplifying its aspect to conform to the new aesthetic. Buildings by architects of the old classic school have come to appear more like the appearances of the new simplicity which have arisen. And so we do have some improved effects? I think we all like "deflowered" classic much better than we like the old ornate classic.

So far, so good. And that good is directly due to our new movement. Someone has said, and I think very well said, that radical liberals do their work not so much by growing strong in themselves as by making all others more liberal. Now that much has already happened to our credit. Today we have much in the appearances of the world as direct consequence of the thrust and power of this new idea. But it is not unreasonable to suppose that having that now, we are going further afield with it and putting definite working principles even into our schools. Yet, I wonder whether we are going to have any schools in the near future in the same sense as of old or at present. And I wonder too whether we are going to have cities in the old sense in which we once had cities. Personally I believe both schools and the city to be distinctly dated. The great city, haphazard at best might be possible for what existed at the time, has become scientifically impossible. The horse and buggy, foot-work . . . the enemy just outside the gates? Well once upon a time, close the gates and the enemy could not get in. When life was primitive and things very different mechanically the overgrown city had validity as a necessity. But what validity has the overgrown city now? If we were less habituated, if we were less like sheep, if we had not been made, by years of habitude to imposition, to like it, we could not stand it longer. It is all one's life is worth now to live in any great modern city. Someone has said that to cross the street in New York now, one must have been born on the other side. To get into the now senseless aggregation and to get out of it again takes too much life out of the man. We should soon have in authority developed minds that comprehend the modern sense of spaciousness so characteristic of today now that scientific mechanization is being made available to everyone, rich or poor. We should soon be able to realize that the door of this cage—this thing we call the great city—is at last—open. The door is open and we can fly. We can go from the cage and it can go from itself never to return. We should realize too that gathered together now, in cities, we are frightfully vulnerable; we can easily be destroyed in masses. The enemy still exists; peoples still hate one another so destructive forces are more than ever at large. Once upon a time we defended ourselves by city walls and gates in the walls. We could shut out the enemy. But we cannot deal longer with the enemy in that simple way. More important than this misfortune there is growing up by way of speed and instantaneous interchange a new sense of spaciousness, a new need for the outside coming into the building and for the inside going out.

Garden and building may now be one. In any good organic structure it is difficult to say where the garden ends and where the house begins or the house ends and the garden begins—and that is all as should be, because organic architecture declares that we are by nature ground-loving animals, and insofar as we court the ground, know the ground and sympathize with what it has to give us and produce in what we do to it, we are utilizing practically our birthright. We can go to any place anywhere then and happily be ourselves. But in the overgrown village called a metropolis, now, we have to watch our step, dodge cars, literally take our lives in our own hands to get from somewhere to anywhere—wasting all of our nervous energy and half our time merely to get there and get back again—get back again maybe—keeping up this senseless urban concentration in a pig-piling and scraping, the basis for which disappeared when all these scientific inventions that now threaten us from above and from every side, were made. Do

240

you not think we could with reason expect our architects to take all this in constructively, so that we could get away from all that or have it on more directly humane terms and as soon as possible? By no means is it possible for us to satisfactorily make over our great cities. Reflect that congestion has only just begun! The motorcar Englishman will soon be three out of five. No, by no means is it possible for us to "make over" the old style buildings still called "classic." A fundamental new thought with scientific constructive insight into the nature of the thing to be done and the way of the doing, must save modern humanity from the torture of its self-inflicted misery: that thought is ready to go to work as organic architecture.

It is not enough merely to be sincere about this thing. I think the time has come when one must be intelligent; you, young architects— so many of you there against the walls—you must be able to grasp the meaning of this crisis and learn to proceed from generals to particulars to solve these entirely new equations. Then this movement toward an organic architecture will be a genuine, upward, forward movement of life itself because as its center line, I am sure, henceforward lies the truth of any culture of indigenous character for any people, and any- where. I am sure it applies in England just as it applies in the United States.

I am chagrined somewhat, to come back here—as I have already said—only to see that nearly everything we have above ground has proceeded from London, has come to us from the United Kingdom; nearly all of our abuses of such culture as we have, nearly all of our bad architecture and a great many of our bad personal habits. Pro- fessional humility and overworked pronunciation among them. But I am happy to say that I now see that a great many of our good things came from you too. I could not deny that nor wish to do so. I am glad to say that our English inheritance is the best thing we have, provided we can understand it, see it in perspective—and not be too "awfully had" by it. That is an English expression, is it not? I once heard some- body say in Tokyo: "You know, my dear, I was *awfully had* yesterday, yes, yes *had* awfully." You see I remember it! Now I think we Usonians have been "awfully had, my dear" by our educational, Oxfordian,

Cambridgeistic servility concerning "you all" and what you have got in the way you have it. I think Usonians now have something which you in England have yet to get. I think you need that something most of all.

Standing here as I do again today, I am really an emissary of the ground, preaching the salt and savor of a new and a fresh life. I urge you to be a little less self-consciously educated and conservative, to be a little more liberally reasonable, and all of you—every architect included—should—daily for seven minutes if possible—do a little more serious and a little deeper thinking on the subject of what constitutes organic character in economics, in statesmanship, in architecture, yes and why not in salesmanship? True architecture my noble lords, ladies and gentlemen . . . is poetry. A good building is the greatest of poems when it is organic architecture. The fact that the building faces and is reality and serves while it releases life, makes daily life better worth living and makes all the necessities happier because of useful living in it, makes the building none the less poetry, but more truly so. Every great architect is—necessarily—a great poet. He must be a great original interpreter of his time, his day, his age. This afternoon I went to the Architectural Association and spoke to 250 or more young people, just one little handful among all those young architects you are making to help carve out your future for you. There they were. They were being educated—and how? I do not mean this as a reflection upon them or their teachers in particular, because that condition is one that is now found throughout the world. It is worse in Usonia than it is in England. It is worse with us than it is with you because there is less excuse for it with us.

But what should those boys be doing now if this movement toward organic expression of organic society is to grow? Where should they be? Not there at all. Having ground they should make a plan and working drawings for the work they want to do and the way they want to do it. Somebody should give them that piece of ground; there are so many splendid pieces lying waiting, just for them, here in England. The boys should then go out on that ground and inspired by it—build. And during the building while scheming and scheming while building,

242

meantime designing and drawing, learn something actual with the sweat of the learning on their sun-tanned brows. That, I take it, may not be "education," but it would be culture. And culture is far better —now.

Today, I think, our Usonian educational system and the thing we call culture are not even on speaking terms with each other. And since you, our England, has been our teacher how can it all be different here with you? I have said that it is quite unlikely that a man can be a gentleman and a good architect too, and that is probably true, if we take the accepted sense of the term "gentleman" and the new sense of the term "architect." But you do not see that out of all the professionalizing in this world and out of no professionalist, no life can come now? He—poor man—is *ipso facto*. He was made what he is by what was, but he cannot leave that now, to experiment. He cannot go forward, any more than government can do so. Government—by nature—must be *ipso facto* also. Both, as they stand, and if they are to stand at all, can follow but cannot lead. We in our country for instance have expected our President to have ideas and have browbeaten him senselessly—ceaselessly—because he cannot think of anything we would like to save us. Senseless hatred from those he sought to save was Franklin Roosevelt's fate and I suppose it will be the fate of anybody in a similar position today. Nations have run out of ideas because the individuals composing them have none.

Now you may properly ask where is all this fresh impetus to come from? Where are we going to find this salt and savor of life that comes fresh from the ground with the needed ideas, coming with capacity for broader applications of those new ideas in order to make of life the thing that really life ought to be under this democratic ideal that we profess and wear as a label? You in England probably have more of the democratic instinct or, let us say, the actual practice disguised by certain superficial dissemblances, than we have in the United States. Of that I am not sure, but I do feel—since knowing you better— that it is possibly true. Why then do you not trust life? Why does not great England on behalf of this great upward swing of life, on behalf of this desire to serve and intrepret and develop humanity with fresh integrity; why does England not trust life? After all, it is a good and lordly gesture, is it not? Yes, it would even be a "gentlemanly" thing to do.

Awfully painful this assumption that life is a thief and a liar until it somehow, to your satisfaction, proves itself innocent. That is no proper attitude for gentlemen to take. But it seems to me to have become your attitude. And your attitude is adopted nearly all over the world, as I have seen it. When I got here I was immensely disappointed to see the fear that exists among you. Where is the great old England, standing up, afraid of nothing, magnanimous, splendid, not afraid of life, because she was living? If she still lives why be afraid of anything today, even of a great idea? Certainly not afraid of an aeroplane carrying bombs. After all, airplanes are only a stunt. They can do a deal of damage and perhaps kill a great many women and children, if the world really has sunk so low that warfare must consist in killing women and children. If so then why not kill them all? But I digress a little now; I should not have touched upon this, I know. It was only that I hoped to find something among you over here, that I know *is* here but see submerged for the moment. I know it is here because I am one with it, I know that what I feel, what I desire, what I love and hope for, is just as English as it is Usonian. It is probably also German, probably Italian too. And I happen to know that very largely, way in underneath, it is Japanese. So what? The ideal of an organic architecture for an organic society as the center line of a new culture is inevitably a great peacemaker in the world, because it is genuinely *constructive*.

I have sometimes been called an iconoclast but no such term properly applies to me. I never wanted to destroy anything living nor wanted to take even the dead away unless death became a threat to life. I have had a better thing in a better way in my hand to plant, with the planting of which the living dead interfered. That reasonable destruction by order of nature is the only justification there is for destruction. Perhaps it is all the justification we need.

I am speaking of this new movement, tonight, as the ideal of a life organic, of buildings as organic, of an economic system truly organic. A statesman would be a great architect in this sense of knowing life at its best to be organic. I am speaking to you, therefore, of a great humane ideal. If we are to be served by it, if we are to see it grow, continue to move and come forward, let us divest life and the movement itself, especially of all these equivocal appearances either "left" or "right," and let us get youth to work at it as the center line runs—true. And youth never was nor ever will be a matter of one's years.

Now I have talked enough. Really talking is of very little value, I feel. I am always ashamed to be doing it publicly but . . . still . . . I do it. After I have given a talk of this kind I go home depressed thinking to myself: "Here I am at it again trying, trying, trying, and what is the use?" That, "what is the use" is too English I think. You English listen, you approve, you say, "Yes, that is true," and you do nothing at all about it because a deep pessimism concerning life seems settling down among you if you don't watch out.

I rather gathered from Mr. Wright that cities are a bad institution and that what we ought to do is to go out into the country and live there. Should not we by that means destroy the country and, without making it exactly like a ribbon-developed road, make it lose the character which we want it to have?

That is a sensible question and the supposition that the city is a bad institution now is a natural one. But, as for destroying the country, of course we are not talking about such buildings as now constitute the city moving to the country. God forbid! We are talking about the countryside itself developing into a type of building in which will lie naturally building becoming part of the countryside, building belonging there naturally with grace. Such buildings will exist. There are already a few of them. I too should hate to see these London buildings of yours in the English countryside. English life is all cooped up in them for all your little garden plots outside. These buildings of yours look to me far too pessimistic. They have no appropriate sense of the countryside and lack any modern sense of life whatever. If London were to be preserved as a museum piece by parking its insignificant undesirable portions it would become a great treasure for the future. I should dislike to see it destroyed bit by bit by builders. I should like to see the slums and insignificant parts removed and the precious, historical aspects of old London itself preserved for posterity in a great park, when the people, having learned how to build, go further afield, and all the countryside of England becomes one beautiful modern city, in the new sense, wherein the country was the more beautiful because of the buildings, yes, even the factories. Then they could come back to London and see it for what it once was. That is possible.

What would you do if you had to build something new in an old city? Would you put your own architecture into it or would you think of something which would fit what was there already?

I think that question deals with the problem of the moment: how to continue, in this transitory period, to live in an old city without destroying it with new ideas or abortive old ones. If I were asked to build a building in London as I have said, I should not know what to do. But if I built at all I should try to build something at least not outrageous, something which would least insult and mortify my sense of London. Just what that would be, how do I know! All that is possible now, in the buildings you build in your city, is a kind of merciful mitigation. Nothing thoroughbred of strength and purpose and character can be city-born nowadays. But you can do something to ease off dying and make this old city quite comfortable while it approaches inevitable dissolution.

How would you suggest bringing the countryside into a garden that is a plot 60 or 100 or 200 feet wide? That is a problem which in England is a very great one, as we have everywhere the development of very small plots.

The plot of 60 by 100, or any line-up of plots, is a hideous thing, making larger life impossible at the beginning. Why should there be such small plots, even in England, for anybody? As for us if everybody in the United States of America had an acre of ground at his disposal, we should not fill the state of Texas alone, and you would be surprised, I am sure, how much everybody might have if you took the population of England and worked out how much ground area would be available to the family provided it was all properly available. When people are huddled together as they are in London it seems as though there was not enough room in all the world for them. But not far away from here, at Richmond, there is a 1,000-acre park! I sat next a gentleman the other day at dinner who spoke of his 4,000-acre estate. There is plenty of room in the British Isles for British life and British scenery be none the less desirable.

Is not this ideal of yours entirely against the basic principle of humanity? Is not the basic principle of humanity to herd? Surely human beings still have the desire to herd and not to spread themselves as far as they can from their fellow human beings?

Did I say "as far as they can"? But I think the young gentleman asked a very sensible question. He asserts the herding instinct of humanity as "basic." He thinks we are still like sheep and still have these animal attributes. So we have. But I believe culture—in spite of urban education—has done something for us, and think that culture should and will go on to do more by way of agricultural training. If we are to grow and develop as human beings, by way of that spirit which has been a gift to us, we shall grow less and less like animals and in the light of modern times do less and less "herding." This new philosophic principle of reality, and these great opportunities now for the first time given to humanity by science, resulting in this gorgeous sense of speed and space, is so loved by us, even though we are animals, that by way of these scientific gifts we are going to seek to herd more intelligently, and so, herd less and less. I do not say that we should go as far from each other as possible, but I do say we should go sufficiently far for this modern sense of space and life to be ours, at no one else's expense.

Is it not inevitable that organic architecture will also develop a body of pattern and that there will be dogmas and principles which are not altogether obvious and must be inculcated into students? If the movement is not to dissipate itself in a hundred and one directions, must not it be given some direction and some basic structure?

247

That is a moot question, and I think an easy way to answer it is by saying: Yes and No. We were all, in Britain as probably in Usonia, educated as eclectics and that inbred eclecticism is become our special touch upon life. And so, general and specific imitation is yet inevitable. People *will* take these ideas and principles and exploit them on the one hand and formulate them for academic training on the other hand. Academies will soon be making *a* style where only *style* itself is needed. In fact, "they" have already done so. But what we have to keep in mind is that we no longer want a style, if that is what you mean by "basic structure." Humanity needs style all the time, therefore needs individuality perpetually fresh and new with every instance in any and every generation in every nation on earth. The law of change is immutable law; the only law we have not taken into account. It is the only law we have not learned to consider and respect when we proceed to make FORM. We have tried to stem and hold in check the tides of life. Now, why go on with it? Why not see that if pattern is to be made at all it must be free pattern, the one most suited to growth, the one most likely to encourage and concede growth to life? That means, I think, the end of the word "institution" as we have it set up. The moment we have any vested or sentimental interest we feel we have to protect it, to guard it, to fend off its enemies by holding it tight. Our thinking, our philosophy, everything we have, is like that *"to have and to hold."* I am sure you would be surprised to see how effective it might be to reverse that process. If education would learn to do that by way of some true human culture, forgetting its "to have and to hold" precepts and practices, allowing organic culture to come through with its great liberal sense of life, you would find that life can be trusted, perhaps that life is all that can really be trusted. And how interesting you would find its variety of manifestation!

We young people, after a very lengthy training, come out of our schools possibly with some feeling that it has not all been as satisfactory as we should like it to have been, and we go, for instance, to work under a borough engineer or someone like that. While serving the community as far as we can in our position, how are we, after all this education, to uneducate ourselves in order to serve the community better?

There is only one way to uneducate ourselves. Of course, all things with us are literally and mentally now in pigeon-holes or compartments. For an instance we have the engineer, the architect, the landscape architect, the interior decorator, etc., etc. But, under this thing that I have been talking to you about, a man soon gains a sense of the whole and a feeling of complete responsibility as a unit in the whole develops in him, not to be pigeon-holed. The only way he can "uneducate" himself is by going to work with this new sense growing up in him, getting out to work somewhere where life is actual, not theoretical. In that way, holding to the larger view, he will be likely to forget everything he was taught because what he was taught just would not work.

If you tonight, and on the other occasions when you address numbers of people who are interested in building, achieve in each person a realization of the organic principles of building and life, how would you suggest that we can in this country bring about that realization among the millions of people who have not met you and are not at present architecturally minded? How can we achieve, in a country such as this, within our lifetime, what you would wish to bring about?

Why worry about one's lifetime or too much about the future? Everything that *is, is* right now. If opportunity is mine and I do well with it, next to it another will come to me. The future—beyond that part of it that is seen today—is something we cannot assure nor should we think too much about it. We should consider our present; we should act in the present for the future, the present being the future so far as we can now see. I think we should not be too much concerned about how long growth is going to take or about how difficult it is going to be either here and now or hereafter. If we see it as good it is for us to *act,* now. . . . If my words have conveyed my thought and inspired one single mind tonight I shall be satisfied. One mind is enough.

You have inspired me tonight. You have given me a feeling of space, a feeling that I want to expand and feel things as you feel them. Some day I hope to be given a commission to build something. Assuming that I get that commission, I shall first of all have to please my client and give him what he wants. What I want will probably not be what he wants. If I can get a combination of the two, I shall then be faced with the task of getting my scheme passed by the local authority. Those two obstacles are paramount amongst the difficulties which we architects over here have to face. I am sure that in your early buildings you have faced similar difficulties.

I have and, while vexatious, they are really only difficulties to be overcome.

What I want to know is how you were able to break away originally from what had gone before and evolve the new style of architecture in face of what I call these difficulties.

First, to go back to your fear of your probable client. It *is* a reasonable fear and one which stands as a specter before many a young man throughout the world today. Fortunately, it did not exist for me. I had to break away from nothing. Things were as they were, I was as I was, and I built as I wanted to build. My client came to me to build for him, so he was mine too. I do not think any architect *could* build for a client across the grain or against his own knowledge or feeling or goodwill. Nor is that to be your job, as I see it. In a case of the sort I think you should say: "I am sorry but I cannot build for you," and wait until some right opportunity does come. Then it will surely come. No man can build a building for another who does not believe in him, who does not believe in what he believes in, and who has not chosen him because of this faith, knowing what he can do. That is the nature of architect and client as I see it. When a man wants to build a building he seeks an interpreter, does he not? He seeks some man who has the technique to express that thing which he himself desires but cannot do. So, should a man come to me for a building he would be ready for me. It would be what I could do that he wanted. I have opened the door and shown many a man out of my office when I found he sought mere novelty and did not understand what I would be doing for him. Only the other day it was the name that interested a client. He was not up to this organic endeavor in building, I knew. And I knew that building for him would be only putting something into his hands that he could not properly live in. So do not despair of the break-away on any account. Every man has his own and his own will come to him, though he may have to wait a long time in England!

Architects are the only people who are taught to plan; no other people in the community are taught anything about planning. It should form a small part of everyone's general education, especially in the case of people who take up politics. I think a Prime Minister or a President who does not know how to plan in the abstract cannot possibly be expected to be able to plan for a community, and I think that the fact that architects are the only people who have any knowledge at all of planning is very unsatisfactory from the point of the community.

I think that is a fact and very unsatisfactory. I believe every man or woman should have included in his or her culture—I will not say their education—some knowledge of planning and of reading a plan. Any really cultivated man or woman should be able to read a plan as easily as a book. When that is the case ideas will flow more freely. What we have been talking about tonight presupposes architecture as the center line of any truly indigenous culture. That being so, it should be just as natural for young boys and girls to learn the nature of the plan and themselves to plan as it is for them to learn to play the piano or the harp, or read Dickens or even read Walt Whitman.

England and America are democracies and we like to think that they are free countries, yet our building is regulated and can be hindered to a large extent by by-laws, regulations and all sorts of conditions. Germany and Italy are under dictatorships; yet we see splendid building schemes going on there and being completed in a very short space of time. Can you suggest a reasonable compromise between those two states of affairs?

I could suggest a basis for compromise, but I do not think that would settle the matter. The building codes of the democracies embody, of course, only what the previous generation knew or thought about building, and the ensuing generation finds the code a stumbling-block. When I was called to build the building in Tokyo I could not get a permit to build it. Nor could I get a building permit to build any one of the buildings you have seen in the film tonight. With regard to the building you have just seen finished, the S.C. Johnson Wax building, I could not get full permission to build that either. And we are just building in Philadelphia a little group of houses called the Ardmore Experiment. That experiment could not be passed under the building codes, so we managed to have the code abrogated. It is sometimes necessary to say: "After all, buildings are for life and life goes on. If you want to confine all that the next generation or this generation is going to know about building to what the past generation knew, go ahead and stop our building." But they do not quite like to take that responsibility. We are a little more liberal in Usonia, probably, than you feel you can afford to be here. But this anachronism of which you speak, however, does not arise entirely from the fact that we are democracies and other countries fascist. It arises because we are not genuine democracies: we are in too many ways undemocratic in thought. Democracy is on our lips, an oration on the pages of school books. But we put little of it into active practice. And the illiberal administration of these building codes is due directly to the antiquated educational processes that have produced the men who made the codes.

The desire to hold to rules and regulations that prevent progress is not characteristic of a democracy but, of course, committee work is slow work at best and democracy is a kind of committee at work. Dictatorship is free to abrogate and to say: "This is a good idea; let us have it," and you might wish you hadn't got it. But under the system that you have in England and even the one we have in America it is only rarely that our "rulers" dare to say that, until the matter goes to committee. They, and we, seem to think their countries are democracies when rule is by committee . . . an idea of democracy extremely peculiar, as you will see if you analyze it. Even so . . . No, I do not think hindering codes are a question of dictatorship as against democracy, but are a matter of present confusion of ideas in our democracies. And fear of any individual's free-will (except the dictator's) on the part of dictatorships. Really there is no good reason why a democracy should not have, and be free to will and to possess the best. Is not democracy the highest form of aristocracy that the world has ever seen—the aristocracy of the man, the individual, his qualities as a man making him the aristocrat? Let us put that kind of democracy into practice somehow in place of snobocracy and the code will be no impediment to better building. It seems a long way to go.

You mentioned in your lecture that there was one justification for destruction, namely, building something better. Do not we come up against that same moot point—who is to decide what is something better? A certain friend of ours on the continent thinks he has been doing that for some time.

Yes—who is to decide what is better? Well, in a democracy the man decides his own for himself. I would not say that any tribunal would be competent to pass upon the "better" for him. Nor do I think it should be a case of "tribunal," a matter of judgeship or of judging. The time comes when nature herself, the nature of things coinciding with the nature of the man, cries out, demands and determines in its own way. For instance, I think we are there now in this matter of architecture, because of circumstantial changes brought to pass by science.

Do not you think we should design buildings to suit the people who have to live in them and not to please ourselves?

Yes, but as we see suitability, if we are consulted. People who live in buildings know strangely little about buildings, as a rule. They think they know what they want. Sometimes they do. If they come to you, wanting you, believing that you know, they do know that much. But, if they come to you to tell you *how* to build what they want, that is something else. That could not work. In building according to this ideal which I have just propounded I am sure it would not work. Any architect builds a building to please his client, certainly; otherwise why is he architect and the man his client? But were you as an architect to go out seeking a job, go after a piece of work, try to persuade a man to let you build a building for him, then perhaps you would have to please your client against your will, do what he told you, and serve you right, too! But to put yourself there in his power is unethical, of course.

To think and plan nowadays an architect has to have a thorough knowledge of the very complex technique of building, which is becoming more and more complex. Can the average intelligence master all that, or must specialists be employed?

The matter of "experts" seems embedded in "the system" as it exists today. The specialist has arisen because the capitalistic system which we practice needs cogs to make its wheels keep turning. It is true that buildings have become extremely complex, but they have become complex because the system creates its own complexities and confusions. There is no very great difficulty in creating an organism, an entity, in the way of a building in which all needed services are incorporated features of the building. But that type of building, call it creation, cannot be under any "specialistic" system such as that to which you refer. Such creation must occur by single-minded mastery on the part of the creator of the building, and that alone is organic building. We cannot in organic building have a group of specialists; we have to relegate the expert to the back-yard of the building . . . or to oblivion. I like what Henry Ford said about the expert—"if he had an opposition which he wished to destroy he would endow it with experts." I believe that today the expert is the absolute enemy of the thing about which I have been talking to you, and that the more you let him come in and the more you think you are going to get from him the worse off you will be. So I believe an architect should learn the principles underlying the installation of electricity, he should know what constitutes good plumbing, he should be able to invent and arrange and bring all this together as a complete organism. We are talking of an entity when we speak of an organic building; we are not talking of a shell being set up and appurtenance men cutting it half down in order to get their work into it —then the plasterer coming in, daubing it all up—the painter coming in to patch up defects, and so on.

Think of those old five-process buildings! Now we are building one-process buildings and have dispensed with some of the appurtenances; for an instance the heating is underneath the floor now. It had become so difficult to build a building that it was almost impossible to think of building one. And this new thought that I am bringing to you tonight demands first a general simplification in the process of building. The architect must learn to think "in simples" before he can build a modern building worth building.

Much as we might despise and condemn most of the buildings in the suburbs of London, the people living in them think that they are wonderful; they love their houses. Do you suggest that we should take the liberty, the burden and the responsibility of advising them that they are quite wrong, to satisfy our own ideals of what a house should look like?

If I thought the houses were quite wrong, I should certainly tell the people living in them so, if they asked for my opinion. But I do not think I would walk in on them, just to tell them so.

THIRD EVENING

First of all as "hors d'œuvre" I shall show you some more of the apprentice Jimmie Thompson's film of our work at Taliesin North and West. The modern world is become so picture-minded that it is difficult to get much understanding of anything without pictures. (*The film being shown.*) The pictures on the screen now show you what we call the Taliesin Fellowship, and show first of all the desert camp on a great Arizona mesa which the boys, together with myself, are now building to work and live in during the winter-time. We work in Wisconsin for

255

only seven months of the year—summer—and for the other five months —winter—we leave that region, where it becomes about 30° below zero and go out to where the sun is shining in the vast desert of the great far West. We have only half-finished building the buildings you see now. Many of the building units have canvas tops carried by red-wood framing resting on massive stone walls made by placing the flat desert stones into wood boxes and throwing in stones and concrete behind them. Most of the canvas frames may be opened or kept closed. In addition to my study which you see to the left there is a large general workroom and there are thirty cubicles for the boys. Instead of sculpture, as you see we have used native rocks written on centuries ago by the American Indians and which we found on our own piece of ground. The camp has grown out of that ground, according to the spirit of environment and climate, although perhaps you may not feel it in that way as I do when you look at it in these pictures. Here comes a detail of the furniture. The furniture goes with the buildings—spawned by it really —but unfortunately, as you have seen, although their skins are, the costumes of our people living there are not yet got into line with the structure. The canvas overhead being translucent, there is a very beautiful light to live and work in; I have experienced nothing like it elsewhere except in Japan somewhat, in their houses with sliding paper walls or "shoji."

The film now shows you the native background for our camp buildings, the wonderful skylines with the finest sunshine anywhere unless in Greece. The great cacti you see standing about like monuments are called saguaro. They are one of the few prehistoric plants still existing; they were there when the ichthyosauri were there too. Some of them, still growing, are about six hundred years old.

The pictures now are—in summer—of our real home, Taliesin, Wisconsin. Every boy there has to take his turn at the work which has to be done about the place, and the girls do the same. A boy may be in the kitchen one day and next day driving a tractor, the next day laying stone, but nearly every day he spends some time in the drawing room making plans. It is amazing what the boys accomplish with just a little direction. The leadership rotates from fortnight to fortnight and so all the seniors take a turn in leading the others. We have as little organization as possible—too little, I suppose. We are trying to develop initiative in these young people. We build all the time that we are not drawing or maintaining ourselves and we find it, as a way of life, very interesting. Some of these youngsters will refuse tea in the afternoon in order to keep on working when they are especially interested in what they are doing, as they usually are. It is that special interest in his work which I think immensely important in the education of an architect, getting a feeling of the stone and wood and a sense of construction into his hands on the way to his mind.

Music is a great feature of our lives and, as you see in this portion of the film, we have a little quartette now playing Bach as they often play Beethoven—the two greatest architects I know anything about. All that we ask is action, more action and then some more action. It need not be violent, however, as you see we all enjoy ourselves as work goes along, and part of it takes place in the drafting room every day or any evening.

Taliesin itself is a natural house built of the stone of the region, as you now see, and surrounded with hollyhocks. I believe the hollyhock is considered a weed; at any rate it seems to volunteer all over the world. I have been told that it originated in Asia Minor and in Southern Europe but I think the English have made it feel more at home than has any other nation. Most of our ornaments at Taliesin are ancient Chinese like those you are seeing now. They seem to have the modern spirit which characterizes modern buildings and the more ancient they are the more of that spirit they seem to have! There is room for an argument there, I suppose. Continually we try to keep awake an enquiring, experimental frame of mind. The girls work just as the boys do; we try to make no distinction between them at work although that is some-times difficult.

I do not want you to have the idea that Taliesin is a school, or a community. It happens to be our home and where we work, and these young people are my comrade apprentices: no scholars. They come to help, and if they can learn—well, we are very happy. There are very many things to do because we have several hundred acres of "farm," and in addition we are practicing architects; we are building at the present time some fifty or sixty buildings all over the United States, so that we are fairly busy. But at the same time we were building this camp in Arizona and extending our own home at Taliesin, we were building the Johnson administration offices, an enormous air-conditioned building, modern in every sense; you will see something of it later, and a number of modest-cost houses as well.

The film stops and Mr. Wright begins his lecture.

The modest-cost-house movement is now the thing we are engaged upon for most of our time. It is really amazing to find how low-cost housing in America is the crying need of the hour; I imagine that we could keep on building such houses indefinitely. I feel that it is the most important field that we have and it has been neglected by our architects. I therefore undertook to build a little $5500 house in Madison, Wisconsin, and I succeeded in building it without an extra, with nothing whatever for the owner to pay in addition to his $5500. This "Jacob's House" was a floor-heated laminated-wood-wall house abolishing the hollow spaces made by most wood construction and which, as you know, are an invitation to vermin to come and live with you. Once there, it is hard to get rid of them. The cellular spaces also make the building good kindling wood for fire. We have, therefore, made a thin but solid wall house and by the configuration of the laminated wood walls get strength enough to carry the roof. Most of these houses are of one story but they could be two stories if necessary and are simplified—greatly in plan—all appurtenances made one with the house.

Having built this house some of my colleagues, I am told, said that this was just a stunt and that I would never build another. But, being of the opinion that to build these houses is the one most important thing in our country for an architect to do, I pledged myself to do forty of them. We are now on our twenty-seventh, and I want to assure you that there is nothing more interesting or more important in this world today than trying to put into the houses in which our typical best citizens live something of the quality of a genuine work of art; but nothing is more arduous, nothing is more exhausting and difficult. It would be an exaggeration to say that into one of these little low-cost buildings goes as much thought and effort as goes into a building like the Johnson office building which cost a million dollars. But in any case the effort is disproportionate to the reward as architects practice now. If I were rich or well endowed I would go on building these houses for the rest of my life because from them, I am sure, would begin to flow the better public and industrial building we need so much. But I think something might be done to make an architect's service better worth while on both sides if the importance of it were realized.

Tonight we shall attempt to go on with the practical applications of this new ideal which I have been trying to lay before you. I want to say that I went in so strongly for designing these small houses because I believe that to be one of the most practical of all applications of architecture, in noble sense, today. And it is quite surprising, as well as gratifying, to find how architecture-conscious our young people have become in Usonia concerning this deeper thought in architecture. I go about somewhat among our youngsters, refusing to go more than seven or eight times a year. I have gone to our various universities to talk directly to them about this matter of a center line for indigenous culture and have tried to explain it as simply as I could. The response—I may truly say—has been tremendous. They one and all seem hungry for something, they do not know what but know they are in shallows now. They all feel that what grandmother had and the way grandmother had it was all right because grandmother was all right, but—not just the thing for them now. And that applies to buildings just as much or even more than anything else. Still more than all does it apply to the life that is just in sight.

Here, owing to the young minds of our nation, you will soon find practical applications of the idea from coast to coast—from Canada to the Gulf. Many examples are already to be found in every state of our Union. Perhaps in England your young people are only just beginning to feel the impact of modern science where and as they live, of mobilization—the motorcar, telephone, telegraph, the radio and television, flying and all these other modern agencies which have made our life in America hold such potentialities, a great spaciousness, a change in human scale which is still resisted by all the ideals which we possessed concerning buildings and life in them. But the young have begun to understand that "the door of the cage we call a city has been left open," and they can go out as they are qualified to go. In our United States of America we are beginning to find practical realizations of freedom in the fact that spaciousness is the great modern opportunity, that human scale *is* grown entirely different and that we no longer need—nor will we—live on little plots of ground with our toes in the street and a little backyard behind us with a few plants in it, shaking hands out of the windows on either side with neighbors good and bad. I have said that an acre to the individual should approximate the minimum and if there are seven in a family that family should have seven acres. An approximation we are trying to bring home to the people of our United States. A practical effort of great importance, I feel sure.

It is difficult to get this application or any keen realization of it because of education, the school training of most of our architects, as I have before said again and again—being backwash. We are just a little newer England, East of Buffalo. New York, that's all, with other nationalities thrown in for good measure. But our old Colonial traditions, fine as they were, were soon, so far as the country went on westward, exploited and exploded. We no longer wear the knee-breeches and the silk stockings and the buckles with the lace at our wrist and neck that went with our forefathers' buildings. Wherever and whenever we build them I wish that we might be compelled to do so. It would be much more consistent with what is being done in certain parts of our East. But really Usonian life has gone far and away by the East now and if English travelers want to see "America" as it really is they must forget all about that. Now, America begins *west* of Buffalo. The greatest and most nearly beautiful city of our young nation is probably Chicago. Eventually I think that Chicago will be the most beautiful great city left in the modern world.

For practical applications of our ideal of an organic architecture these grand western plains with their great sense of space afford us room enough in which to carry out, letter and spirit, my own practical proposal of Broadacre City. To introduce Broadacre City as a "practical application to date" now, may take us too far afield into the future —reserved for our last lecture. But it seems important now. . . . The Broadacre City proposal suggested a new human spacing—as already said—the acre to the individual. To accommodate everyone in our nation on that scale—let me say again, would require only one single state. We should have to take the state of Texas, but the state of Texas would accommodate everybody that we have with a minimum of an acre of land for each and leave the rest of Usonia empty of people. While the proposals cannot be carried out in our lifetime at least it is not, therefore, unreasonable to suppose it practicable to educate people to again proceed in that manner to the ground. I do not believe in a "back to the land" movement; I think that any backward movement would be folly; but if we can go forward to large-scale practical application now with all that science has provided for us—or laid up against us—going forward intelligently to the new forms which *must* be made for the accommodation of life so that men may live more generously, more spaciously and more fully, we shall be dealing—practically—with the actual problem of construction now on our hands. And that is why I shall introduce Broadacre City to you here tonight. The future we see is our present. Any reference to Broadacre City is a kind of preachment I suppose. I think that I received the urge to preach from England, because my forebears were preachers going back to the days of your Reformation. I am aware that it is a bad thing, but here it is and there you are. So if I am to tell you tonight how far we have got with our ideal—I must hold up Broadacre City to you—a little. You will all hear more about it within a year or two.

I have just spoken to you of the modest-cost house. We have got that movement toward Broadacre City to show already. We never know just where the next development in that connection is going to be. It happens to be at the moment that we are building in Broadacre style a group of eight houses on forty acres, and for whom, do you suppose? For the university professors of the State University at Lansing, Michigan. I call that heaping coals of fire on my own head but practical progress; our professors—philosophy, etc., etc.—are getting Broadacre religion too! In Wheeling, West Virginia (old Colonial stronghold east of Buffalo) we are to build another group which we will call Usonia III. Taliesin is Usonia I and Lansing is Usonia II.

Again, I do not know whether some of you here tonight for the first time are familiar with this word "Usonia" for our country. "United Statesers" doesn't sound well and we are not really entitled to call ourselves "Americans," because we have not a monopoly of that title. The South Americans, as I found when I was in Rio de Janeiro several years ago, resent our use of it; the Brazilians say that they are the Americans. We have therefore to settle a dispute to find a good name for ourselves. Your Samuel Butler called us "Usonians." I think Usonian an excellent name, having its roots in union, as we have our national life in it. So I use the term and hope to get the country used to it in good time. Well—to get back again to practical application of the idea, these various little centers springing up in the Broadacre style are the newer Usonia, expressing the inner spirit of our democracy, which by and large is not yet so very democratic after all, as you may know. I believe there is more the feeling and practice of democracy here in England than with us.

But we are comrades now with England: no longer the little one lost on the prairies, we are coming back to stand shoulder to shoulder with you and I hope we are going some day to take you somewhere in Usonia to see this new expression of life in a democracy—Broadacre City.

If we have found it so very hard to cut through the crust of dead tradition, so hard to throw traditions away in order that the great Tradition may live; you may have some idea how hard it will be to establish such reintegration of life as Broadacre City means. When we try to move we encounter the resistance that will reach you too, indeed I am not sure it does not reach us from you. Were it not for current popular education, Oxfordization in our country, we should be miles along the road toward the realization in that idea of perhaps the greatest architecture the world has ever seen and probably the grandest expression of human life, too, the world has ever seen. But that realization cannot take place except by inches, little by little, overcoming the cultural lag, the educational tenets of yesterday imposed upon life today. In education today what have we—actually—to help realization of Broadacre City? Well, our own country is filled—and this is incidental to my topic Broadacres, although it may not seem to be—with young but helpless white-collarites all walking the streets looking for a job and not knowing a job when they see it unless it happens to be one of those particular perquisites of education such as selling bonds or stocks or being made agents for selling something somehow, somewhere or becoming an acceptable son-in-law. It has never occurred to these young men, our better-educated young men, scholars and gentlemen at that, to go back to their own countryside, or to go out to the old farms, to go again, enlightened now, to native ground to make life there so beautiful as they might, making their land and buildings and way of life there homely and surpassingly lovely. Were they so minded that would mean the beginning of the actual building of Broadacre City if they would qualify. There in the beauty of vernal countryside today they might so easily have on liberal terms anything a great city has to give them except the gregarious pressures of humanity upon humanity, and such excesses of the herd instinct as are there inevitable. But, tragic as it all is, we must face the fact that even the United States of America now no longer owns its own ground. Its ground has gone into the hands of brokers, banks, insurance companies and other money-lending institutions of our country, until today to find any true popular ownership of ground is rare indeed unless we can get it back again to the people by some such plan as Broadacre City presents.

That senseless unthinking drift toward urbanization, that ceaseless drift from the green country to the hard pavements and overgrown factory industry—that it is that stands principally in the way of what we want to do in Usonia now and where we want to go from where we are, that is to say to Broadacre City. Because of this seemingly hopeless drift toward destruction at the depth of depression—1932—we began to work out at Taliesin this better way of life, a free and a better pattern for living it in a democracy—based upon a true capitalistic system. We thought we ought not to talk much about these things until we could really say what might be a better way of doing the thing we talked about, and so we began a great model, really a cross-section of our complete civilization studying that in much detail. We conceived and modeled in this way better ways of doing nearly everything to be done in it than ways being followed then or now. Soon, however, we came up against the fact that it is useless to attempt to free humanity by way of architecture (organic) so long as humanity itself is inorganic, therefore in jail. So long as nothing else—social—is free, the social mind being essentially in darkness and the economic system knowing only the profit system, nothing of the nature of money, we were faced with one tremendous obstacle after another. Who knew the nature of money? No one seemed to know. Was that ever taught us in school? It seems to have been accepted as an abstraction even by kind old Karl Marx.

And we found that we must have ground free in the sense that Henry George predicated free ground—I am not speaking of the single tax—and we found that we must have not only free ground but free money, that is money not taxed by interest but money only as a free medium of exchange, and as ground would be free to those who could and would use it. Then we ran against another dark-place iniquity, lurking there: the ideas by way of which society lives, moves and has its being, all become speculative commodities. A little further on we began to realize that everything we had to live on—this, remember, was during the 1929-1935 depression—was some form of *speculative* commodity. We found that life itself with us had practically become a speculative commodity; yes, the matter had gone down so far as that. Of course, having everything in life down on the level of speculative commodity, you would naturally enough have a nation of gamblers; and you would have gambling not only as the principal money-getting device but the great romance of being of a whole people. And that is what the capital-ist system (call it capitalistic but it isn't really) became in America. It is very largely so today, perhaps not knowing how to become essen-tially capitalistic or probably now unable to become so.

An organic architecture may belong to a genuine capitalist system, the base of that system broad upon the ground, but it encounters all this imposition, these gestures, these pretenses, these general inhibi-tions, these sanctified falsifications—because that is what they are—of

264

the main issue, that issue being a better life for a better man. Now, we realized soon that one cannot spend one's life building buildings for humanity, loving humanity, loving the art of building and inspired by modern opportunity, seeing what it might be and what it might do for humanity, without realizing the iniquity of these establishments or institutions about which I have just been speaking. And I assure you I am not talking out of books; nor am I advancing theories. I am giving to you as simply as I can with the usual bristling personal pronouns the result of a prolonged practical unscholarly effort on our part to build a better basis for building in a better way a better life for a democracy. I am telling you how these certain things we encountered make it unlikely that any such effort should ever generally succeed until changes are effected in our so-called "System" by more intelligent education. I bring that point up tonight because it is really practical, and the sap in the veins of any organic architecture of creative scope and character. How, I ask you, are we to build great free buildings, buildings out of the ground into the light with a new fine sense of spaciousness—apostrophe to freedom for a free people—unless life is itself—free? How are things in detail, economic and social, to be able to add up to a free life and make it happy to live in modern circumstances, realizing the advantages modern science has given us—the enlarged scale of living, the swift clean beauty of speed, of the richness of broadened community contacts and a general or common interest the world over? Nothing does happen or can happen in one corner of the world at any moment today which may not the next moment be known everywhere. A single decade is today the equal of a past century in point of elapsed time.

Organic architecture in the Broadacre City plans perceives that all our scientific progress has its great romance, its possible beauty. But these must make their way to our lives as a blessing instead of a curse dead against almost everything we call culture and especially against the current of popular education. Again our major effort encounters the terrific cultural back-drag of the scholar. Is the back-drag justified in the United States of America? Is it even justified longer in old England? It is perhaps justified—temporarily—in Russia, where it is seen in most painful state today. There in the U.S.S.R. we have a great nation, the majority recently serfs. A nation 91 percent, I believe, illiterate, therefore young and able now to emancipate themselves. I suppose they are doing what they please, asking for what they want and getting it. Serfs mainly, before they were liberated, they had had less than nothing, eating out of the hand of a superficial upper crust of culture which finally, as it went on, had nothing of great Russia herself in it: becoming merely an eclecticism imported from the European common stock. Those pilastered buildings with lofty ceilings hung with glittering glass chandeliers, Greek statues on balustraded Renaissance terraces with baroque sculptured fountains playing against the tonsured green, in short a form of grandomania which had seized the Western world for five centuries, examples of which you see all over the "great" cities of our civilized world. And dire poverty beyond conception ate out of the hand of that spurious thing. But what do they want now that they are free? What is it "they" are determined to have? Well, they are now determined to have just that very same thing. Talk to them of simplicity? No. Talk to them of organic architecture? Why . . . they would reply, "No, give us this thing that we want." And we find it in the classic! So Russia is getting a revival of the Renaissance now, that was a greater degradation of life than any imposition she revolted against. Every subway station on the underground railway in Moscow more or less resembles a palace with glittering chandeliers, when the subways are popular. Everywhere you go in Russia, soon you may see that kind of thing again especially in the great palace dedicated to WORK. Economic and social freedom here outran culture, hence their own desperate cultural lag.

But really how much better off are we, the great enlightened! How far have we gone, my lords, ladies and gentlemen, with the realization of this great new simplicity I have been putting up to you? Has this new demand for integrity of the form and character of the thing that we must live in and the way that we must now live in it gone much further on with us? Life has not yet gone very far forward with us when we are still back with the Franco-Georgian tradition, and with these great old Renaissance palaces you treasure. Again I ask where did you get them? Ask yourselves where they came from to you in England. I know, as every architect who thinks must know, that buildings of that insane period are no longer treasures, that they were a mere mask upon a meretricious life and are in no sense revealing or evolutionary where modern life is concerned except as a horrible example. We know, if we care to know, that they lack integrity in every sense.

Now, concerning the practical applications of this movement—and it is a world-wide movement at last—I have justly said that many of the buildings built in its name betray the movement. Nevertheless it is a nobler human movement toward a finer integrity on earth than we have had before—this movement that so inevitably has from the very beginning encountered the resistance of the trained, habituated mind of the popular scholar. But, worse than all, it has encountered this self-satisfied superficial bugaboo of "cultivated" taste. I want to reiterate and emphasize that the better buildings of the movement reject that matter as first rejection of all. It is not that the architects of organic buildings do not value good taste: we do believe in developing it, conserving it and respecting it but only when it is in its place—a minor place now, because we believe that if ever this complete circle, science, art and religion as one, is to be struck—we shall have to stop dividing life all up on the surface from the outside and give far less respect to merely taste-built buildings at present and in future. Let us have what good taste there is, but first, I say, let us have the right-minded application to structure of the right idea in the right circumstances. Then by the instinct that is taste carry the expressions of life we call art as high in the scale of things beautiful as you please, beautiful as you know how to make them. God knows how beautiful buildings can be made now, as compared with those either standing or yet to stand inspired by any erudite trifling with outworn, outmoded traditions, whatsoever.

I think I have drifted afield (one of the risks of extemporaneous discourse) and left largely unsaid what I started to say of what has been accomplished to date in the designs of Broadacre City. I shall have to take that up as "continued in our next" because I have talked too long already. But now, I am willing to stand here and "take it from you."

Why do you consider that Chicago is going to be the most beautiful city in the world?

First of all because it has a generous park system, the greatest on earth. You may drive nearly the whole day without going away from the boulevard and park system of Chicago. And the parks are as well looked after as your own London parks which is very well indeed. Another reason is that, thanks to an architect, Dan Burnham, Chicago seems to be the only great city in our States to have discovered its own waterfront. Moreover, to a greater extent than any other city it has a life of its own. Chicago takes pride in building things in a big substantial broad way. Even when the city goes in for gangsters it does so on a big scale, although I think you'll find more gangsters in New York City than in Chicago and a more dangerous gangster mind there too. I deplore its narrow provinciality but I like to go occasionally to New York. But, well, I like Chicago.

Mr. Frank Lloyd Wright has said that houses should be built in order that people might live happily in them and that those houses should be suited to the needs of the family. A working-class family with several children who have to live in three or four rooms can still be very happy, and, since they live in such a small space, they become like sailors on board ship; they learn to respect each other's requirements, and when they go out into the world they are good-natured and have very many qualities which stand them in good stead. I doubt very much whether it would be any advantage to them to have an acre or two, because they could not keep it in order. If the population of England was spread out at the rate of an acre per head, England itself would be ruined as a playground for those who live in the towns and take their holidays enjoying the country; there would be semi-suburban conditions all over the kingdom. It is different in America, with its large areas.

Another point is that there is no better man than the Cockney

TALIESIN NORTH, DRAUGHTING ROOM, SPRING GREEN, WISCONSIN

BROADACRE CITY, CITY DWELLERS' UNIT, MODEL

soldier and no one who can bear hardship with greater fortitude and cheerfulness. I think that is due to the fact that he has lived what I may call a battleship existence through living in crowded quarters; his wife can lean out of the window and talk comfortably to her neighbor. There is much to be said for such a life. People who may be perfectly happy in such conditions may be led into desiring to have a motorcar and into feeling that they must spend something every time they want to have some pleasure, and I do not think that that is at all necessary. In Colonial times in America the family lived on the farm and made becoming hats out of coon-skin with the head in front and the tail hanging down the man's back, and they had buckskin coats and trousers.

Yes Sir, and with that coon-skin cap modern architecture may be said to have begun for the United States of America.

I think that we should have people who will go back to the land and live on farms, making everything for themselves. It means that the women will have to work from morning till night, but they can do it easily if their minds are not on other things. The men will have to work all day as well, and they will not be able to afford to buy newspapers or have a radio or anything of that kind. Provided they are willing to do without those things they can live in the country.

Is that drudge-a-day life the beau ideal, then, of modern civilization—the battleship existence of which you speak? If it is then I think the speaker perfectly right, and suggest that the more we can compress our people the better; the less space we give them the more effective the result will be. And in that case I really do not see why they should need as much space as they have got now; why not put the pressure on still stronger and deprive them of still more, so that they may fight even better? Because they have not known a better life, probably will not know it in this generation or the next, or the next, I suppose where ignorance is bliss, 'tis folly to be wise!

The existence the speaker describes is, however, to me a negation of life rather than any affirmation of it. I deplore the circumstances in which such lives must be spent. It is just that kind of thing that the modern movement and life itself go up against. It is true that human life may be satisfied or habituated under pressures to adapt itself to whatever circumstances, even the bombing of women and children as modern warfare. But is life to end there? Why did Englishmen go to the new country we call ours now? Why have we this great new nation and this new country? It is because, long ago, Englishmen said No to that idea of yours, sir. Some of them would not accept it. Were they worse men than the Cockney soldier? Even the slums, on your assumption, may be very fruitful. Maintaining them might produce excellent results of which we are not yet aware. Perhaps were we to abolish "the battleship-life" of the slums it would do a great deal to abolish war, which would be a great disaster to the human race, would it not? Perhaps the admirable Cockney is a soldier just because of his "battleship existence." Perhaps humanity itself now labors under fearful threat of war because of this ideal disciplinary character of the "battleship-life" lived by citizens in tight quarters and in slums.

I feel, however, that to be humane we must stand for the philosophy of freedom rather than for any philosophy of battleship sacrifice whatever, because what has the fighting Cockney soldier achieved in life, so far, by his fighting except *the need for more Cockney soldiers*?

What worth having has civilization to show gained from these human sacrifices? What? Unless more and more airplanes flying overhead destroying women and children in masses, now legitimate as modern warfare? I can think of nothing more degraded in this world.

I suggest that Mr. Wright's remarks on Russian architecture are rather unfair in view of the fact that the architects of any experience in Russia today are a legacy from the Czarist régime, and that the younger element have not had the experience yet whereby they can produce this new architecture.

I would not wish to say anything unfair to Russia. I admire the spirit of the Russian people, and I believe in the potency of that spirit. I know but little concerning their politics or policies. But I was there two years ago talking with the younger architects, making their acquaintance, and then learned a little of what was going on. It seems their leader, Stalin, said: "Yes, we want simplicity in building for a better life, but remember that this generation fought the war of the revolution; give them what they want now. We will tear it all down again in ten years." I think that, too, is in a way, a fine spirit in advance of our sentimentality that would preserve it indefinitely. Nevertheless I do not believe such temporizing with the future—right.

With the idea of an acre for each person there will be a good many people in agreement, but it would be interesting to know what kind of community life people will have in these circumstances. People cannot merely subsist for themselves; they must have some kind of community life, and I should be interested to know the kind of community life which Mr. Wright has in mind. In Northern Ireland the farms are very small and the people there breed pigs and have sold them with some difficulty in the past, but now the State has worked out a means of educating them in the breeding of their pigs, in the buying of their pigs and in selling them through central agencies, and now the only reason they have for going into the country towns is to go to the "pictures," or to buy a pair of braces, or something like that. The old community is going and a new order is being superimposed on these people. It is very much a matter for a town planner or architect to try to find out what kind of community life these small scattered farmers in Northern Ireland will live, and the same problem will arise in a community where there is an acre to each person.

We who eat pigs should have a care for the breeders of pigs, but we live in a period of transition, and it will take many decades of transition for the outlines of what I have given you as Broadacre City—pigs in place—tonight, to become visible. You must not think the kind of buildings we now have are going to remain, or that community needs as they are now will remain as they are now. They are all going to change as a new and finer type of building in a freer community we do not yet foresee except that it will be more *of* the country, is growing up. The more of such buildings we have in the country the more beautiful community life will become and the less you will be aware of the fact that buildings are there at all as intrusion.

As for the definite future pattern of the community life in such circumstances, who knows just what any community life of the future is going to be like? The old relationships are bound to change. The motorcar has already vitally affected the rural community life of our States. Even Northern Scotland won't escape in due course. Nearly every man in the States will soon have a car, and today I know of no pig-farmer (we call them dirt-farmers) in my own neighborhood who has not his family motorcar, and perhaps two. I know of none who have no telephone. All have a radio. I know of some who do not care, now, to leave the farm to go into a town to eke out the remainder of their days. The Usonian farm—notwithstanding its mortgage—is by way of becoming the little principality, the unit most desired in our life, just when it is being taken away from the farmer. To say that it has already become so would be untrue. But definitely that is the direction in which things are moving, with no aid from architects and only a makeshift economics. A realization is growing that community life in the sense that it is now lived in small hamlets, villages and cities is going to be no longer necessary, nor as charming as it used to be when it becomes unnecessary. Ease of intercommunication is making ten miles today what two city blocks used to be. As I have said, many times, an entirely new space-consciousness is entering into all of life, town or country. A new human scale has come in that is bound to change community life, changing everything within it. So what community life? If you had parking space and driving space enough for everyone in London even now there would be no London at all, because all there is of London would barely provide the parking space and driving space essential even now. Reflect that the motorcar Englishman has only just begun on London. What will your own urban community life be like ten years from now? What will be the community twenty-five years from now? As architects we must look beyond the tolerances and ignorances of the moment, rural or urban, and try to see the future. If we are not able to see beyond the present and to plan accordingly for the future, I think community life, pigs and goods plus God or leisure, will remain a battleship-life and we shall stay where we are—eventually to fight for existence in trenches in our city parks or rot in bombproof cellars.

Mr. Wright said in his lecture that he would leave London as it is, and yet in reply to the last question he said that existing buildings would disappear. That seems a little inconsistent.

I do not see inconsistency. The better parts of London, like so many of our great cities, constitute now the greatest museum piece in the world. Great cities, or the more valuable and historic portions of them, might be just that, were we to keep them as they are as we decentralize. I suggested, our last session I believe, that London, its insignificant parts and slums removed to make room for trees or grass, would make a wonderful park in which the citizens of the newer London might take their recreation, certain parts still habitable. It would not be possible to rebuild London, because a habitable London on modern terms would disappear in the process; there would be no London, so why not leave historic London as historic London?

So I see no inconsistency in what I have said. London buildings, not valuable history, are unfit to go to the country; the dreary miles of gloomy dwellings seem to me more like miserable coops for humanity than buildings with a modern sense of life and space. So destroy all those. Let them disappear because, nevertheless and notwithstanding, there is plenty of room in England for a Broadacre City. I do not believe the assertion that there is not enough room in England for the modern life of which I have spoken. I will mention again the thousand-acre park nearby at Richmond, and the incident of sitting at dinner next a gentleman who mentioned his four-thousand-acre estate. There are thousands such, where natural beauty would be enhanced not destroyed. I would not destroy the beauty of such estates by taking buildings into them, as London building is now or as London builders are. But I do advocate on the part of architects the development of a fresh sense of the ground, developing landscape rather than destroying it by way of building. There is such a thing as that—I build it, but it is hard to explain in a few words just how I do it. I know such union of countryside and building is coming, and to the enhancement of each, I believe

It seems to me that if you take away these buildings which you say that you will rebuild, you will destroy your museum piece.

No, I would destroy nothing but London's shame. I suggest you maintain all that is truly "historic." I would destroy the rows and rows of commonplace houses in which people try to live, not those where there was once a glorious life. I would preserve the better houses and palaces, historic old streets and lanes and public buildings and churches.

But if you take away all the squalor and unpleasantness of London, and leave just the historic buildings, what is left of London?

Enough. We occasionally go to the graveyards of our ancestors, so why not to the remains of their cities? But vision which will cut through the weight of their past to the freedom of our future does not come in a moment.

I am not satisfied with the answer given with regard to communal life. If the people of England are to be dispersed over the country in the way suggested, it will require the area of a square with sides 260 miles in length, which will take up most of the country, and even if they are dispersed they will require to join in communities of some kind if any of the country is to be left free. There are some places where houses cannot be built, as on the tops of mountains.

The mountain sites would make the nicest building sites. And I doubt the gentleman's arithmetic. I advocate building (perhaps high buildings) on those portions of the land least useful for other purposes. It is possible to build a building anywhere in this new sense of organic building. You could not build Georgian or Elizabethan or Tudor houses there, but you could build wide-spread ground-built houses such as I have described, or upstanding slender isolated ones.

But let's say, to help along the argument, that the country is coming to the citizen instead of the citizen going to the country. I do not wish to "disperse" any city; decentralization is not dispersal—that is wrong . . . it is reintegration. And whether you believe what I have been saying or do not, the great implements science has put into the hands of humanity are themselves carving out this new city that is to be everywhere and nowhere. They are going to build something like Broadacre City. Architects are not going to build it, I fear, because I see that as they are educated they are not competent even to see it. And so these natural agencies, these tremendous scientific forces, will build it without them but will not lack master builders.

Dispersal is not going to take place, I think. The matter will be more a process of the gradual absorption by integration of inevitable consequences. Little by little people are going to become more and more dissatisfied with increasing urban pressures. Mass education is going to lose its hold on the people as organic culture comes to take the place of such sterilizing education. When culture does come changes are going to take place rapidly because any true form of culture now will work with the law of change, not try to stand against it or fall to its knees shedding tears.

I would ask you all why civilization is everywhere so jittery and miserable today? Is it not because there has been no great vision, no real thought, which wisely accepted the law of change and went along with it, making patterns for life so free that to the life concerned the law of change need not mean unhappiness and torture? The time must come to take this inexorable law as a matter of course into the philosophy and the concrete forms expressing our era. I am one of those who firmly believe that that time is here.

I want you to go a little further than that and come down to practical details. These individuals may be happy on their acres, but they will have to cooperate among themselves.

Yes they will—why not?

But having got the people where you want them. . . .

Not, sir, where *I* want them, but where *they* want to be. If more practical education has not first taken hold of the man to teach him somewhat of the ground and make him a lover of the gifts of the ground (he is a ground animal), nothing much can be done with him except deport him or build a skyscraper in some country park letting

277

him live in that to cooperate in the style to which he is accustomed, all of which is practical enough in the new scheme of Broadacre City, itself a pattern for a free communal life.

When these people are where they want to be, they will have between them some sense of cooperation. Music, the theater and art all need cooperation in some form or other.

Yes—naturally. But in future more on the air or chiefly perhaps, because people may not want to leave their complete homes to go to something which they can enjoy much better at home.

In the film we saw your boys playing music on the hill, and they seemed to like it better than the radio.

We could not have music on the radio unless we continued to make it ourselves. I think we need and will always have both at home. But, inevitably, there will develop a new form of community life, but just what it will be except as Broadacre City tentatively outlines it as free to grow, who can say? Not I. Who is going to say how humanity will eventually be modified by all these spiritual changes and physical advantages, sound and vision coming through solid walls to men, each aware of anything in or of the world he lives in without lifting a finger, making it unnecessary to go anywhere on earth unless it is a pleasure to go. The whole psyche of humanity is changing and what that change will ultimately bring as future community I will not prophesy. It *is* already greatly changed. I see this more plainly in my own country than you can see it in yours. The result of our education is the folly which does not wish to see change nor allow for it as a law of growth. So the young man today is helpless. Knowing nothing of the changing life of organic growth spiritual or material—he is a parasite. Not born a parasite, perhaps, but if he is not so born he is made one to breed one. What then are we to do with community life, say, in a parasitic world for parasites? Well, I can't say. But community life will take care of itself given these amplified, enlivened, widened horizons and conditions I see as inevitable. And for one I believe that community life to come will be much more alive just because it will be less an escape from life.

278

I do not think you or I can know all the details. All either of us need know is the general direction and after that what is coming next in sight.

What part is the appeal to romance going to play in the architecture of the future?

From my point of view as a modern architect, the center of what we call romance has shifted; I find it lying no longer upon the periphery of things. So it is no longer much concerned with taste. I find it as a new sense of reality, a new adventure in thrilling search for reality. If there is anything more romantic than that, it has not appeared in my life, and I do not think that it will appear in yours—the hazards, the great rewards, the incomparable beauties, the unreasonable punishments, all go to make life romantic. No longer escapist gestures, no longer taste-built, taste-formed ideas, but an earnest lifelong search for that thing growing out of the nature of the thing, not from anything applied to that thing from without.

And now I must ask, at long last, to make an end of this discourse. I have allowed you to go far afield from the original intention for conversation number three and cut well into number four.

FOURTH EVENING

At our last session—the third—we went so far afield with our discussion and got so far into the future that the topic intended for tonight —"The Future"—has been about exhausted. So I shall have to, probably, "sum up." But, as before, we shall begin by showing another and the final installment of the James Thompson Taliesin film. We preface the pictures of our latest buildings as designed at Taliesin by showing you the boys (and girls) working on the farm while carrying on their work in the draughting rooms. As you see, architecture is not simply a drawing-board matter with us; it is a way of life. By doing this outdoor work the boys (some girls too) get the nature of ground into their system and find sweat on their brows excellent for promoting ideas. When I am myself weary of ideas and seem getting a little stale, I go out and pound stone on the new roads, work on the buildings or go out in the fields. I come back refreshed—better able to carry on. We have a 200-acre farm upon which we all work. I have been told that we at Taliesin have been accused of being "escapist," but this rigorous sort of thing as you see it on the screen doesn't look especially escapist, . . . or does it? These pictures appear here preliminary to the conversation that is coming, but they are really collateral. At this moment you see apprentices painting the rebuilt barn by spraying it with red paint. The red barn is one of Wisconsin's greatest assets in her landscape. Nearly all the barns in Wisconsin are similar red (oxide of iron). Now you are seeing the work of rebuilding going on after the dam conserving our water power was washed out and we had to rebuild it. We do not so much mind if something does occasionally fail, because it gives us opportunity to do it over again, and do it better the second time. We learn that way. I am happy to say that although all these Taliesin young people are using machinery and edged tools, sometimes doing things not very safe, during all the six years we have been working there have been no casualties of moment. That speaks well for the correlation of these youngsters. And we are all "self-starters" at Taliesin; we take care of ourselves lengthwise and crosswise, heating, lighting, transport and water system, and have little or no paid help. We feed ourselves, from the ground partly, and entertain ourselves. And we provide for the coming winter in summer. One reason why men from the north are conquerors of the men of the south is because they are perpetually surrounded by circumstances which are inimical to life and have to fend for themselves, meantime providing for themselves when winter comes. The north can never "let go" as the south may, because emergencies are always to be met. On the screen now is a building in The Glen, Bear Run, Pennsylvania. The house is called Falling Water. Concrete cantilever slabs projecting from the rock bank over the stream carry the living space out over the waterfall. The structure has the usual sense of space. The slabs appear rather gentler than usual because all edges of

280

the copings and overhangs and the slabs of the eaves are all rounded. The slabs are genuine reinforced slabs throughout, doing the work they seem to be doing. Natural stone has been used together with them. The building is very much part of its site. When building such structures it is our custom always to send one of our apprentices to the building on which we are engaged, and there they gain actual experience as work on the building goes along in the draughting room and in the field.

Next we come to a wooden house on a Californian hilltop, built with thin but solid walls of laminated wood, the conformation of the walls devised for strength, the Hanna House—we call it Honeycomb House because the structure was fashioned upon a hexagonal unit system. The hexangle is better suited to human movement than the rectangle.

Next comes one of our houses on Long Island, near New York, cypress-wood boards and battens inside and out, red brick walls likewise. We have used no plastering here. We have eliminated plastering from our buildings wherever possible, using wood boards or plywood instead. Sometimes synthetics are used, and increasingly steel and glass.

Here you see the latest prairie house, the Johnson house at Racine, Wisconsin. We call that house "Wingspread." A house with a great living room with tall chimney standing up through the center, wings extend from it in four directions; to the left you see the wing (a mezzanine coming into the open living room as a balcony) with rooms for the owner and his wife and his young daughter; to the right is a wing on the ground level for the four boys, a playroom at the far end; another wing is for the servants and their activities and still another for guests and automobiles. The clear-cut sweep of the building is like the many other houses I have thought appropriate to our Mid-western prairies. The ground below the many projecting trellises is planted with wild grape vines. The outside woodwork is 2-inch cypress plank, while the brick walls are red and the stone a pink Kasota sandstone. There is the usual feeling of breadth and human spaciousness about it all, and from the house itself the surrounding landscape looks particularly charming. No one noticed that we had a particularly beautiful site until the house was built. Then they began to realize how beautiful it really was. When organic architecture is properly carried out no landscape is ever outraged, but is always developed by it. The side walls of the swimming pool are undercut. The average swimming pool looks to me like a glorified bath-tub. There is less sense there of the water than of the basin it is in. With the pool sides undercut you see no walls in the pool but only the water and reflections. This house—"Wingspread"—has something of the clean-limbed sense of power adapted to purpose which you find in a well poised plane or ocean liner, but it is no mere aesthetic, it is constitutional, I assure you. This probably is one of the most complete, best constructed and most expensive houses it has ever been my good fortune to build.

Lastly, you are seeing construction photographs of the windowless, floor-heated completely air-conditioned office building of the S. C. Johnson Wax Company at Racine, Wisconsin, here shown ready for the glass tubing to go in on the skeleton frames. We had to carry out tests before the Wisconsin Building Commission would let us go on with this structure. The dendriform columns you see now are being tested for the Wisconsin Building Commission. They proved to be about six times stronger than needed. I believe this also is one of the best built buildings, technically, anywhere in the world. And I regard it as not only a thoroughly modern piece of work but more nearly exemplifying the ideal of an organic architecture than any other I have built. But perhaps that is only because it is the latest one. There is no feeling of weight when you are inside, mass has vanished, no sense of being enclosed either as you have not been cut off from outdoor light or a sense of sky anywhere.

Now to go on with our last "conversation." Perhaps what you have seen on the screen has given you a little idea of this new way of building about which I have been talking; this feeling for a building as something out of the ground for the life lived in it, a building conditioned by the nature of the materials and the purpose of the thing done, as something actually having a fresh integrity—not theory but practice.

Before we started to look at the screen this evening I said we had dealt with the subject matter of the lecture proposed for this evening, at the last session getting so far afield into the future that perhaps we ought to come back tonight, bring out the keg of nails and with a heavy hammer drive home some technical details. I was again somewhat shocked this afternoon when an ornamentally bewhiskered young man who came to the hotel to interview me, said that he had heard me accused of being "escapist" and would like to have me affirm or deny it. Well, it is probably time I put up some defense, but really I don't know exactly what an "escapist," in his sense of the term, is, nor what it means to be one. I might call him one if I knew. But if he means escaping from the oppression of the dead past into a life more suited to the living present, I plead guilty to the soft impeachment. The basis of the "escapist" accusation may be that at Taliesin we live a pretty self-contained life, devoting ourselves to a life of our own in our own way; you have just seen something of its character on the screen. And if that is escaping from life then I do not know what life is. We intend to head straight into it, all courting it, not afraid of it but eager to explore reality. In fact, I believe Taliesin to be a little research station on the way toward just that—*reality*. We at Taliesin see reality as romance today. We have already found that romance lies no longer on the periphery of life as we see it now man-made, but is something deeper to be independently found within life by living it. I daresay that that is an escape too, but, if so, let's all escape! But, rather, I guess the accusation had reference to some cult of the mind because sentimentality went too far and the "anti's" want to go too far the opposite way now.

Well, during the preceding several evenings I have said a great deal (but finally you have done considerable talking yourselves) about an architecture in the equivocal circumstances in which we live at present; now we have with us or against us—really—in every branch of culture the precious aesthetic, the high sentimentality in false consideration for the old, the consequent foolish academic unwillingness to bury the dead. Now why this universal reluctance to let the dead past bury its dead? I confess to being in love with fine sentiment myself, but I deny that I am therefore either escapist or a sentimentalist. Since coming to London I have found, as I expected, that the cultured Englishman is the best comrade and most charming company in the world, and I find this dear old London of yours full of pathetic charm and a lively antiquarian interest. I have not been through a museum of any sort for many years and I like it. As such I do not want to see London changed much. I should hate, too, to see this fine museum piece of yours patched up. Why not save it as it is? Why let architects or bombers destroy it?

There was a pleasant little fracas at the English Speaking Union the other evening between your Professor Richardson and others (myself on the side lines). Question: whether London was in more danger from builders or bombers? I took the stand, then, that it is really immaterial. I don't think it matters so very much because I believe London is in danger from neither; London is only seriously in danger from this thing we call Life, life itself, because, let us face it, my lords, ladies and gentlemen, architectural London is senile. London is senile. How can we deny it longer? Now had you a grandmother hopelessly senile, what would be your attitude toward her? It would be one of amelioration and of mitigation, wouldn't it? That should be your humane attitude, and you probably would not embalm her and preserve her in a glass case if she died. As I see it something like that should be your attitude toward London—amelioration, mitigation, honoring old London and leaving it at that, but at last and soon preserving the best of it as memorial in a great green park.

This may seem on the face of it, too simple a solution of all these vexing technical difficulties with the conflicting interests of human nature. But decentralization and reintegration is the one eventual, *inevitable* solution not only for London but for every overgrown village in the world today. I know it is hard to accept what I am saying as true, but I am sure that if you do not take the matter of getting away from London into your own hands the natural mechanistic, scientific forces which are carving out the future whether your architects like it or not (of course they *won't* like it) will build you a city of the future more akin, I believe, to Taliesin's proposal for a Broadacre City as we discussed it or tried to—somewhat—at our last evening together, than anything we have yet had opportunity to consider as a definite modeling of an advanced idea of good modern life.

Yes, tonight we will recapitulate and—as usual—reiterate. There has been much reiteration in these talks, necessarily. Not one of them has been intended as a proper lecture upon the subject of architecture. Every one of them has been as spontaneous a discussion of its need and place in society as anything may be, not enough studied, but felt very deeply indeed. I stand here before you now for the last time, feeling more deeply than ever about what I have just said to you, about the city for one thing, and also concerning the nature of life in this jam it has got itself into all over the world today. We "humans" are really in a dreadful fix. We are not even so well conditioned as to be between the devil and the deep sea for all our military pomp and show—perhaps because we have gone so far with just that—that we are so utterly bewildered we don't know where we are. The young people whom I meet and talk with as I have gone about our country somewhat, your country too, now, young "educated" people, talking to them as I am talking to you (educated people) now—are all bewildered, eager to know direction forward as I am sure you are. They are pretty sure there must be a better life for them somewhere just as you are sure. As I have said, all of them are educated in the style of some façade and very far indeed beyond their capacity, in Usonia, undoubtedly no more so than in older countries like yours. And all for what? Surely it cannot be that they are educated just for more cannon fodder? Surely it cannot be that they are educated merely for false gods to make just another cog on the too many wheels of a capitalist system which—let us face that fact too—is really no capitalist system at all. I wish we had a true capitalist system! I believe in a capitalistic system which has its base laid broad upon the ground, its apex high as you please. But here we have one with its apex on the ground and its base well up in the air; something has been going wrong for democracy! For all the swarming everywhere there is no real potence. The potential forces of peace are far greater than those of war, but they have never yet been marshaled in all the colorful beauty of their charm. Love for Joan of Arc will far outlive hatred of Napoleon.

I know little about politics. I confess that I respect politicians not at all. But as an architect studying structure I find it deplorable that no sense of structure as something organic exists today in their minds to make them statesmen so as to help save the life of the world. And I am certain if that sense of structure does not get into action among you soon where will civiliatizon be found? At an end.

Scholarship aside, we can readily understand how architecture got into the fix it is in today when we realize that architecture has been for 500 years merely the application to construction of the revival of some kind of superficial aesthetics, and I believe that same thing goes all the way along the line of our education where our culture ought to be. We have got into the fix we are in in the States because—as I have insisted —the "aesthetic" we accepted came along to our shores as the "Colonial tradition," having in it no knowledge of organic principles, knowing nothing at all upon which a new life on new ground in new circumstances could fashion the new forms it needed to be something organic in character itself. Some form of Colonialism was all we had for culture and you got what you had in much the same way that we got ours. This "ism" went round about the world (and pretty much the same) as some kind of renaissance of many another renaissance . . . many too many. So for 500 years at least, that mere application of taste to circumstances from the outside in pagan sense, in all the affairs of life has been what the world of architecture and no less therefore the affairs of men has had to live and grow upon.

In the meantime, what great creative work have we to show as an actual working basis for the life which we have led or as proof of its validity? Not much. No, it was truly an escapist life we have led. We will find there in that life just application of the word "escapist" if the word has any meaning at all. All of our culture has been this poor second-hand attempt to, on the left or on the right, escape from the actualities of existence by way of taste-created fashionable *illusions*. Spurious education has confirmed the fashionable illusions from generation to generation, confirmed them by book, by order and by reward. Economically, as architecturally, nearly everything with which we started to build the democracy of our United States—like our inherited cultural lag—was a feudal hangover, some unsuitable hangover from feudal times. We began with the great idea of making life an even break for every man, giving every man an equal opportunity before the law. I think it must have been an error when it was written into the

Declaration of Independence that every man was born free and equal, because that is pure nonsense. . . . I think that what was meant was that every man is born free and equal before the law. . . . That being so, it did not take long for these hangovers of a feudal age now so freshly set up as the economic basis for the new democracy to allow the wolf and the fox and the rat in human form to be the winners in that new set-up, and they are quite completely the winners now. So were we headed off from any expression of a democratic life very quickly, doomed to defeat even before we began. No wonder we are now stalemate, out of work and utterly bewildered.

Yes, some thinking, some real thought, must enter not only into architecture but also into this thing which we call the economic basis of social life.

No longer satisfied—as bystanders—with looking in from the outside we must enter within as masters by way of some sense of structure such as I have been reiterating during these four evenings. Some deeper thought on our part, even though we are educated, must get inside, penetrate, and from the inside work out the practical new forms suited to genuine democratic life, rational structural forms that will make democracy not something upside down or leave it something merely on the lips, but make it an actual way of life and work, *alive,* and affecting, throughout, every human being today right where he stands.

Occasionally I scan the newspapers and have noticed the way in which democracy is being held up as opposed to fascism. But I think the more you analyze communism, the more you analyze fascism and democracy, the less you will be able to see any substantial differences between them in practice after the theory has evaporated. Now something radical is missing in all this hullaballoo of the *hoi polloi* "press," and so "radical" we must now be. We need honest radicals. England I am happy to say has been hospitable to such. But to mention the word in our pseudo-capitalistic country is like waving a red flag; educated people expect everything to come tumbling down upon them. Ten-to-one they will call the police, "disperse you" or have you arrested. But let us be rational . . . radical only means trying to find out what lies at the root—the word "radical" means "of the root." How much do we of today know of the root? Notwithstanding our "penchant" for history how much have we been taught of roots, the roots of our economic order for instance? Professors in Usonian universities who begin to meddle at the root of anything like that may lose their jobs. Many of them, meaning no harm and not wishing to injure life or humanity, but hoping to benefit it, seek by research to find out something about roots in order that they may teach, but they encounter this opposition from their employers—the system—in a free country, in our own democracy! I know a number such.

None will say that is admirable, but is it even sensible? Is it longer tolerable? What has brought all this prejudice and fear down upon our heads like tons and tons of collapsed bricks? Why have we not yet the courage of the free? Why are we not yet able to see for ourselves and to stand alone? Why do we not know the nature of these vital things we have been discussing, the inner nature of this thing which we call architecture for one instance? All other life-concerns are the same as that great one or would be in any true democracy! What is architecture anyway? Is it a vast collection of the various buildings which have been built to please the varying tastes of the various lords of mankind? No. I think not. I know that architecture is life; or at least it is life itself taking form and therefore is the truest record of life as it was lived in the world yesterday, as it is being lived today or ever will be lived. So architecture I know to be a great spirit. No, it is not something which consists of the buildings which have been built by man on his earth. Architecture is that great living creative spirit which from generation to generation, from age to age, proceeds, persists, creates, according to the nature of man, and his circumstances as they both *change. That* really is architecture.

Now in this broad sense do the professors handling the subject for us know much about it? Do they do much for us? We are talking about architecture now as something which has again to come right-side up— for a right-side-up society. Architecture is something we must have right-side up or miss the beat of the rhythms that life has to bring to us, or forever lose something vital and valuable; something for which all that science has been doing so much to accomplish at such frightful cost to us, cannot compensate. Science has done more than much to accomplish miracles which might bless our lives but which are now becoming curses, because culture without creative architecture cannot come along with them to make them blessings. Without creative architecture as the center line of all culture we cannot utilize what science has already done, nor show how to use bountiful scientific results intelligently in even a material way, to say nothing of using them creatively and beautifully.

What prevents this realization and the cultural utilization of science in creating a better tomorrow today? What prevents true statesmen (architects of the social order) from arising among us at a time like this? Why are peoples the world over at the mercy of scheming industrialists and wily politicians? Why do national intrigue and financial plotting come to be accepted as normal statesmanship? Why is it now accepted by civilized nations that women and children may be mass-murdered in their own homes by wholesale mechanical "improvements" as an accepted form of warfare in modern civilization? That murder is lower than anything degraded I can think of in past history. That crime being tolerated by civilized nations you may see what the status of thought or thinking in such life as ours has come down to be. No nation, no, nor any combination of nations being able to say No to such desperate degradation, what future can we hope for? Well . . . economically our so-called capitalist system may need such degradation and worse to keep going on. That alleged system is of course primarily a matter of money—but, believe it or not, nobody, the "system" least of all, really understands money. During the breakdown in the United States—they liked to call it a depression there, but it was a breakdown—I do not think anyone in our country (or in yours, either) ever heard during that dreadful time one single enlightened official suggestion as to the why or wherefore of the circumstantial mystery called money, nor listened to any sensible remedy in the circumstances. And this was so simply because "they" did not understand the nature of the thing—money. No, "they" did not and do not even yet understand the nature of money. Dear beneficent old Karl Marx and noble Henry George did not understand it either; they accepted it as established abstraction or as something from God. And we have so accepted it. I only mention money as one instance of the lack of any *sense of structure* in economics or society and in this search for organic structure for which I am pleading in architecture. Nowhere is any such thinking in simples operative and effective as we might truly call *practical* today.

Now this costly confusion because of the recent terrible breakdown of all the old theories, economic, social, aesthetic, certainly calls for something from within to come forth and indicate a better way of use and wont; promulgate a way according to nature which primarily will not be afraid of the law of change because that law must be recognized as the necessary inevitable *law of growth.* I believe that what has done most damage to youth in their euphemistic educational training in both our cultural and economic system, is the fact that the "isms" of institutionalism have become habitual and we must fight the "istic" of the "ites" who are all against the vital laws of organic change instinctively—the cowards regarding all changes whatever as enemies. So indeed we are become now all somewhat afraid of change and feel secure only if we know we can keep hands on what we have as we now have it. The more money power we get and keep the more we become stupid stand-patters rather than promulgators of the good life for its own sake. Let our universities realize and teach that *the law of organic change is the only thing that mankind can know as beneficent or as actual!* We can only know that all things are in process of flowing in some continuous state of becoming. Heraclitus was stoned in the streets of Athens for a fool for making that declaration of independence, I do not remember how many hundreds of years ago. But today modern culture has made no progress in that direction because we took no heed of that courageous declaration and because we became so institutional, so limited in outlook, so filled with fear of life rather than inspired by willingness to trust it, that I am afraid deep distrust of life now is stronger in the United States of America and in England today than ever before. We are afraid . . . cowards . . . yes . . . because we are so busy having and holding (or trying to) that we have not got hold of something deeper and substantial which we must now find, or watch ourselves disappear as a civilization. It is that same something which we must find that I have kept on trying to drive home to you in all these informal egotistic talks. It is that same substantial something which organic architecture has found and although we have so little of it to show, it is finding its place and planting, little by little, round the whole world. But, except for rare exemplars, what can we do with an organic architecture in general as the architecture of a whole people so long as we have no whole people, but have only a society so superficial as ours has become; so ignorant of cause and effect as to be afraid of everything life really is? I have learned in my lifetime that there is only one trust worthy of any man and that is trust in life itself; the firm belief that life *is* (worlds without end, amen) that you cannot cheat it nor can you defeat it. So far as what education chooses to call culture goes we have been trying all these centuries to beat life and to defeat it, pretty nearly succeeding too. "Authority" has seldom trusted life at any time. We certainly have not trusted life in architecture, nor have we trusted it in economics, and we have not trusted it in politics or statesmanship. We have not trusted it anywhere, no—not even in religion! We talk about God, and we have built all these great architectural sacrifices to God, God being anything other and elsewhere than the life we know and the daily life we live. No wonder we are as we are and not as we must be in order to go on alive—or go dead, to Heaven! And it is of no little significance that one must be dead to go there.

As I go back to my home and to my knitting, go back to Taliesin trying to put these simple things of the spiritual life on earth into objective concrete form, trying to bring out subjective truth to make forms and patterns for living more worthy of life, I can only leave with you what I have been saying these past several evenings to help overcome this terrific cultural . . . architectural lag that our science exposes and shames, every nation the same so it seems to me.

The cultural lag has been greatly aided by our wily, wanton, prostitute, social sentimentality. Nor can any aesthetic whatsoever, no matter how mechanistic and hard it may imagine itself to be, save us now. We have to get people, states and buildings *thought-built*! Unless the things of life concerning culture, a natural architecture being first among them, are now thought-built from within, I think we are at the end of the last chapter in . . . is it a great civilization I wonder? Are we perhaps at the tail end of something, dwindling to a conclusion? How many of you can feel that unless we find this upward way from within, life is on the upward rather than the downward grade? For myself, I feel we *must* learn the nature of this organic character and integrity in all that we do *now* or perish. If we do not soon learn to call that learning "culture" we shall soon learn to call what we now call culture, a curse!

Here these suggestive democratic preachments, I am afraid, come to an end. We have no time tonight for many questions. In any case I am not going to let you take me so far afield as you did at our last meeting. But if I have said something tonight which you think not true perhaps you will tell me. I have—all along—seemed to belittle the nature of our time and the great achievements of science, but I have intended to do neither because I believe human nature still sound and recognize that science has done a grand job well; but well I know that science cannot save us. Science can give us only the tools in the box, mechanical miracles that it has already given us. But of what use to us are miraculous tools until we have mastered the humane, cultural use of them? We do not want to live in a world where the machine has mastered the man; we want to live in a world where man has mastered the machine!

At least, or at long last, I have brought you this message; what we call organic architecture is no mere aesthetic nor cult nor fashion but an actual movement based upon a profound idea of a new integrity of human life wherein art, religion and science are one: form and function seen as one, of such is democracy.

Well . . . if you are not ready with questions tonight, I think I would better go. . . .

Thanking you, my lords, ladies and gentlemen—all of you out there, from the bottom of my heart for giving me such indulgent, appreciative audience . . . good-by and good hope!

AFTERWORD

I know that many young architects are going to be disappointed because I have not gone into the technique of building more exactly as I might easily have done; have not spoken more of the plastic as distinguished from the old structural principles of construction and given them details of the principle of continuity as the physique of a true aesthetic; of building with our new materials—steel and glass, which are changing not only the face of our world, but its very skeleton. So many moot points in their minds I have purposely neglected because it seemed to me these lectures should be concerned more with the place and character of architecture in modern life than in any way to practice it.

SOME ASPECTS OF THE FUTURE OF ARCHITECTURE

SOME ASPECTS OF THE
FUTURE OF ARCHITECTURE

THE chapter on the past and present of architecture ended with the ideal of an organic architecture—the new reality.

If architecture has any future more than revival or passive reform, we must speak of future architecture as organic. It is apparent that the pagan ideal of architecture—we call it classical—has broken down. In practice, then, speaking out from experience in the field, what does this term, organic architecture, mean? Already it has been said—*lieber meister* declared it—and biology knows and shows us that "form follows function." But the physicist cannot interpret the word "organic" as it applies to architecture. Not until we raise the dictum, now a dogma, to the realm of thought, and say: *Form and function are one,* have we stated the case for architecture.

That abstract saying "Form and function are one" is the center line of architecture, organic. It places us in line with nature and enables us sensibly to go to work. Now accepting that fundamental concept of architecture as interior discipline, how can we work it out in actual practice?

Let us rebuild a building with phrases as I have built one with bricks and mortar and men. I have built one, as I believe, naturally.

"Form and function are one" is the thought in the back of the mind that will now shape an attitude towards everything in our sight, including Mr. and Mrs. Domestic Client and progeny, or, it may be, towards the capitalist-captain, the unfeeling corporation, or the baron.

Before we begin to build, however, what is the "nature" of this act we call architecture? That quest will discover certain elemental truths with which building, as organic, is concerned. Form and function being one, it follows that the purpose and pattern of the building become one. They are integral. This, in a sentence, is the ages-old thesis, which, made new, we call the norm of organic architecture. This new integrity, "from within outward," is now evident as the modern architect's guide and opportunity. "Out of the ground into the light" is opportunity. The nature of materials is also his opportunity and no less limitation. All three opportunities are limitations but they are a condition of success. Human nature, too, is one of these materials, served by the building and serving it.

With the purpose or motive of the building we are to build well in mind, as of course it must be, and proceeding from generals to particulars, as "from-within-outward" must do, what consideration comes first?

The ground, doesn't it? The nature of the site, of the soil and of climate comes first. Next, what materials are available in the circumstances—money being one of them—with which to build? Wood, stone, brick, or synthetics? Next, what labor, or means of power, is available and advisable in the circumstances? Manual, machine, or both? The labor union or the factory, or both? Always with this "from the nature within" in mind, working in imagination towards a significant outward form, we proceed always within the circumstances.

Here we come well in towards the processes of thought that properly employ science in the erection of an organic building. But, still, the most desirable and valuable element in creation is lacking. It, too, is primary. We call it "inspiration." It seems to us a mysterious element. But it is of the "from within outward" and it is a qualification that gives finality to the whole structure as creative. To give life to the whole is "creative" and only that. We imply the structure of that life when we say form and function are one, or organic.

What, then, is life?

To answer that question the organic structure must now appear not only as "entity"; entity must appear as individuality. We are concerned with organism. We may say the organism is a living one, only when all is part to the whole as whole is to the part. This correlation, such as is found in any plant or animal, is fundamental to the life of organic architecture, as it is to any life whatever. But more important, and what finally makes any building live as true architecture, this building we are building must finally come to terms with the living human spirit. It must come alive where that spirit is concerned. Now what is this "*living*" human spirit?

First, it is a quality of the mind really informed with a sense of man's universe. It is a mind wholly in life as life is in it. It is the spirit in life for what life may be. It desires living to the utmost. Such spirit is seldom lost in any part of the whole. Such a mind never for long loses the direction of the center line of "sentient entity." The "living spirit" would, at least, be the spirit capable of that. Let us call the living spirit, then, the new-old integrity that in architecture, as in all else, is the bridge by which man's past reached the present and by which his present will reach the future, if his present is to have any future at all. If our present in architecture contains any future worthy of the living human spirit, it will cross over this bridge. I am trying to present that architecture here in words as architecture "organic": the living expression of living human spirit. Architecture alive.

As already said, such architecture is and, as a matter of course, must be actual interpretation of social human life. Such living architecture is a new integrity in these modern times. It enters a distorted world where capital has got ahead of labor; where individual qualities of the personality are rendered invalid by new dimensions for money.

We shall go on in thought now with this building we started to build.

We start with the *ground*.

This is rock and *humus*. A building is planted there to survive the elements. The building is, meanwhile, shelter and human dignity, though inevitably destined to succumb to time in due course.

Why should the building try to belong to the ground instead of being content with some box-like fixture perched upon the rock or stuck into the soil, where it stands out as mere artifice, regardless where it stands up and "off," as "Colonial" houses do, and just as all houses not indigenous must do?

The answer is found in the ideal stated in the abstract dictum, "Form and function are one." We must begin upon our structure with that.

The ground already has form. Why not begin to give at once by accepting that? Why not give by accepting the gifts of nature? But I have never seen a "Colonial" house that did or could do this. Inevitably that house looks as though it hated the ground, with vast vanity trying to rise superior to it regardless of nature, depending upon a detachment called "classical" for such human values as habit and association of ideas could give to it.

Well, then, rejecting the "classical"; what of the ground?

Is the ground a parcel of prairie, square and flat?

Is the ground sunny or the shaded slope of some hill, high or low, bare or wooded, triangular or square.

Has the site features, trees, rocks, stream, or a visible trend of some kind? Has it some fault or a special virtue, or several?

In any and every case the character of the site is the beginning of the building that aspires to architecture. And this is true whatever the site or the building may be. It is true whether it be a dwelling among Wisconsin hills or a house on the bare prairie, the Imperial Hotel at Tokyo, or a skyscraper in New York City. All must begin there where they stand. For our "case in point" we shall take the Imperial Hotel at Tokyo and try to put into words something of the thought process that tended to make that structure organic.

A social clearing house, call it a hotel, became necessary to official Japan as a consequence of new foreign interest in the Japanese. A new hotel becomes necessary, because no foreigner, no matter how cultivated, could live on the floor, as the Japanese do, with any grace or comfort. It was also necessary for another reason: a Japanese gentleman does not entertain strangers, no matter how gentle, within his family circle. So the building will be more a place for entertainment with private supper rooms, banquet hall, theater and cabaret than it will be a hotel.

No foreign architect yet invited to work in Japan ever took off his hat to the Japanese and respected either Japanese conditions or traditions. And yet those aesthetic traditions are at the top among the noblest in the world. When I accepted the commission to design and build their building it was my instinct and definite intention not to insult them. Were they not a feature of my first condition, the ground? They were. The Japanese were more their own ground than any people I knew.

So while making their building "modern" in the best sense, I meant to leave it a sympathetic consort to Japanese buildings. I wanted to show the Japanese how their own conservation of space and the soul of their own religious shinto, which is "be clean," might, in the use of all materials, take place as effectively for them indoors in sound masonry construction when on their feet as it had taken place for them when they were down upon their knees in their own inspired carpentry.

I meant to show them how to use our new civilizing-agents—call them plumbing, electrification, and heating—without such outrage to the art of building as we ourselves were practicing and they were then copying. I intended to make all these appurtenance systems a practical and aesthetic part of the building itself. It was to be given a new simplicity by making it a complete whole within itself.

Mechanical systems should be an asset to life and so an asset to architecture. They should be no detriment to either. Why shouldn't the Japanese nation make the same coordination of furnishing and building when they came to be at home on their feet that they had so wonderfully made for themselves at home on their knees?

And I believed I could show them how to build an earthquake-proof masonry building.

In short, I desired to help Japan make the transition from wood to masonry, and from her knees to her feet, without too great loss of her own great accomplishments in culture. And I wished to enable her to overcome some of the inherent weaknesses of her building system where the temblor was a constant threat to her happiness and to her very life.

There was this natural enemy to all building whatsoever: the temblor. And, as I well knew, the seismograph in Japan is never still. The presence of the temblor, an affair of the ground, never left me while I planned and for four years or more worked upon the plans and structure of the new hotel. Earthquakes I found to be due to wave movement of the ground. Because of wave movement, foundations like long piles oscillate and rock the structure. Heavy masses of masonry inevitably would be wrecked. The heavier the masonry the greater the wreck.

The feature of the ground that was the site itself was a flat 500 by 300-foot plot of ground composed of sixty feet of liquid mud overlaid by eight feet of filled soil. The filling was about the consistency of hard cheese. The perpetual water level stood within fifteen inches of the level of the ground. In short, the building was to stand up on an ancient marsh, an arm of the bay that had been filled in when Tokyo became the capital of the empire.

But the mud beneath the filling seemed to me a good cushion to relieve earthquake shocks. A building might float upon the mud somewhat as a battleship floats on salt water. Float the building upon the mud? Why not? And since it must float, why not extreme lightness combined with the tenuity and flexibility that are a property of steel instead of the great weight necessary to the usually excessive rigidity which, no matter how rigid, could never be rigid enough? Probably the answer was a building made flexible as the two hands thrust together, fingers interlocked, yielding to movement yet resilient to return to position when force exerted upon its members and membranes ceased. Why fight the force of the quake on its own terms? Why not go with it and come back unharmed? Outwit the quake?

That was how the nature of the site, the ground, entered into the conception of the building. Now, to carry out in detail these initial perceptions.

I took a preliminary year in which to acquire necessary data, making tests for the new type of foundation. Finally flexible foundations, economical too, were provided by driving tapered wooden piles, only eight feet long, into the strata of filled soil, pulling them out and throwing in concrete immediately, to form the thousands of small piers or concrete pins two feet apart on centers upon which the jointed footing courses were laid. Nine pile drivers dotted the ground, each with its band of singing women pulling on the ropes lifting and dropping the drive-head—twelve ropes, one for each pair of hands.

The good sense of careful calculation so far: now what about the superstructure?

The building was going native, so intensive hand methods would have to be used and native materials too. The nature of the design therefore should be something hand methods could do better than machinery. It was impossible to say how far we could go in any direction with machines, probably not very far.

Evidently the straight line and flat plane to which I had already been committed by machines in America should be modified in point of style if I would respect the traditions of the people to whom the building would belong. The Japanese, centuries ago, had come nearer the ideal of an organic architecture in their dwellings than any civilized race on earth. The ideals we have been calling organic are even now best exemplified in their wood and paper dwellings where they lived on their knees. As I have already said, I wanted to help the Japanese get to their feet indoors and learn to live in fireproof masonry buildings, without loss of their native aesthetic prestige where the art of architecture was a factor. Trained by the disasters of centuries to build lightly on the ground, the wood and paper homes natural to them are kindled by any spark. When fire starts it seldom stops short of several hundred homes, sometimes destroys thousands, and ends in complete destruction of a city. After the irresistible wave movements have gone shuddering and jolting through the earth, changing all overnight in immense areas, islands disappearing, new ones appearing, mountains laid low and valleys lifted up taking awful toll of human life, then come the flames! Conflagration aways at the end.

The cost of metal frames and sash at that time was prohibitive, but the plans were made for an otherwise completely fireproof build-

IMPERIAL HOTEL, EMPEROR'S ENTRANCE, TOKYO, JAPAN

ing and the designs were so made that all architectural features were practical necessities.

The flexible light foundations had saved one hundred thousand dollars over the customary massive foundations. Now how could the building be made as light and flexible? I divided the building into sections about sixty feet long. This is the safe limit for temperature cracks in reinforced concrete in that climate. Wherever part met part I provided through joints.

To insure stability I carried the floor and roof loads as a waiter carries his tray on his upraised arm and fingers. At the center all supports were centered under the loaded floor-slabs; balancing the load instead of gripping the load at the edges with the walls, as in the accepted manner. In any movement a load so carried would be safe. The waiter's tray balanced on his hand at the center is the cantilever in principle.

This was done. This meant that the working principle of the cantilevers would help determine the style of the structure. So the cantilever became the principal feature of the structure and a great factor in shaping its forms throughout as the floor-slabs came through the walls and extended into various balconies and overhangs.

Tokyo buildings were top heavy. The exaggerated native roofs were covered deep with clay, and the heavy roof tiles laid on over the clay would come loose and slide down with deadly effect into the narrow streets crowded with terrified humanity.

So the outer walls, spread thick and heavy at the base and tapering towards the top, were crowned there by a light roof covered with hand-worked sheet copper tiles. The light roof framing rested upon a concrete ceiling slab extended outward over the walls into an overhang, perforated to let sunlight into the windows of the rooms beneath.

Now as to materials. What would be desirable and available? Again we go to the ground.

A stone I had seen under foot and in common use in Tokyo building was a light, workable lava, called oya, weighing about as much as green oak and resembling travertine. It was quarried at Nikko and was floated down on rafts by sea to Tokyo and then by canal to the site.

I liked this material for its character but soon found that the building committee, made up of the financial autocracy of the empire, considered it sacrilege to use a material so cheap and common for so dig- nified a purpose. But finally the building committee gave in and we bought our own quarries at Nikko. We used oya (the lava) throughout the work, combining it with concrete walls cast in layers within thin wall shells of slender bricks.

Large or small, the pieces of lava could be easily hollowed out at the back and set up with the hollow side inside, as one side of the slab-forms for casting the concrete. In this way the three materials were cast solidly together as a structural unit when the concrete was poured into them.

Copper, too, was a prominent feature in our list of available hand-worked materials.

Thus the "Teikoku" (Imperial Hotel) after these measures were taken became a jointed steel-reinforced monolith with a thin integral facing of lava and thin brick, the whole sheltered overhead by light copper tiles. The mass of the structure rests upon a kind of pincushion. The pins were set close enough together to support, by friction, the weight calculated to be placed upon them. To the lengthwise and cross-wise work in this particular structure all piping and wiring were made to conform. Both were designed to be laid in shafts and trenches free of construction. The pipes were of lead, sweeping with easy bend from trenches to shafts and curving again from shafts to fixtures. Thus any earthquake might rattle and flex the pipes as they hung but could break no connections. Last, but by no means least, an immense pool of water as an architectural feature of the extensive entrance court to the hotel was connected to its own private water system. This was to play its part in conflagration following in the wake of earthquake.

During the execution of these ideas I found the language a barrier. Men and methods were strange. But the "foreign" architect with twenty Japanese students from Tokyo and Kyoto University courses in architecture, some of whom were taken to Taliesin during the preliminary plan making, and one excellent American builder, Paul Mueller, made up the band that built the Imperial Hotel. Hayashi San, the general

306

manager of the Imperial Hotel, was in direct charge of everything. The principal owner, the Imperial Household, was represented by Baron Okura. And there was a board of directors composed of five captains of Japanese big business—ships, tobacco, cement, and banking.

The original plans which I had worked out at Taliesin for the construction I threw aside as educational experience for the architect only and worked out the details on the ground as we went along. Plans served only as a preliminary study for final construction.

Those Japanese workmen! How clever they were. What skill and industry they displayed! So instead of trying to execute preconceived methods of execution, thereby wasting this precious human asset in vainly trying to make the workmen come our way, we learned from them and willingly went with them, their way. I modified many original intentions to make the most of what I now saw to be naturally theirs. But, of course, curious mistakes were common. I had occasion to learn that the characteristic Japanese approach to any subject is, by instinct, spiral. The Oriental instinct for attack in any direction is oblique or volute and becomes wearisome to a direct Occidental, whose instinct is frontal and whose approach is rectilinear.

But, then, they made up for this seeming indirection by gentleness, loyalty, and skill. Soon we began to educate the "foreigners" as they did us, and all went along together pretty well.

As the countenance of their building began to emerge from seeming confusion the workmen grew more and more interested in it. It was a common sight to see groups of them intelligently admiring and criticizing some finished feature as it would emerge to view. There was warmth of interest and depth of appreciation, unknown to me in the building circles of our country in our own day, to prove the sincerity of their pleasure and interest in their work.

Finally, out of this exercise of free will and common sense, with this unusual Western feeling of respect for the East and for Japanese life and traditions in view as discipline and inspiration, what would emerge?

A great building is to be born; one not looking out of place where it is to stand across the park from the Imperial Palace. The noble surrounding walls of the Palace rose above the ancient moat. The gateways to the Palace grounds, guarded by blue-tiled, white-walled buildings nesting on the massive stone walls, were visible above the moat across the way. It was architecture perfect of its kind and as Japanese as the countenance of the race. I conceived the form of this new associate—the Imperial—as something squat and strong, as harmonious with this precedent as the pines in the park. It should be a form seen to be bracing itself against storm and expected temblor. Appeal has already been made to imagination in a realm scientific; but pure reason and science must now wait there at the doorstep.

Wait there while something came to Japanese ground—something not Japanese, certainly, but sympathetic, embodying modern scientific building ideas by old methods not strange to Japan. No single form was really Japanese but the whole was informed by unity. The growing proportions were suitable to the best Japanese tradition. We have here in the individuality of the architect a sincere lover of old Japan, his hat in hand, seeking to contribute his share in the transition of a great old culture to a new and inevitably foreign one. Probably the new one was unsuitable. Certainly it was as yet but imperfectly understood by those who were blindly, even fatuously, accepting it as superior to their own. A great tragedy, it may be.

Looking on then as now, it seemed to me as though tragedy it must be. The Far East had so little to learn from our great West, so much to lose where culture is concerned.

I might ameliorate their loss by helping to make much that was spiritually sound and beautiful in their own life, as they had known it so well, over into a pattern of the unknown new life they were so rashly entering. To realize this ambition in concrete form, apparent in a structure that acknowledged and consciously embodied this appropriate pattern, was what I intended to do in this masonry building 500 feet long by 300 feet wide. It was a world complete within itself. It now may be seen. It is known far and wide as it stands on the beaten path around the world. Said Baron Takahashi to a conscientious objector from America, "You may not like our Imperial Hotel but we Japanese like it. We understand it."

Two years later—1923—in Los Angeles: news was shouted in the streets of awful disaster. Tokyo and nearby Yokohama were wiped out by the most terrific temblor in history. Appalling details came in day after day after the first silence when no details could be had. As the news began to add up it seemed that nothing human could have withstood the cataclysm.

Too anxious to get any sleep I kept trying to get news of the fate of the New Imperial and of my friends, Shugio, Hayashi, Endo San, my boys and the Baron, hosts of friends I had left over there. Finally the third or fourth day after the first outcry, about two o'clock in the morning, the telephone bell. Mr. Hearst's *Examiner* wished to inform me that the Imperial Hotel was completely destroyed. My heart sank as I laughed at them. "Read your dispatch," I said. The *Examiner* read a long list of "Imperial" this and "Imperial" that.

"You see how easy it is to get the Imperial Hotel mixed with other Imperials. If you print the destruction of the new Imperial Hotel as news you will have to retract. If anything is above ground in Tokyo it is that building," I said, and hoped.

Their turn to laugh while they spread the news of destruction with a photograph across the head of the front page in the morning. Then followed a week or more of anxiety. Conflicting reports came continually because during that time direct communication was cut off.

Then—a cablegram.

"FRANK LLOYD WRIGHT, OLIVE HILL RESIDENCE, HOLLYWOOD, CALIFORNIA.
FOLLOWING WIRELESS RECEIVED TODAY FROM TOKYO, HOTEL STANDS UNDAMAGED AS MONUMENT TO YOUR GENIUS HUNDREDS OF HOMELESS PROVIDED BY PERFECTLY MAINTAINED SERVICE. CONGRATULATIONS.

OKURA."

For once in a lifetime good news was newspaper news and the Baron's cablegram flashed around the world to herald what? To herald the triumph of good sense in the head of an architect tough enough to stick to it through thick and thin. Yes, that. But it was really a new approach to building, the ideal of an organic architecture at work, that really saved the Imperial Hotel.

Both Tokyo houses of the Baron were gone. The splendid museum he gave to Tokyo was gone. The building by an American architect, whose hand he took to see him through, was what he had left in Tokyo standing intact, nor could love or money buy a share in it, now.

When letters finally came through, friends were found to be safe. And it appeared that not one pane of glass was broken in the building—no one harmed. Neither was the plumbing or the heating system damaged at all. But something else was especially gratifying to me. After the first great quake was over, the dead lying in heaps, the Japanese came in droves, dragging their children into the courses and up onto the terraces of the building, praying for protection by the God that had protected the Teikoku. Then, as the wall of fire that follows every great quake came sweeping across the city toward the long front of the Imperial, driving a continuous wail of human misery before it, the Hotel boys formed a bucket line to the big pool of the central entrance court (the city mains were disrupted by the quake) and found there a reserve of water to keep the wood window frames and sash wet to meet the flames. The last thought for the safety of the Imperial had taken effect.

Early in the twentieth century, a world in itself, true enough to its purpose and created spontaneously as any ever fashioned by the will of any creator of antiquity, had been completed within a sector of the lifetime of its one architect. Such work in ancient times generally proceeded from generation to generation and from architect to architect. Strange! Here expert handicraft had come at the beck and call of one who had, up to that time, devoted most of his effort to getting buildings true to modern machine processes built by machine.

Here in the Far East a significant transition building was born. Are really good buildings all transition buildings? But for the quality of thought that built it, the ideal of an organic architecture, it would

310

surely have been just "another one of those things" and have been swept away.

While the New Imperial only partially realized the ideal of an organic architecture, the pursuit of that ideal made the building what it really was, and enabled it to do what it did do. The fact that were I to build it again it would be entirely different, although employing the same methods and means, does not vitiate my thesis here. It greatly strengthens it.

Now let us glance at what followed this natural approach to the nature of a problem as a natural consequence. Opposition, of course, followed until finally Baron Okura took full responsibility and saw the building through. There was the unfriendly attitude of Americans and Englishmen. Though none too friendly to each other, they opposed this approach. They had owned Tokyo up to now because, where foreign culture was being so freely and thoughtlessly bought, they were best sellers. The Germans were there, strong too, but they were almost out of the running by now. My sympathetic attitude, Japan for the Japanese, was regarded as treason to American interests. I encouraged and sometimes taught the Japanese how to do the work on their building themselves. The American construction companies were building ten-story steel buildings with such architecture as they had hung to the steel, setting the steel frames on long piles which they floated across the Pacific from Oregon and drove down to hard pan. I suppose they were built in this fashion so the steel might rattle the architecture off into the streets in any severe quake? These companies were especially virulent where I was concerned.

The Western Society of American Engineers gratuitously warned me that my "scheme for foundations was unsound." The A.I.A.— American Institute of Architects—passing through Tokyo when the building was nearly finished, took notice and published articles in Tokyo papers declaring the work an insult to American architecture, notifying my clients, and the world generally, that the whole thing would be down in the first quake with horrible loss of life.

Finally, when the building was about two-thirds completed, it came directly to the directors from such sources that their American

311

architect was mad. Now every director except one (my sponsor, the Baron), so worked upon continually for several years, became a spy. The walls had ears. Propaganda increased. General Manager Hayashi was "on the spot." My freedom was going fast and I worked on under difficulties greater than ever. Hayashi San, the powerful Okura, and my little band of Japanese student apprentices were loyal and we got ahead until the final storm broke in a dark scene in a directors' meeting. Then the Baron took over the reins himself to see me through with my work, and the building of the New Imperial went forward more smoothly to conclusion.

I have learned that wherever reason shows its countenance and change is to take place, the reaction in any established order, itself not organic, is similar. Therefore organic architecture has this barrier to throw down or cross over or go around.

As for government, I should say here that no permit to build the Imperial Hotel was ever issued by the government. I explained to the proper Imperial Department our intention, registered the drawings. The result was visitation by Japanese authorities, more explanations, head shakings. But the attitude was entirely friendly and sympathetic in contrast to the attitude that might be expected in our own country. Finally we were told no permit was needed, to go ahead, they would watch proceedings and hoped to learn something from the experiment. They could not say that most of the ideas did not seem right but, having no precedent, they could not officially act. They could wink, however, and "wink" the government did.

This "wink" is the utmost official sanction organic architecture or any thought-built action of the sort in any medium may expect from a social order itself inorganic and in such danger of disturbance if radical examination is permitted that even an approach in that direction is cause for hysteria. Institutions such as ours are safe, in fact remain "institutions" only upon some status quo, some supreme court, which inevitably becomes invalid as life goes on.

Now—so far as the architecture of the future is concerned, what is to be deduced from this particular and by no means typical instance?

Let us take an example with a broader application. The problem of the moderate cost home for that unfortunate—the "average American."

Suppose, then, we consider briefly a much broader application of the principles of an organic architecture: the moderate house for the citizen in moderate circumstances. For some reason—probably not a good one—five or six thousand dollars seems to be as much as the better part of the average citizenship of the United States can afford to pay for a house and the lot he builds one on. This lot is usually a fifty-foot lot for some other reason, certainly not a good reason. He may secure sixty or seventy feet, and has been known in rare instances to acquire title to as much as one hundred feet on some street front where sewer, water and gas, or electricity are available. The "lot"—the word is short for "allotment"—varies in depth from 125 to 200 feet, with a sixteen-foot "alley" at the end opposite the street end. Each lot on each side must range lengthwise along neighboring lots, so privacy is unlikely or impossible to any great extent. Corner lots are exposed to the street on two sides, with more taxes to pay accordingly and even less privacy than the inside neighbor has.

The result is a row of houses toeing an imaginary mark called a building line—a line predetermining how near the street the houses may come; and sometimes they must stay away several feet from the neighboring depthwise lot line. Oftentimes not: the feeling being pretty general that when a man buys a piece of ground it is his for better or for worse, not only from side to side but from the center of the earth to the top of the sky, although the "top of the sky" has been the subject of recent regulation.

Fortunately the owner's imagination, though ambitious, is limited. And he can go about as far as his neighbor goes and no farther. That is about all the actual discipline there is. Within that limitation each proceeds to be as original—"different" they call it—as each can be, with the net result, of course, that all look monotonously alike in their attempts to be "different" because the thought involved never changes. To be perfectly sincere—no thought at all ever enters into the affair from beginning to end. There is only habit, fashion—a certain association of ideas and the idiosyncrasy called "taste." The citizens talk of comfort and convenience without knowing very well what either really means. They spend two-fifths of the cost of the whole house to do as well as their neighbors in appearances, or to outdo them. Emulation or competition are in it all, but constructive thought does not enter. A certain shrewd common sense has to serve as it may, and such taste as may be.

Then the department store delivery wagon appears out front and the furnishings begin to come in from the chief source of furnishment. Countless items in the prevailing mode, all bought in some big establishment with the help sometimes of the interior decorator, whom even the undiscriminating are learning to call "the inferior desecrator."

So the interior is Marshall Field, Wanamaker or Kaufmann's at this level, instead of the Montgomery Ward and Sears Roebuck of the next level down—say the three thousand dollar bracket—house and lot. Now it is well to realize at this point that these houses so furnished are usually investments. They are homes, that's true, but they are homes afterward. Nothing must be done that detracts from the likelihood of profitable resale—on occasion. And American life is continually making that occasion for some reason, probably a good one this time.

A privy used to grace the backyard; perhaps there was a small stable for a horse and buggy, which necessitated a driveway along the north side of the house. And there was (still is) a north side which the sun never sees because the streets are all laid out square with the points of the compass—they had a reason for this but I could never find out what it was except that it was a surveyor's convenience. This scheme (or lack of one) gave every house a hot front or a cold front. The south belonged to one front alone. The morning sun shone in the east windows—the afternoon sun in those to the west. No one questioned the inevitability of all this, and only rarely is it ever questioned now. The net result of all the placing and fixing (and fussing, too, because they were awfully fussy about this) were the long rows of houses, all facing the street to the north or south or east or west, and set back to give thirty percent of the ground to that street for general effect.

314

This dedication to the street is a marked characteristic of all American towns.

The "backyard" thus left was divided from the neighbor by a fence or hedge, or none. Modern plumbing came to take the privy into the house. The motor car came to add the so-called garage to every house in place of such stables as there were, and privacy was something none understood though some few did desire it. It would take too long to say how all this came to be. Of what use to say it now?

Into these inorganic circumstances so curiously, unthinkingly compounded to confound simple living comes this organic $5500.00 house with the automobile as much a feature of life as the bathroom and the kitchen. When error has confused an issue hopelessly it is time to begin again. What can this house do to have a better beginning? Go to the country or go out in regional fields where ground is not yet exploited by the realtor. That is all. And it must go because to this house a garden is no backyard affair—an acre is necessary. The street cannot be desirable so far as this ground consideration is concerned except as a way to get to the place as unobtrusively as possible.

What, then, is desirable to this new house?

Well . . . *first*, free association with considerably more ground than the old house was allowed to have.

Second, sunlight and vista, a spaciousness conforming to the newly developed sense of space demanded by modern facilities. No north front because the house will not be set square with the compass.

Third, privacy, actual, not imaginary or merely makeshift.

Fourth, in the arrangement of rooms a free pattern for the occupation of the family that is to live in the house. As the families vary, so must the house. The rooms should be as much as possible on a single level for several reasons, all good.

It would be ideal to have all these requirements meet in some integral harmony of proportion to the human figure; to have all details so designed as to make the human relationship to building not only convenient but charming. For this building which we are considering is intended not to make shift with life but to give life more easy conditions that will cherish and protect the individual—not so much in

315

fostering his idiosyncrasies and sentimentalities as in protecting his vital necessities and fine sentiment. Above all, we must see this new house as the cradle of continuously arising generations. So, while appeal to reason is intrinsic, it is insufficient. There must also be beauty —beauty of which man himself is capable, the utmost beauty of which he is capable without getting himself into trouble with the installment system and the tax collector. We are hinting at a new simplicity of appearances where this new home is concerned.

We must achieve that new simplicity too, as well as establish a finer logic of use and want, but the new house won't pay two-fifths for it. It will pay nothing at all. Now, here we are with the acre essential to an individual human life on earth. The acre is level, with a few trees in one corner or more, but an acre fit for a garden. The house sees that garden to begin with, arranging itself about and within it so as to enjoy the sun and view and yet keep privacy.

The living room is where the familiar life is lived, so it must take first place. It is a room common to all, with a big fireplace in it.

Because of modern industrial developments the kitchen no longer has a curse upon it; it may become a part of the living room by being related to another part of that same room set apart for dining. An extra space, which may be used also for studying or reading, might become convenient between meals. In such a house the association between dining and the preparation of meals is immediate and convenient. It is private enough, too.

Next in importance to this decentralized central unit is the toilet unit, the bathroom. Only it should now be a triplicate bathroom, one section for man, one for wife, one for offspring. The fixtures are placed to have the economy of close connection but the three bath compartments themselves are large enough for dressing rooms, closets for linen, etc., even wardrobes, with perhaps a couch in each. The bedrooms adjoining this unit are small but airy. Both bedrooms and the triplicate bathroom would be alongside the garden, easy of access from the living room.

The indispensable car? It is still designed like a buggy. And it is treated like one when it is not in use. The car no longer needs such consideration. If it is weatherproof enough to run out in all weather it ought to be weatherproof enough to stand still under a canopy with a wind screen on two sides. Inasmuch as this car is a feature of the comings and goings of the family, some space at the entrance is the proper space for it. Thus the open car-port comes to take the part of the dangerous closed "garage."

While the car is yet far from being well designed, it has more in common with our sanitary appliances and modern kitchens than the older cars could have with the older houses. The proportions and lines of this organic house are those the industrialists are trying so hard to get into their products, succeeding only superficially in doing so. But they are doing so sufficiently to make congruous the house, car, kitchen and bathroom. Furniture too is coming to reflect this new sense of unity and congruity. They are calling it modernistic, or streamlined, or just modern.

Except for the more advanced triplicate bathroom unit, not yet executed, I have been describing here a particular house, the house of Herbert Jacobs built at Madison, Wisconsin. It was let by contract for $5500 to Harold Grove.

What I want to say in words the house itself alone can say. But perhaps enough has been said to suggest the ideals and processes of thought at work that are giving us an indigenous and, probably, a greater architecture in every respect than has existed before.

I could go on with many instances in the widely varying fields of our American activity and show how a new development in building design is bringing order out of chaos. I could show pretty clearly how a new technique of building is growing up into the American scene— a new technique as well as an integrity of design that does bring to the house builder and home owner the benefits of industrialism and the efficiencies of the factory. Instead of the criss-cross of the open field we are developing building schemes that utilize the economies of standardization without its curse, using the simple unit system applied to building, meaning buildings put together upon a horizontal and vertical unit system much as a rug is woven on its warp. The implications are as aesthetic as they are scientific and economic.

I hope enough has been said to indicate that organic architecture has already gone far enough, that standardization is no real obstacle to freedom of individuality. Standardization is not a real obstacle in spite of the international style, the "permanent wave," the realtor, and "housing."

A future for architecture depends upon a new sense of reality, a different success ideal, a deeper social consciousness, a finer integrity of the individual—that there may be promoted the integration of a whole people with their own soil or ground. This will in turn bring about freedom from a false economy. It will bring about the end of labor, money, ground and buildings as speculative commodities. It will bring about the rise of cultured sentiment to take the place of educated sentimentality. It will abolish commercial standards that are only profit-taking. It will close institutes, museums and universities until new ones may be created to bring culture to youth by way of action in an atmosphere of truth and beauty. It will train youth to want and utilize its own ground. There is also necessary a new type of architect and a new structure of government that governs only where individuality may not exist. Such a government will function as a business of the whole people in matters common to the whole people, and only so, instead of as a policeman and a politician. A further essential is a popular realization of organic structure as the basis of all culture in the development of the whole life of a whole people. Such a future as this must grow slowly. Finally the abandonment of ultra-urban life is necessary. A new type of city must be realized. There will be organic structure in government, organic structure in society, organic structure in the economics of both.

THE LANGUAGE OF AN ORGANIC ARCHITECTURE

THE LANGUAGE OF AN
ORGANIC ARCHITECTURE

ORGANIC (or intrinsic) architecture is the free architecture of ideal democracy. To defend and explain whatever I have myself built and written on the subject I here append a nine-word lexicon needed, worldwide, at this moment of our time.

The words.

1. NATURE. Why? As in popular use this word is first among abuses to be corrected.

2. ORGANIC. Ignorant use or limitation of the word organic.

3. FORM FOLLOWS FUNCTION. Too many foolish stylistic constructions are placed upon the slogan.

4. ROMANCE. A universal change is taking place in the use of this word, a change to which organic architecture has itself given rise. No longer sentimental.

5. TRADITION. Confusion of all eclectics, especially critics, concerning the word.

6. ORNAMENT. The grace or perdition of architecture; for the past 500 years "applique."

7. SPIRIT. Any version or subversion of the word by the so-called international style or by any fashion promoted by experts.

8. THIRD DIMENSION. Where and why the term was original. What it now means in architecture.

9. SPACE. A new element contributed by organic architecture as style.

When the nine words I have listed here are added together (they often are) a degradation of original form and intent which no vitality can bear, is widespread. Due to much prevalent imposition the gutter seems the only visible destination of an original idea of architecture that is basic to democratic culture: an ideal that might become the greatest constructive creative philosophy of our day if only understood and well practiced. That philosophy is surely the center line of integral or democratic culture in these United States if and when we awaken to the true meaning and intent not only of organic architecture but also of the American democracy we are founded as a nation to maintain. So I shall try to explain these nine terms. All are on the center line of both architecture and democracy. Current trends of standardized education today tend to turn young lives more and more toward sterility. Elimination of creation in favor of any cliché that will best serve mechanization. Mediocrity serves it best because mechanization best serves the mediocre. Present tendencies toward the mediocre international style not only degrade organic American architecture but will eventually destroy the creative architect in America, as elsewhere.

DEFINITIONS

1. NATURE means not just the "out-of-doors," clouds, trees, storms, the terrain and animal life, but refers to their nature as to the nature of materials or the "nature" of a plan, a sentiment, or a tool. A man or anything concerning him, *from within*. Interior nature with capital N. Inherent PRINCIPLE.

2. The word ORGANIC denotes in architecture not merely what may hang in a butcher shop, get about on two feet or be cultivated in

a field. The word organic refers to *entity*, perhaps integral or intrinsic would therefore be a better word to use. As originally used in architecture, organic means *part-to-whole-as-whole-is-to-part*. So *entity as integral* is what is really meant by the word organic. INTRINSIC.

3. FORM FOLLOWS FUNCTION. This is a much abused slogan. Naturally form does so. But on a lower level and the term is useful only as indicating the platform upon which architectural form rests. As the skeleton is no finality of human form any more than grammar is the "form" of poetry, just so function is to architectural form. Rattling the bones is not architecture. Less is only more where more is no good.

Form *is* predicated by function but, so far as poetic imagination can go with it without destruction, transcends it. "Form follows function" has become spiritually insignificant: a stock phrase. Only when we say or write *"form and function are one"* is the slogan significant. It is now the password for sterility. Internationally.

4. ROMANCE, like the word BEAUTY, refers to a *quality*. Reactionary use of this honorable but sentimentalized term by critics and current writers is confusing. Organic architecture sees actuality as the intrinsic romance of human creation or sees essential romance as actual in creation. *So romance is the new reality.* Creativity *divines* this. No teamwork can conceive it. A committee can only receive it as a gift from the inspired individual. In the realm of organic architecture human imagination must render the harsh language of structure into becomingly humane expressions of form instead of devising inanimate facades or rattling the bones of construction. Poetry of form is as necessary to great architecture as foliage is to the tree, blossoms to the plant or flesh to the body. Because sentimentality ran away with this human need and negation is now abusing it is no good reason for taking the abuse of the thing for the thing.

Until the mechanization of building is in the service of creative architecture and not creative architecture in the service of mechanization we will have no great architecture.

5. TRADITION may have many traditions just as TRUTH may have many truths. When we of organic architecture speak of truth we

speak of generic principle. The genus "bird" may fly away as flocks of infinitely differing birds of almost unimaginable variety: all of them merely derivative. So in speaking of tradition we use the word as also a *generic* term. Flocks of traditions may proceed to fly from generic tradition into unimaginable many. Perhaps none have creative capacity because all are only derivative. Imitations of imitation destroy an original tradition.

TRUTH is a divinity in architecture.

6. ORNAMENT. Integral element of architecture, ornament is to architecture what efflorescence of a tree or plant is to its structure. *Of* the thing, not *on* it. Emotional in its nature, ornament is—if well conceived—not only the *poetry* but *is the character of structure revealed and enhanced.* If not well conceived, architecture is destroyed by ornament.

7. SPIRIT. What is spirit? In the language of organic architecture the "spiritual" is never something descending upon the thing from above as a kind of illumination *but exists within the thing itself as its very life. Spirit* grows upward from within and outward. Spirit does not come down from above to be suspended there by skyhooks or set up on posts.

There are two uses of nearly every word or term in usual language but in organic sense any term is used in reference to the inner not the outer substance. A word, such as "nature" for instance, may be used to denote a material or a physical means to an end. Or the same word may be used with spiritual significance but in this explanation of the use of terms in organic architecture the spiritual sense of the word is uppermost in use in every case.

8. The THIRD DIMENSION. Contrary to popular belief, the third dimension is not *thickness* but is *depth*. The term "third dimension" is used in organic architecture to indicate the sense of depth which issues as *of* the thing not *on* it. The third dimension, depth, exists as intrinsic to the building.

9. SPACE. The continual becoming: invisible fountain from which all rhythms flow to which they must pass. Beyond time or infinity.

The new reality which organic architecture serves to employ in building.

The breath of a work of art.

If what I have myself written upon the subject of architecture and any one of the 560 buildings I have built are studied with this nine-word lexicon in mind, I am sure we will have far less of the confusion and nonsensical criticism upon which inference, imitation, doubt and prejudice have flourished. Isms, ists and ites defeat the great hope we are still trying to keep alive in our hearts in face of prevalent expedients now sterilizing the work of young American architects and rendering our schools harmful to the great art of architecture although perhaps profitable to science commercialized. If organic (intrinsic) architecture is not to live, we of these United States of America will never live as a true culture. Architecture must first become basic to us as creative art, therefore beneficent the world over. Present tendencies in education are so far gone into reverse by way of museum factotums, various committees and university regents spending millions left behind by hard working millionaires that owing to fashions of internationalism promoted by the internationalite we will have seen the last of the architecture of great architects not only in our democracy but all over the world beside where there is danger of the machine becoming a pattern of life instead of life using the machine as a tool.

Because our Declaration of Independence saw democracy as the gospel of individuality and saw it as above polemics or politics, probably a definition of the word democracy should be added to this lexicon of nine words. Therefore a tenth:

Democracy is our national ideal . . . not yet well understood by ourselves so not yet realized. But we are a new republic professing this ideal of freedom for growth of the individual. Why not cherish it? Freedom is not to be conceived as numbered freedoms. If true, freedom is never to be conceived in parts. Freedom is of the man and is not accorded to him or ascribed to him except as he may require protection. For that purpose government—as protection—exists, not as a policy maker. Democracy is thus the highest form of aristocracy ever seen. Aristocracy intrinsic.

A gentleman? No longer chosen and privileged by autocratic power he must rise from the masses by inherent virtue. His qualities as a man will give him title and keep it for him. Individual conscience will rule his social acts. By love of quality as against quantity he will choose his way through life. He will learn to know the difference between the curious and the beautiful. Truth will be a divinity to him. As his gentle-hood cannot be conferred, so it may not be inherited. This gentleman of democracy will be found in any honest occupation at any level of fortune, loving beauty, doing his best and being kind.

Anyone may see by our own absurd acts and equivocal policies how confused we are by our own ideal when we proceed to work it out. But the principles of organic architecture are the center line of our democracy in America when we do understand what both really mean.

Only by the growth and exercise of *individual conscience* does the man earn or deserve his "rights." Democracy is the opposite of totalitarianism, communism, fascism or mobocracy. But democracy is constantly in danger from mobocracy—the rising tide of as yet unqualified herd-instinct. Mechanized mediocrity. The *conditioned* mind instead of the *enlightened* mind.

Taliesin
May 20, 1953

PHOTOGRAPHERS' CREDITS